Ultimate Techniques & Tactics

James Parinella
Eric Zaslow

Human Kinetics

Library of Congress Cataloging-in-Publication Data

Parinella, James.
   Ultimate techniques & tactics / James Parinella and Eric Zaslow.
      p. cm.
   Includes index.
   ISBN 0-7360-5104-X (soft cover)
   1. Ultimate (Game) I. Title: Ultimate techniques and tactics. II. Zaslow, Eric. III. Title.
   GV1097.U48P37 2004
   796.2--dc22

                                           2004001618

ISBN: 0-7360-5104-X

Acquisitions Editor: Ed McNeely
Developmental Editor: Susanna Blalock
Assistant Editors: Anne Cole, Wendy McLaughlin, Cory Weber
Copyeditor: John Wentworth
Proofreader: Coree Clark
Indexer: Sandi Schroeder
Graphic Designer: Nancy Rasmus
Graphic Artist: Francine Hamerski
Photo Manager: Dan Wendt
Cover Designer: Keith Blomberg
Photographer (cover): Scobel Wiggins
Photographer (interior): Tom Roberts unless otherwise indicated. Photos on pages 13, 165, 167, 173, 179, and
   182 © Human Kinetics.
Art Manager: Kareema McLendon
Illustrator: Brian McElwain
Printer: Versa Press

Human Kinetics books are available at special discounts for bulk purchase. Special editions or book excerpts can also be created to specification. For details, contact the Special Sales Manager at Human Kinetics.

Printed in the United States of America   10 9 8 7 6 5 4 3 2 1

Human Kinetics
Web site: www.HumanKinetics.com

United States: Human Kinetics
P.O. Box 5076
Champaign, IL 61825-5076
800-747-4457
e-mail: humank@hkusa.com

Canada: Human Kinetics
475 Devonshire Road Unit 100
Windsor, ON N8Y 2L5
800-465-7301 (in Canada only)
e-mail: orders@hkcanada.com

Europe: Human Kinetics
107 Bradford Road
Stanningley
Leeds LS28 6AT, United Kingdom
+44 (0) 113 255 5665
e-mail: hk@hkeurope.com

Australia: Human Kinetics
57A Price Avenue
Lower Mitcham, South Australia 5062
08 8277 1555
e-mail: liaw@hkaustralia.com

New Zealand: Human Kinetics
Division of Sports Distributors NZ Ltd.
P.O. Box 300 226 Albany
North Shore City
Auckland
0064 9 448 1207
e-mail: blairc@hknewz.com

Ultimate Techniques & Tactics

Contents

PART III *BUILDING A SUCCESSFUL TEAM*

Preface

Ultimate is a way of life. College students sing cheers on their way to a national tournament; professionals mingle on the sidelines in recreational leagues; parents play in the mixed division while their toddlers frolic on blankets off the field; travelers meet new friends during pick-up games in foreign lands. No one who has ever played this game fails to recognize the special character or "spirit" of the sport. However, many longtime players remain unaware of subtle aspects of the game, as yet unawakened to the structure of the sport itself. These players enjoy the sport as much as anyone but find themselves eternally relegated to the "minor leagues," unable to tap their true potential as athletes. This book will help you master the sport of ultimate by giving you an understanding of the main structures of the game and the basic principles from which the guidelines for solid play are derived. More than a handbook of techniques and guidelines for good play, more than a repository of knowledge and a shared common reference, this book is also a synthesis of concepts gleaned from years of playing.

The sport of ultimate began in 1968 at Columbia High School in New Jersey, and over the few decades that followed, it has grown to a sport played by over 100,000 people in over 50 countries worldwide. Although there are now national and world championships, and although ultimate is a medal sport at the World Games, the sport is still in its youth. Ultimate is just beginning to become visible in high schools and elementary schools nationwide. Teams are sprouting up in schools and recreational leagues, and coaches with limited playing experience are volunteering their time to help the sport grow at the grass roots level. For coaches looking for a comprehensive explanation of how the sport works, there's precious little written instruction material, and what is written lacks cohesion. Each article represents a different viewpoint with no underlying fundamental principles carrying over from one to the next. Teams attempting to improve have had to fashion a game plan piecemeal from these writings, rely on word of mouth, or try to invent their own strategies. This book has been written to fill a need in the disc community for a clear and consistent explication of the sport today.

Because ultimate is a young sport with strategies not yet fully developed or universally accepted, virtually every ultimate player can learn something from this book that could make the difference in a close game. (Indeed, the authors have learned from each other preparing this book.) Many experienced and otherwise highly skilled players feel that they or their teams don't know "how to win." This book can help them plan their season and develop confidence that their games are sound. Intermediate players, especially those in isolated markets, get a chance to study many strategies that they might otherwise see only once a year, if that. Coaches of beginning teams can search through the universe of known strategies to learn the reasoning behind the fundamentals and pick the formations most suited to their players. And while many of the concepts explained here have been published or put online, everything appearing in this book has been developed anew; never before have the various topics been collected and tied together.

Although virtually anyone who wishes to learn more about how to play ultimate will benefit from this book, intermediate to advanced players and teams will benefit the most. This book will help them be more successful in achieving their goals. Additionally, coaches of beginning to intermediate teams can use the book as a reference and as a general coaching guide. These coaches are typically volunteers who give their time to spread the sport they love, and they simply want to teach as much as possible.

This book continually comes back to the six basic principles of good ultimate: focus, weight, space, communication, efficiency, and possession. Explicit instructions are provided for many situations, as well as outlines on how these principles are at play; thus, the reader is given the background necessary to make appropriate decisions in new situations. The authors have each played the game for over 20 years at all levels and have spent much of this time analyzing it. This book is the culmination of what we have learned through their experiences, observations, and insights.

Spirit of the Game

The ultimate community has created and nurtured a notion called the "Spirit of the Game." This special aspect of the culture and etiquette of the sport takes many forms. It's on display when teams cheer each other after games; when a player takes back a poor call; and when national championships are held without referees. No one who has played the game would describe ultimate as "just another sport." Ultimate's unique quality and fiercely loyal community exist in no small part because of the Spirit of the Game.

The Spirit of the Game is reflected in the rules as well. Fair play is one of the underlying tenets of ultimate. Not only is it explicitly written into the rules that intentional violations are forbidden, but the culture of the game actively dissuades such behavior. Players and teams can soon develop bad reputations if they push the rules. It is every player's responsibility to play by the rules, even as impartial observers are given more authority on the field. No tactic or technique shown in this book violates the rules in any manner. In fact, whenever possible, you are warned about subtle ways that unsportsmanlike opponents might bend the rules and are suggested ways to handle these transgressions. It bears repeating—play fair, play hard. There's no place in ultimate for cheaters.

Of course, any player improves naturally through practice and competition at increasingly high levels, but the rate of improvement can be enhanced through guided learning, focused practice, and continual review. This book contains detailed expositions of proper tactics and effective techniques for good play, which you can use in structuring your own education within the sport. Try picking an aspect of your game and reading about it in the book. Then, at the next few practices, try the recommended technique, noting differences from your own. For example, you might discover that you've been dropping a few too many routine passes. After reading the chapter on catching, you might realize that your technique produces a jarring motion while your hand grasps the disc and find in the text a less jarring catching procedure that you resolve to adopt. Such a diagnosis and prescription can quickly lead to improved performance.

After a few practices using an approach recommended in the text, you'll be able to assess how well it works for you. Did the technique help your game? Why or why not? Sometimes, a nontextbook method might work as well for you. Compare how your approach differs from the technique advocated in the text. How are the principles of the game applied in the two techniques? Can you find a composite approach that works best for you? Repeat this process with other facets of your game. By going through this process, you can develop important adjustments in your game and a better appreciation of others. In addition, this knowledge will be useful down the road—when critiquing teammates, teaching youngsters, marking an unknown player, and in other unforeseeable ways. More important, this exercise teaches you how to learn about the game itself (and anything else, really).

The same process applies to your team. Form a book club with team members. Pick out an aspect of team play that needs work—zone defense, for example. Read the part of the book that deals with this aspect of play (chapter 10) and design a practice to focus on this area. After practice, discuss your team's weaknesses and strengths, how they compare to the ideal, and what steps might be necessary to fix the problems. Maybe the cup in your defensive zone was excessively porous. After reading the zone chapter and discussing it with your teammates, you might find that the problem is caused by poor coordination between the middle-middle and the short-deep. After some practice in this area, your zone soon improves. We hope your teammates are as committed as you are!

This book does not attempt to reveal every secret of experience or to explain in detail every possible offensive stack or zone variation. The basic skills are reviewed only briefly so space can be devoted to topics more suited to the advanced player. Many examples of the more subtle individual techniques are given, as attention to detail is one of the characteristics of successful ultimate players. For team skills, a broader picture is painted so that as strategies continually evolve, the reader can keep up with innovations elsewhere in the game.

Developing a great team requires a collective effort and a holistic approach to the game. A dropped pass or errant throw occurs not in isolation but in the context of 14 on-field players and many more on the sideline. In most cases, it takes more than one error to cause a turnover, and it behooves a team to recognize all the factors contributing to the gaffe. For example, a simple drop might be the result of (1) an improperly angled cut that allows the defender to trail very closely, (2) a flight trajectory that's not optimal for the improper cut, or (3) a lack of focus by the receiver caused by his thinking the defender in hot pursuit. Understanding field situations such as this one, in the context of the basic principles stressed in this book, is a process of analyzing the pieces (such as, the mechanics of the catch) and synthesizing them into a comprehensive picture. The best teams are composed of players who understand and acknowledge their share of responsibility in every play on the field. If you watch a great game of ultimate, you'll notice players far from the disc (even those on the sidelines) apologizing after a turnover.

The book is divided into three main parts: Individual Skills (offense then defense), Team Skills (defense then offense), and Building a Successful Team. This mirrors the order in which a player becomes interested in the game. Most new players immediately want to know how to throw the disc and how to become more involved in the offense. Next, they want to prevent their opponents from catching the disc. Once they're comfortable with their individual skills, they gain interest in learning how to play as a team. It's only after these individual and team skills have been refined do the players want to know how to work as a team on and off the field. (As a team's offense is often a response to the structure of the defense, it makes sense to consider defense first.) Then, getting in shape becomes important, as do the subtler aspects of team building. Around this time, players also come to an understanding of their own capabilities and weaknesses and learn how to get the most out of themselves.

Useful drills are presented where appropriate to allow for hands-on practice of the skills in the book. Sidebars describe tips, suggestions, and specific situations on which to focus. Diagrams show on-field positioning and motion, and action photos complement written descriptions of hard-to-visualize tactics.

On a more general level, the organization is similar to the learning process of analysis and synthesis. We dive into a new topic by following a few basic rules. We learn more through experience and the effort of analysis how to apply these rules in new situations. Eventually we modify these rules and synthesize them into a more complete and cohesive set.

Besides being the first book published that details advanced strategies of ultimate, this book has several unique aspects, including useful tips, pitfalls to avoid, rules of play, practice drills for developing skills, diagrams to illustrate techniques, sidebars describing specific tactics, a full training regimen, and a glossary of terms.

How will this focus on principles help you learn? Consider errors on the field. These errors can be (1) fundamental, individual errors such as drops, bad decisions, or poor throws; (2) team-level errors, such as when no one is open or two players miscommunicate; or (3) acceptable errors, such as when a reasonable risk is taken without success. This book will clearly identify the root cause of errors, helping players to eliminate errors of the first kind and teams to reduce errors of the third kind. With fewer fundamental and acceptable errors, the risk level of many plays decreases, meaning that team-level errors are curtailed as well.

Winning ultimate demands not only that players (and teams) work hard and learn the game—it requires them to imbue themselves with the proper attitude. Resolve yourself to becoming a good player. Good players chase down swill. Good players clear out. Good players cut when they're tired. Good players remember the defense. Good players call for help when they need it. In fact, "good" players are great players. Great teams also require great teammates. Become a great teammate. Be ready to play on time. Critique but don't criticize your teammates. Apologize for your mistakes. Take yourself out of the game when you're tired. Eschew pride.

Every player can get better. We hope this book gives you the skills you need to ensure your own progress in whatever aspect of the game you wish to improve. We'll see you on the field!

—Jim and Zaz

Acknowledgments

I'm grateful to everyone I've played with and against over the years. I'd especially like to recognize Lance and Todd Williams for getting me hooked on the game; Alex de Frondeville, Dennis McCarthy, and Phil Price for their friendship and for being such integral parts in my still-developing understanding of the game; and the teams Earth Atomizer and DoG for having the brains and guts to try new ideas and for giving me such great memories. Seeing my parents become fans and giving me their support has meant a lot to me. I owe so much to my wife, Jackie Bourgeois, who—along with her other great qualities—patiently answered my many queries about this technique or that tactic. Finally, I'd like to thank my son, Christopher, just for being the happy, lovable little guy that he is.

—Jim

I would like to thank my family and my many teammates and friends who have inspired me with their passion, dedication, and great play. Zeph Landau, Dave Meyers, and John "Bar" Axon bring friendship and fun to serious competition. I am lucky to have been led by the examples of Lenny Engel and Steve Mooney. From Moo Disc to Boston Kremes to DoG and Machine, I owe many my gratitude. Finally, thanks to Lizzie for her magical combination of silliness and sagacity.

—Zaz

Both authors would like to thank Adam Goff for reading an early draft; Zeph Landau and Phil Price for their careful read and many suggestions; and Marshall Goff for the use of his photographs. We would also like to thank the Ultimate Players Association (UPA) for doing so much for the game and for making it easier for us to give something back. Finally, we'd like to thank every ultimate player who thinks about the game and wants to get better. This book is for you.

Key to Diagrams

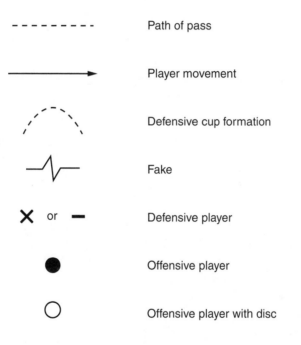

- - - - - - - -	Path of pass
———————▶	Player movement
⌒	Defensive cup formation
╱╲╱	Fake
X or ▬	Defensive player
●	Offensive player
○	Offensive player with disc

Note: Throughout the text, male gender voice is used to refer to players on offense, and female gender voice is used to refer to players on defense.

PART I

Individual Skills

Principles of the Game

How can a mechanic understand how a car with thousands of parts works? How can a doctor understand the operation of all the parts of the body? How can a physicist understand the myriad ways that particles can interact? How can a chess player find a great move among billions of possibilities? How can an ultimate player make the perfect cut in any situation? What enables human beings to wrap their finite brains around an infinite number of situations is *the ability to comprehend complex structures in terms of organizing principles.*

Central to great ultimate is the ability to understand the game in "real time," to be able to see a field situation and choose a course of action in the midst of play. Often, only a half-second window of opportunity appears, so a player must be able to analyze the situation and capitalize on it instantly. This is the case in such situations as making poaches, recognizing cutting opportunities and mismatches, and capitalizing on an off-balance or out-of-position defender. Because there are so many ways in which players can position on the field and so many variables affecting play—including players' skill levels, types of players, and weather conditions—there's no way to study every possibility and be prepared to perform the appropriate action. Instead, you develop an understanding of a set of principles that you can apply to most situations on the field.

As a comparison, think of how the golden rule (do unto others as you would have them do unto you) serves as a guidepost for moral behavior. One principle applies to a multitude of situations. It works the same way in ultimate—once you have learned a governing principle, you can apply it in many different situations. In this opening chapter, we'll review the basic principles of playing ultimate. These principles will make better sense and mean more to you as we present examples in this chapter and those that follow.

Reacting in real time requires a combination of understanding and coordination. Reading a book can aid understanding and give tips on how to train coordination, but there's no substitute for practice. In this chapter, we'll focus solely on understanding the game of ultimate in terms of organizing principles. We have arrived at the principles we discuss—focus, space, weight, communication, efficiency, and possession—through years of playing and making many, many mistakes. We hope you can benefit from learning these principles without having to duplicate our slow process of developing them.

Focus

The legends of every sport—Tiger Woods, Wayne Gretzky, Michael Jordan, Lance Armstrong—share an uncanny ability to focus. Some call this focus "playing in the zone." No athlete can play in the zone all the time, but the great ones seem to get there more often. Bill Rodriguez, the most winning ultimate player in history, has said, "What separates good players and great players is not skill but focus." Focus is the most important principle in the game. It drives you through training, throwing, catching, decision making, listening, sprinting, and every other aspect of the sport.

If you want to enter or remain in the upper echelon of the game, you must train your mind on the task at hand. When diving to make a catch, any attention to extraneous details (spectators, flair, anticipated pain upon landing, fear of contact with other players, thoughts of the throw you'll make after the catch, and so on) reduce your chance of success. A defender who gets distracted and loses sight of her offender might be a step too late to make the block. You need to focus on yourself, your opponent, and your interaction with the rest of the players. Is someone yelling at you

Focus is the most important principle of the game of ultimate.

© Marshall Goff

to switch? Is there a teammate behind you who is in better position to cut? Likewise, when training, you must maintain focus during your sprints or lifts; when the mind wanders, the body opts to rest. On the sideline, while resting, you can contribute to your team's success by cheering for your team, analyzing the opponent's strategies, constructively criticizing (and accepting critiques from) your teammates, and discussing tactics with your captain. A player who has fully committed to the team knows that dedicating the whole of the mind's attention to the team's collective goal is the best way to contribute.

There are a few mantras involved in focusing, all of which involve the same concept. Play ultimate; be just playing ultimate. (Anything else is irrelevant.) Stay in the moment. (Don't drift; don't worry about the future or past.) Let your body do it. (You've trained your body to run, catch, and throw—don't mess things up by overthinking. "Focus" does not equal excessive mind activity.) Stay in the game. (Be ready to grind it out, even if you can't find your A game.)

Throughout the book, we'll emphasize the importance of focusing. Training and learning are not useful without careful attention to how they are applied.

Drill: Focus

You can practice focus at any time of the day. If you're walking down a path (or even standing still), focus on a sign 100 yards away. As you move, keep your eyes and attention fixed on the sign. Don't let your mind wander. Don't think about the act of focusing. Don't become self-conscious. Don't think about how this focusing drill will affect your game. Devote all your attention to the sign. Don't think about how the sign was crafted, what it's made of, or what it says—train your attention only on its existence.

How did you do? The drill is difficult to do well, especially at first, when your attention might scamper off like a dog at a squirrel convention. You'll need to practice to maintain focus; try holding your focus a little longer each time you do the drill.

Space

The principle of space includes considerations of field sense and timing. In any sport involving motion, you need to understand where to direct your movements, what pitfalls might befall which maneuvers, where the opportunities on the playing field lie, and how to capitalize on the opportunities presented to you. The principle of space requires you to understand how much space you need for an offensive play, how likely it is that a defender will encroach upon that space to disrupt the play, and how much time you need to make the play. Such factors are especially important in field sports such as ultimate because many players are moving over a large area at once.

The easiest offensive play in ultimate is a throw to an open receiver in an empty part of the field. How do you arrange this scenario? Collectively, an offense needs to work as a team to maximize the space available to players; players must then capitalize quickly on the sudden availability of space. Individually, players must learn to recognize defenders who are out of position and find the easy cuts that result. Throwers need a clear sense of available, and desireable, throws. They must be able to recognize an opportunity before it's gone.

Conversely, a defense wants to limit the availability of space for the offense, taking away precisely what the offense seeks. The principle of space dictates that players in team defenses cooperate to cover the greatest possible territory. Individually, players must constantly reposition to minimize free space available to the offense. They must vie for the inside position when defending against floating hucks.

As we'll see, a strong sense of field space contributes to many aspects of good play in ultimate.

Weight

Motion demands balance. Off-balance players have compromised control over their bodies. Beyond balance, a proper command of your weight allows you to direct your force during throwing, running, and jumping. We collect all such aspects of motion under the principle of weight.

A good understanding of weight and balance is fundamental to any sport. In ultimate, the speed and stability of throws depends on skillful weight-shifting by the thrower. Defenders must maintain proper balance, with weight centered over the hips, to be able to respond to the jukes and cuts of offensive players. A cutter can capitalize on a defender's improper footing, using the body to keep the defender at bay. A thrower can break a marker who has lunged from the waist instead of moving with the legs. A marker can take advantage of a thrower who has overcommitted to a single option. In all aspects of gameplay, the ability to control and adjust weight and balance is fundamental.

Communication

Every team sport demands constant communication among players. Listen to the on-court chatter at an NBA game. Watch the organization of volleyball players as they reposition for every touch. Imagine football players trying to move the ball without calling their plays. Communication makes for team harmony. Without good communication, there *is* no team, no whole greater than the sum of its parts. Communication enables a group of seven on-field players to act in unison on offense and in concert on defense. It allows a global, coordinated effort that greatly increases the chance of success. Put plainly, without communication team strategy can't exist. Any breakdown in communication weakens a team.

Ultimate, too, requires communication to achieve synchrony. Communication allows markers to hear threats they can't see; allows throwers to signal to teammates via on-field audibles; allows

Ultimate requires constant communication between team members on and off the field to achieve success.

© Marshall Goff

sideline players to alert on-field players to defensive lapses; allows cutters to tell loitering offenders to get out of their way; allows markers to tell teammates when a stall count is high; allows struggling defenders to call for help; and enables defenses to switch the mark instantaneously in the middle of play. Off-the-field communication—after a game, over dinner, via e-mail—is also important. Communication helps a team achieve its potential. If you fail to communicate a useful thought, observation, or piece of information, you bring your team down.

Efficiency

The principle of efficiency is the Occam's razor of sport. Occam's razor is a principle dictating that things should not be multiplied or divided unnecessarily. When possible, it's preferable to keep things whole rather than break them up and to keep things simple rather than complicate them. In sport, efficiency means that we do only what is necessary to complete the task best. Extraneous motions, words, directions, and other expenditures of energy, are just that—extraneous to the task at hand—and should be avoided. In this way, we get the most out of our limited bodies. Efficiency in words also aids in the flow of communication.

Your energy reserves are limited, so it makes sense to be as efficient in your play as possible. Efficiency leads to clean and simple play, whereas inefficiency can cripple a team in many ways. A cutter who does not quickly clear away from an important space might make it impossible for the offense to advance. An inefficient throwing motion might introduce wobble and imprecision in the flight path or cause a delay in the throw's release. At the least, it diverts energy from the throwing effort. A receiver who takes an unnecessarily long path toward the disc might not get to it in time or reduce the options available to him or her after the delayed reception. Efficiency comes from a clear understanding of your goals and taking the necessary steps toward realizing them. A thrower need only fake out the marker enough to release a pass unfettered. Making wild fakes and pivots without a clear concept of their utility wastes time in the stall count and might create an unbalanced throw, resulting in a turnover, loss of point, and possible defeat.

Possession

Finally, we emphasize the importance of possession—that is, avoiding turnovers. In virtually every game of ultimate, the offense of the losing team has had the disc enough times to score a winning number of goals. This is usually true even if you subtract defensive blocks. In other words, in a very large percentage of ultimate games, the losing team could have won by avoiding preventable turnovers. This is a mind-blowing observation, if you think about it. The hard part is getting an entire team to internalize the principle of possession and buy whole-heartedly into the philosophy. If you can do this, we'll see your team at Nationals.

No individual and no team can be truly successful without understanding the value of possession. Curtailing preventable turnovers and maintaining possession of the disc must always be on an offender's mind. The principle of possession dictates that an offense must maximize its probability of scoring (or minimize the chance of turnover), which means that a thrower must select only intelligent throws. A throw into the end zone with an expected completion chance of 75 percent is not as intelligent as trying to score with two throws of 90-percent completion chance (90 percent of 90 percent is about 80 percent). The principle of possession can overlap with other principles (e.g., an offense that understands space will reduce its turnovers), but because this principle is so often neglected in our sport, we take special care to stress its importance. Value the disc!

The principles of focus, space, weight, communication, efficiency, and possession apply in all team sports. The process of learning to play different sports can be quite similar. Many great athletes are able to transfer knowledge from one sport to pick up another very quickly. Of course, each sport also has its own unique considerations. The pages of this book are filled with explanations of how the six principles apply to our favorite sport—ultimate.

Throwing

Throwers must be poised, in control, and focused on maintaining possession. Flashy, irresponsible throws produce turnovers. Once the disc is in his hands, the thrower looks for the best receiver to advance the disc. Where does he look? If there's no good option, how does he create an opportunity? Once he finds his receiver, which throw should he use? Forehand, backhand, hammer, scoober? Where should he place his throw? What should the flight path look like? How will the throw be affected by wind? All of these questions need to be answered in the context of maintaining possession of the disc and maximizing the likelihood of scoring.

Errors are inevitable; turnovers are not. A thrower should always give himself a margin of error in proportion to the difficulty of completion. Long throws demand more open defenders. An inside-out throw is more difficult to place than a simple throw with the force, so the receiver must be free enough to catch the disk despite some throwing inaccuracy. A certain amount of risk is tolerable in every pass—there are no sure things. A high-reward pass such as a huck or leading break-mark pass can have a proportionately greater risk, but avoid high-risk, low-reward throws at all costs.

Many different situations arise, but several guidelines apply to most throw selections in ultimate. In this chapter we'll review these guidelines and analyze several situations in detail. We'll also discuss the task of handling in general, including objectives, throw selection, and mechanics. After that, we'll discuss the finer points of the most common throws in ultimate.

Four Rules of Throwing

After you receive the disc, don't just launch it to the first cutter you see. Ensure a good chance of completing your throw by following the four basic principles of good passing:

1. Lead the receiver.
2. Make the disc catchable.
3. Put the disc where no defender can get it.
4. Avoid risky throws.

All four rules apply to every pass. Simple enough? You'd think so. Yet only the best teams apply the rules consistently throughout a game. Perhaps many errors could be avoided by keeping one other rule in mind—make sure the receiver is expecting the pass! This is almost always done through eye contact but can also be accomplished through an audible or called play or through a shared recognition of a situation. In any case, this rule is implicit in the principle of communication, and we'll assume it's always in effect.

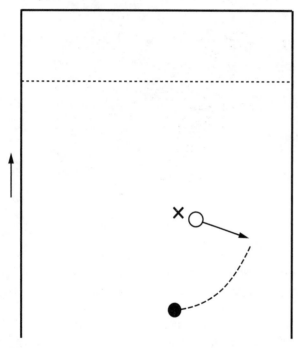

Figure 2.1 The thrower should lead the receiver, arcing the disc so that it comes to the receiver from the far side of the defender.

Consider a cutter running horizontally toward the strong sideline with his defender behind him and no other defenders in the vicinity (figure 2.1). As a thrower, you must throw the pass in front of (that is, on the sideline side of) the cutter's defender so that if both players continue at pace, the defender will still be behind the cutter at the point where the cutter meets the disc (rule 1). If the defender is much faster than the receiver, the throw might need to be thrown more quickly, so that there's less time for the defender to overtake the cutter (rule 3). But such a throw might violate rule 2 or 4 because faster throws must be precise, which means they're harder to catch and harder to throw. In some cases, an open but slow cutter might not warrant a throw, and the thrower will look for a better receiver.

Now consider the same situation, except the cutter is running diagonally (away) toward the sideline (figure 2.2) or even straight down the sideline. The defender must no longer overtake the cutter to place himself in the path of a low, straight pass, even if it leads the cutter. Thus, rule 3 is more difficult to follow. A high pass over the defender's head would generally be more risky, violating rule 4, or float for a long time, possibly violating rule 3 because other defenders might poach and intercept. Instead, a flight path that goes outside-in (that is, curves in to meet the cutter from the sideline side), might be sensible, though for a straightaway cut even this pass is rather risky. If all rules can't be satisfied, don't attempt a throw unless you're way high in the count. Note that certain throws are less risky for some throwers than for others, but don't let strong throwing skills alter your perception of risk—sometimes a throw is too dangerous no matter how strong the thrower is.

The considerations at play in shorter passes are similar for deep throws (hucks) but with a few additions. Deep throws hang in the air a long time, so the thrower must make sure no defender can interfere with the play. Also, long throws are generally much more difficult and thus more risky. But because the reward for a caught deep pass is high (often a goal), a somewhat greater amount of risk can be taken. Again, many throwers err by considering *only* the increased rewards of throwing and ignoring the risks involved.

How about a throw to a cutter running from the center of the field to the break-mark side (figure 2.3)? Generally, the defender is already in the way of the disc (or nearly so), so putting it ahead of the cutter and avoiding the defense is difficult. Matters are made tougher by the presence of a marker trying to prevent the throw. In fact, it might be difficult to satisfy any of the four rules in this situation. Even if you have a potent inside-out throw or great hammer in your arsenal, rule 3 or rule 2 (respectively) might require you to holster your weapon.

As a thrower, play in your head a mental movie of exactly how your pass will be completed. Picture the path of the disc and how it will fare against the wind. Picture the defense trying to block it and how you'll avoid the marker. Picture the reception—which hand will the receiver

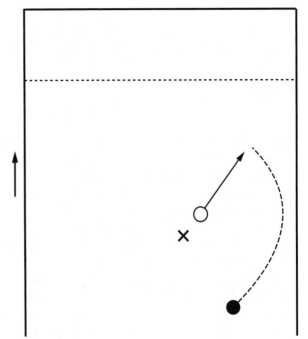

Figure 2.2 An outside-in curve works best in this situation.

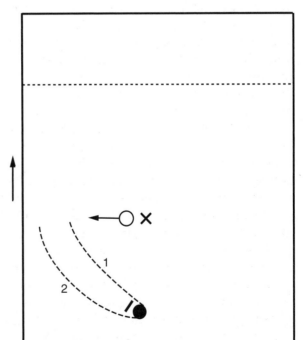

Figure 2.3 It might be impossible to make a catchable throw to this break-mark cut. Path 1 demands a fast throw. Path 2 is a difficult around or overhead throw. Both must break the mark.

use? Will he have to dive or jump? Positive imagery is a powerful psychological tool in sports, boosting players' confidence and performance levels. Forming a mental image of the development and completion of your intended play also allows throwers to apply the four rules of throwing and assess the likelihood of success. As throwers become more skilled, the visualization process occurs subconsciously. Eventually, they can glance at a situation, assess the risk, and make the correct throwing choice in a flash.

Handling

Great ultimate relies on great handlers, but great handling does not mean making spectacular throws to diving receivers in the end zone. A player with the disc must keep his poise. Scared throwers become so wrapped up in the anxiety of causing a turnover that they forget the simple steps toward avoiding one. For example, a scared thrower might make three or four exaggerated fakes without ever having a clear pass in mind. Generally speaking, a fake should misdirect the defender for a reason. A thrower must have a solid idea of what he wants to *do*, not just what he wants to avoid.

Whatever your skill level, as a thrower you must make every effort to be in control, which means staying balanced and unrushed while making your throw, even when under pressure. Maintaining poise comes from hours of practice and an understanding that hurried, lurching throws are likely to cause turnovers.

A downfield player with poor throwing skills should know that his goal after catching the disc is to continue to advance the disc if possible, but otherwise to give it back to a handler. Thus, if you're playing downfield and have just caught the disc, you should establish the appropriate pivot foot, point your body downfield, and look for easy continuation cuts—namely cutters on the strong side. Ideally, the cutter will already be there, ready to receive the pass. If so, the pass is easy to complete because it usually takes some time for the marker to apply any pressure. Passes become much tougher once the mark is on. If you're a weak thrower, look downfield for no more than three or four seconds before turning your weight back toward where the handlers are—typically behind you, if you have caught the disc in the center, or possibly lateral and slightly behind you if you're on the sideline. The timing of when the thrower shifts back to look for dumps depends on the thrower (earlier for weaker throwers), the field position, and the defense. If you have just received a pass on the sideline against a defense that's trapping heavily, you might look to give the disc back to a handler a second or two earlier. As a team, players should come to a clear and mutual decision on these matters ahead of time. Good communication promotes good timing among throwers, receivers, and handlers cutting for dumps.

The situation is similar for any nonhandler who receives a pass, even if he's a strong thrower. It's generally not wise for nonhandlers to spend much time looking for the big gainer. Most offenses work best with handlers in handler position, middles in middle position, and longs in long position. Unless a switch is called, a middle playing the role of handler means fewer options available downfield.

A handler who receives a pass must also have his goals clearly defined. All issues involving handling, as distinct from throwing, are discussed in detail in the next chapter.

Throwing With the Force

The most common throw in ultimate is a forehand or backhand throw to the strong side—that is, "with the force." As a (right-handed) thrower contemplating a with-force forehand, you should be balanced, with your torso, hips, and shoulders directed toward ("facing") the target. Step out with your right foot, away from the marker, and complete a simple pass, preferably curving in to the receiver from the opposite side of the defender because this makes the pass more difficult to block. Throws to cutters coming straight back can be difficult because the proper side is uncertain—a possible cause for miscues between thrower and receiver. An extremely slight curve from the outside of the cutter can be a useful convention.

When throwing with the force, try to step out to release the disc away from the marker's reach. This gives you more room to complete

Learn the technique for a proper throw to improve your chances of completing the pass.

your pass and might position your torso between the marker's body and the point of release. Also, if the marker has to step around your body or your pivot foot, she might become off balance.

Breaking the Mark

A break-mark throw is always a risk and a temptation. The risk of turnover is high because it's more difficult to throw a leading pass to the break-mark side, more difficult to make the disc catchable, and more difficult to avoid the marker. The temptation behind the break-mark throw is that it can result in a string of unmarked gainers and possibly a score. But as a thrower, resist the temptation to break the rules of throwing—only go for a break-mark throw when there's a good chance for a positive payoff.

All of the principles of weight apply to break-mark throws. Stay balanced when you break the mark. Throwers often err by being satisfied with any break-mark release that makes it past the arms of the marker. But a successful pass must get past the mark *and* reach the arms of the receiver. If avoiding the marker means making a hasty, falling-backward release, the pass is unlikely to hit its mark. When passing, remember to keep your head up, establish eye contact, stay balanced, and lead the receiver. To create the space to get by the defender, you might also need to precede the break-mark with a fake or misdirection.

You'll most successfully break the mark with one of three kinds of pass: inside-out, overhead, or around. Overhead passes that break the mark are not much different from those that are with the force. Of course, take care not to telegraph the throw and be sure to release it high enough to avoid the marker's arms.

Inside-out and around break-mark passes have different effects. Typically, an inside-out gainer is easier to throw than an around gainer, but it's less likely to lead to continuing offensive progress down the break-mark side. This is because inside-out throws are typically thrown toward the middle of the field, where forcing defenders are tight enough to their receivers to re-establish a mark quickly. An exception is an extreme inside-out thrown to the far break-mark side. However, this is an extremely difficult throw. Gaining around throws are typically made to neglected, poached, or just plain open defenders on the break-mark side, who are likely to be able to make a continuation throw before the mark is set. These too are very difficult throws, often because of poor leg position and an obstructed line of vision.

In considering an inside-out versus an around throw, a general rule is that inside-out throws are faster throws with less margin of error, whereas around throws are slower throws afforded a greater margin of error. This rule is a simplification, though, and a real assessment comes from considering the mechanics of the throws and the field position of the receiver and defenders.

Inside-Out Throws

When throwing an inside-out forehand under the marker's arms, don't rely on bending from the waist and stretching from the arms to produce a low release. Stay balanced, with knees bent and hips lowered. Lurching down to throw a low-release can produce a jerky motion and lead to an errant pass. The more you can stretch out, the better chance you have of putting an inside-out curve on your inside-out throw. This avoids the defender and prevents the throw from "running away" from the cutting receiver. All of these considerations apply to low break-mark backhands and forehands. Backhands are more difficult throws, however, because the cross-body release of a backhand means there's less arm extension to get the throw beyond the outstretched arms of the marker.

More than the mechanics of the throw, consider the position of the receiver, his defender, and, most important, the marker's stance. Slight variations in the marker's stance can indicate that one throw is significantly easier than another. If the marker is too straight up or too far away from you, then around throws are easier. A highly angled marker is not covering inside-out throws to the middle of the field. (As you observed in figure 2.3, if the marker shifts to take away the around throw (2), the inside-out (1) becomes more free, and vice versa.) A marker who's too close can be stepped around or beaten with a quick release. In making an inside-out, the sharper the angle of the throw (that is, the more inside-out), the harder it is to make. (By nature, inside-out throws are all small violations of the weight principle because the shoulders aren't square to the line of flight.) Another consideration is the angle between the thrower and receiver. The sharper the angle, the less margin for error—first, the throw can more easily zip by the receiver; second, the defender has a shorter distance to the flight path; third, if you have to zip the throw in, you have a small temporal margin of error, too. If you can throw an inside-out at low speed and still avoid the defender, do it!

All of these risk factors must be assessed before making an inside-out break. In most cases, a combination of risk factors must be absent before the inside-out break is a good choice. For example, if your marker is slightly overangled and the defender is trailing the receiver by an extra half step, an inside-out might be worth a try. If favorable conditions apply and you can stay balanced and low on release, you should be able to lead your receiver with a break-mark inside-out forehand thrown at a safe, low speed.

Around Throws

Around throws are typically placed into space for the receiver to run into. If they are not high-release throws, they must be thrown with a long step to get around the mark.

Don't rely on your long arms or on a stretch from the waist to get around the mark. Stretch with your legs, angle your torso, and bend your knees. Getting around the mark is more important here than for an inside-out pass because more effort is needed to get around the marker's body. As a result, you'll likely be less in position to throw a strong downfield pass and will generate most of the power from your swing. This is why around passes are thrown to space.

Sometimes a quick release helps an around pass. The marker's attention is usually toward the force-side release. The legwork of around passes can often signal to the marker that a break is coming (though she might still be unable to prevent it), but if you can sneak a quick backhand around the mark without moving your legs, you might catch her off guard. (Because there's no supporting legwork, this technique applies mainly to short passes.) Be careful, though—smart markers learn quickly.

When throwing around passes, many people make the common error of poor offensive triangulation. Imagine the triangle formed by the point of the thrower, the point of the receiver at the time of release, and the point of the receiver at the intended reception. In easy strong-side throws, this entire triangle (including its inside) remains within full view of the thrower (figure 2.5a). In around passes, however, the marker often stands in the way (figure 2.5b), obstructing the thrower's view of the triangle, in particular the path of the receiver from the time of release to the reception. When view of this path is obstructed by a defender, it's hard to lead the defender accurately. A thrower with an awareness of this problem will shift his head to the outside of the marker's to gain a good view of the developing play (this might also help in establishing eye contact with the receiver), or understand the riskiness of a poorly triangulated release and look for a different throw, thereby reducing the risk of a turnover.

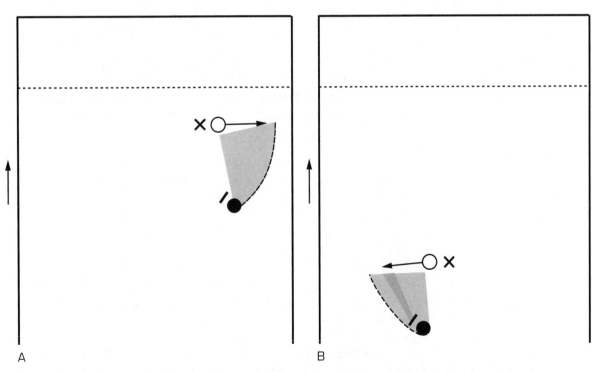

A   B

Figure 2.5 Triangulation on offense: *(a)* The thrower can see the entire development of the cut, throw, and catch (shaded area) of this strong-side pass. *(b)* The thrower's view of the shaded area might be obstructed by the marker.

Against the Trap

When on one sideline with the force toward that sideline (a "trap"), the available offensive space becomes a sliver along the line. Early in the stall count, you might look to continue the play along that sliver, but after a few seconds you'll want to move the disc to a nearby handler, thus initiating motion across the field or at least relieving the trap temporarily. To do this most efficiently, turn your body to face the marker (that is, face directly crossfield) and stay balanced. The handlers will be available for a dump or short downfield pass on either side of the marker. You'll be ready to throw either pass. As a result, the effect of the trap is greatly compromised, and the offense retains possession.

High-Release

Consider a high-release backhand thrown to break the mark (any mark). You must be sure not to jump up or merely fling your arm over the reach of the marker. If you do, the throw will have way too much outside-in curve, hardly any spin, and be extremely susceptible to the wind. It will turn over and die or catch a draft and simply blow away. To avoid this, make every effort to maintain a level throwing plane at shoulder height. The throwing motion should be a swing of the arm with very little bend of the elbow. You'll find that a too-bent elbow leads to a throw that turns over. In fact, you should try to raise your shoulders a bit to produce an inside-out curve, even in this throw to the outside, because so many high-releases turn over. (It's okay to dip the far end of the disc down slightly to get a bit of an inside-out slant; you may need to modify your grip slightly.) In other words, try to approximate a good, inside-out throwing motion in a single plane, even in the difficult context of a shoulder-level release. Finally, keep your eye on the target. For some reason, many players drop their heads when attempting a high-release.

Similar remarks apply to high-release forehands, including the dipping of the disc and the corresponding alteration of the grip. These are delicate throws for low winds only. Practice the mechanics many times before trying them in a game, and even then, think twice before launching a high-release throw.

Swing Continuation

Another throw that breaks the mark is the continuation of a two-pass swing (figure 2.6). Though the throw is quite simple, the maneuver can be tricky. Your goal in this situation is to continue the swing before your marker stops you or the defense becomes wise to the play and disrupts it. So although you're likely to have an open receiver, the trick is to catch and throw the disc with expediency and without error. If you rush, you might throw the disc before finishing the catch, or if you're not careful, you might simply turf the throw. Thus, though the catch-turn-throw must happen quickly, you won't get better results by cutting corners. Instead, focus on the task at hand. While the disc comes to you, prepare for the catch. This means shifting your weight (and hips) so that once you catch it, you'll be able to plant your pivot foot and throw. Also, if you're free enough from your defender, get your momentum moving in the swing direction. (If you release the disc before the third point of contact with the ground, you don't have to slow down.) This preparation must be done in advance, so that when the disc comes, you simply catch it. Once you make the catch, look to the continuation direction to see that the receiver is ready and free. Now, if your marker hasn't caught up, you're ready to throw. (Be sure to give the swing continuation your first look—

there might not be time to complete it if you look elsewhere first.) This catch-turn-throw combination takes some practice, but each component is simple enough and should be recognized as a separate part of the play. The faster your turnaround time, the less likely your marker will be able to respond.

You can hasten the turnaround time at the expense of some legwork but only if the gains in doing so outweigh the loss of positioning. Sometimes you can sneak out a low backhand before the defender even responds. And, to be honest, short but ill-positioned forehands that are released quickly might not be very difficult because short throws can be made entirely with the arms and are independent of what's happening with the legs. Another trick to employ, particularly when a swing continuation seems unlikely, is to immediately look back to the same side. Downfield defenders expecting the swing might give up a with-force opportunity. Or, if you can get your marker to lean toward the force, you might have an easier time swinging around her.

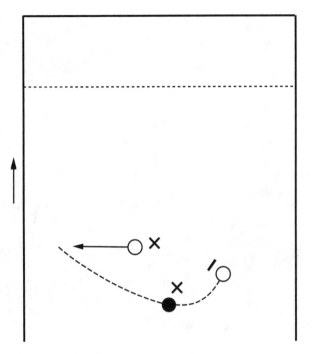

Figure 2.6 Swing continuation.

Overall, the ability to catch from one side of your body and quickly release a balanced throw from the other side gives you a considerable advantage.

The Huck

When throwing a huck, consider that the throw will be in the air a long time, won't be as accurate as a shorter throw, and will take longer to set up and release. Generally speaking, with a huck, the only risk-assessment factor working in your favor is the greater reward that results if successful.

The mechanics of a good backhand huck are similar to those of any other good throw. Let's assume for the moment that the huck will be released without any significant mark to an open cutter. For extremely long distances, your throw should be inside-out, as instabilities can cause most long throws to turn over. Outside-in hucks demand more strength behind them because these throws are inherently less stable. They also might be more difficult to catch if they fall sharply to the ground, so a gentle curve is preferred. Despite their relative difficulty, in practice outside-in huck chances are far more common than inside-out chances, so be sure that you're comfortable with the distance. Also, for cutters moving partially crossfield, an outside-in curve avoids the defender better. For any huck, the disc should remain roughly in one fixed plane during the throwing motion (figures 2.7a-c). Any motion out of the throwing plane will introduce wobble, which affects accuracy and distance. Your throwing plane should be angled appropriately for the curve of your throw. That is, the angle of the disc should come from the angle of the throwing plane. Don't change your grip to introduce tilt; the tilt should come as a result of the throwing plane being tilted. For an inside-out

A   B   C

Figure 2.7 For a long throw, the swing should remain in a single plane of motion, or close to it.

throw, this means leaning over from the torso, whereas for an outside-in, you should adopt a more upright stance than usual. Longer throws also need more spin because spin diminishes during flight, introducing greater instability at the end. To generate enough power and spin, step forward and out and untwist your torso while throwing. The backhand huck is not a violent throw—most of the distance comes from your weight shift and the power that your legs exert in untwisting the body.

Because forehands are released more quickly and at a greater distance from the body, they are easier to release without interference from the mark. However, it's often difficult to produce a forward weight shift when stepping out. Good throwers can step out and forward at the same time, shifting weight with a simultaneous turn of the hip. This, together with the whip of the arm from a forehand throw, can produce enough power for a truly long huck. The forehand snap is more violent than the backhand motion, which makes it far more susceptible to the wind. It takes a great deal of practice to achieve the suppleness and strength of hand needed for a forehand huck into the wind. Less-skilled throwers might be satisfied with stepping out and backward a bit with their nonpivoting foot, then shifting their weight forward during the throw to resemble a pitcher's throwing motion. Note that this takes more time and that the disc is released closer to the thrower's body. Consequently, it's more difficult to avoid the marker's efforts—but if the marker is off and a little extra power is needed, it's okay to try this throw.

Hucks are in the air a long time, so they must be thrown to areas with no defenders anywhere in the vicinity. They should be thrown well in advance of a sprinting cutter who has a defender at his heels. The receiver should run into a gently settling huck and clap it with two hands. Any huck caught by a receiver "skying" (catching over) a defender is a throwing error. The receiver deserves an apology and a thank you.

Know your throwing range and don't attempt throws outside it. If you have to make a great effort to gain the distance you need to complete a huck, you're probably throwing outside your range. Don't expose the belly of the disc to the wind. This invites trouble because even a slight wind shift can carry your throw off target. High throws float, so keep the disc low. Keep in mind that most hucks that end in a cluster of players waiting for the disc to alight fall incomplete.

■ Drill: Practicing the Huck

This drill is good for practicing throwing, catching, and defending hucks. Conditioning and sprinting benefit, too. Form two lines and designate one thrower and one retriever. Player A (offense) cuts deep from line 1. Player B (defense) starts a halfstep back from line 2. The thrower launches the huck. After the catch, players recycle to the opposite line and return the disc to the designated retriever while remaining clear of the next play. After several throws, replace the thrower with someone new.

Now let us return to reality, where markers are present and throws are not released unimpeded. In reality, you can't always release the huck as you would like. This means you'll need to alter the ideal mechanics of the throw, so your margin of error is reduced. You must also get around the mark, so let's turn to this point.

The huck takes more time to release than a regular throw, so the thrower must be sure that the marker is not in position to hamper the release. Many hucks run afoul from the start, when the thrower must make a slight adjustment after a motion by the marker. Slight deviations at the start of a long throw lead to great differences in flight path. These deviations even include abbreviated follow-throughs meant to avoid contact with the marker. Although the follow-through occurs after the throw, most abbreviated follow-throughs are "planned" during the throw and affect the motion before release.

Getting a free huck means much more than getting it past the mark. As a thrower, you can employ many techniques to throw the marker off the scent of the impending huck, including throwing fakes, shifting your weight to the opposite side and then back again quickly, and faking with your eyes. A warning—before releasing the disc, make sure you have not faked your receiver into believing you won't throw it long. He might have broken off his cut if he thought you lost interest.

On the receiving end, good positioning and timing of the jump might be the equivalent of six inches of vertical rise. What this means to the thrower is that the choice to throw to a tall but unopen receiver is almost always a poor decision. Ideally, the reception happens in stride, on the ground, with the defender out of the picture.

The Dump

Resetting the stall count is a crucial aspect of any team's offense. When flow is halting, the offense must reposition the disc, reset the count, and look for new opportunities. In many cases, the dump as a repositioning throw can be a potent offensive tool. Of course, the dump is also a safety against a rising stall count.

More than any other throw, the dump demands thrower-receiver communication, usually through eye contact. As a thrower, communicate to the intended receiver, usually a handler in the backfield, by locking eyes briefly. (In fact, the handler should anticipate when the dump is coming, but eye contact establishes synchrony.) You then take advantage of the space in the backfield by tossing the disc slowly to an area that the receiver can get to before his defender. Because of the large amount of space in the backfield, an open area can be found in almost every circumstance (except, say, for an offense caught in its own end zone). In some cases, the throw is right to the receiver; in other cases the throw is a leading throw to space, over the head of the defender and receiver. In any case, don't throw the dump too fast. All four rules of throwing are in effect here.

The dump pass is often a thrower-initiated pass, which means the throw precedes the cut. A defender in the backfield often faces her offender, with eyes away from the thrower. This allows the thrower to place a dump throw into backfield space, and the receiver responds before his defender, allowing him to retrieve it first. It's important for throwers and receivers to understand (and perfect) the timing of this thrower-initiated maneuver because it's almost unique to the dump.

The timing of dumps is important and should be discussed as a team. If you turn to dump too early, you risk taking the receiver by surprise. As the stall count creeps up, the dump becomes your best option—but once your marker knows you're looking to dump, she can shift her attention toward covering it and work with the dump defender to prevent this last remaining option (figure 2.8). The following dangerous sequence sometimes occurs: (1) look to dump, (2) look away too early, (3) turn back to the dump in desperation, and (4) turn the disc over.

By looking for your dump exactly when the backfield handler (or other receiver) expects it, you'll be able to release the throw before your marker can respond. If she does overcommit to stopping the dump, you can often turn downfield again quickly and find an unmarked option.

For throwing a dump over the heads of the defender and receiver, a high-release backhand is the best option because it travels high and

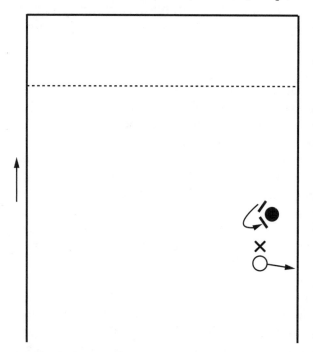

Figure 2.8 If you begin a dump-cut motion too early, you might run out of space by the time the dump is needed. In this figure, the stall count is high, and a slight shift by the marker allows the defender to take away any easy dump option. The only remaining choice might be to go over the head of the defender. If the throw is rushed or if the defender moves close to the thrower, this can be a difficult pass to complete under time pressure.

slowly. Most dump throws are backhands, in fact, because they can be thrown slowly and accurately (the whipping motion of a forehand makes it difficult to throw slowly). In windy conditions, the high-release becomes very difficult, and an upside-down throw might actually be safer.

The Hammer

The flight path of a hammer—high trajectory with a quick descent—makes it a potent offensive weapon when used appropriately. Most often, the hammer is used for throws to the break-mark side, especially in a zone or clam defense, or by a right-handed thrower against a forehand mark. The hammer can sail over a defender and sink into the arms of the receiver. However, be aware that hammers tend to float too long, particularly in a wind. They are also the most challenging throw to catch because they often arrive at an awkward angle, sometimes requiring a Willie Mays, over-the-head type of catch.

Keep your throwing motion in one plane, even for the hammer. This means that in traveling through the throwing motion, the disc slices through the air as an extension of your forearm. You'll have to tilt your torso (because an upright torso results in a vertical blade, for most throwing motions), but you'll be able to release a smooth hammer that comes back down to earth without turning over too soon and floating, giving the defense time to come over and intercede. The hammer should fly with a nearly, but not quite, vertical blade-like trajectory. When a rapid descent is not required, the throw should flatten out at the end of its flight. If you release it too horizontally, it will float (with some exceptions—a high-speed hammer can fly far and true with an upside-down, horizontal profile, but this is an extremely difficult throw to use in a game).

Hammers are most often thrown to an open or poached receiver or one traveling away from the disc. Don't try a hammer to a cutter in full sprint.

Other Throws

When throwing other throws (scoober, push pass, blade, thumber, and so on), heed the four rules of throwing and try to assess the probability of completion. Most of these throws are quite difficult, which is why more standard throws are used instead. If part of your motivation is to look really good on the field, your assessment is likely to be skewed by your ego. Instead try attaching your ego to team success and enjoying the thrill of a shared victory.

Forehands, backhands, and hammers all have different mechanics, but the principles of good passing are universal and constant. Throwers must remain balanced, poised, and prudent about taking risks. Throws must lead receivers, elude defenders, and remain catchable. These points are the essence of good throwing and decision making and are prerequisites for great handling.

Handling

THREE

© Marshall Goff

Until now, we've taken a triage approach to the offense of throwing—survey the situation, and take the best alternative. But a handler who receives the disc has the opportunity, and responsibility, to be creative on offense. This is done in collaboration with the cutters, of course (a pass takes two), but the decision on how to proceed is made by the thrower—and the handler is the player in whom the team has placed the most trust in this matter.

Many teams will play with unequal handlers, such as one who's in charge of jump-starting a sluggish offense with a breakthrough throw and another who is counted on to be more conservative and reliable in his or her choices. Another setup might be a "point guard" type of handler in charge of structuring the offensive flow, with the other handler in a supportive (or subordinate) role.

That said, we should recognize that the choice of how to proceed is usually straightforward for any player, following the guidelines discussed in chapter two. Good offense consists primarily of good cutting that leads to routine throws and catches. But when the offense is not ideal, handlers cannot continually use "dump to handler" as a fallback option—or else the offense goes backward! Thus, we must discuss the unique responsibilities of the handler position and how as a handler you can work to get what you want out of your offense.

Sometimes the offense does not flow smoothly. It's the responsibility of the handler to make a real-time diagnosis of an ailing offense and prescribe an antidote. To do this, a handler must understand how his team's offense is designed to work. Is the intent to clear up deep spaces for long throws? To progress with many small cuts from the front of the stack? To beat a zone with a dump swing? To go through or over the cup? A clear sense of the offense is necessary to recognize what might go wrong, what needs to be fixed, and how to fix it. A sense of defense is necessary for anticipating the motions of the opponents. For instance, a handler who doesn't understand which situations are likely to lead to poaches is more liable to throw into one.

An offense with a keen defensive sense stays out of trouble and anticipates offensive opportunities before they arise. For example, a handler might see that the last back defender is suddenly fronting. He will be ready when his teammate bursts deep. Seeing this opportunity too late might mean not having the distance to lead the receiver.

Many of the responsibilities inherent in marshalling the offense are discussed in this chapter, but it can take years to develop the requisite skills and form a rapport with teammates. In most of what follows, we'll focus on the immediate concerns of the handler. The handler must always be working, with or without the disc. The cycles of play with the disc and without the disc repeat themselves. Let us consider each in turn.

With-the-Disc Play

Suppose you're a handler who has just caught a pass. What you do next depends on what kind of pass you have received. There are three basic kinds of passes—in-flow passes, repositioning passes, and reset passes—which mirror the three aims of an offense: to gain yards, to move to a better position on the field, and to maintain possession. We'll consider each kind of pass in turn.

In-Flow Pass

If you have just caught a leading pass down the line or are otherwise "in flow," then the same principles apply to you as to any other player: Look for the easiest way to continue to gain yards at minimal risk. That is, you should immediately look downfield in the direction of flow. Let's say you're catching a pass down the line, which might be the case if the defense overcommits to covering the dump behind the thrower, giving you the opportunity to go downfield. As you're now in a power position, you should look first for a huck and then down the line, to see if there are cutters ready. If so, take the easy gainer. If not, there's often a viable secondary option, say, a crossfield or up-the-middle pass, before the mark becomes a hindrance, while the offense is still in motion. In general, receiving a pass in flow puts you in a good position with an extremely low stall count. Even if the continuation option is not available, you're still in good position to make a repositioning pass, which might create options for another thrower.

Repositioning Pass

Handlers try to place themselves to receive a pass in a strategic location, with weight and momentum positioned to quickly capitalize on available opportunities. We'll discuss how to set up for such a pass below, when we talk about away-from-disc handler play. For now, let's assume that you have just received a repositioning pass. This might mean that it's the first pass in a swing formation from one side of the field to another. It could also mean that it's a centering pass. It could even be an early-count dump. In any case, any repositioning pass or cut should be made with a specific intent. It's implicit among all offenders that a repositioning pass is made to take advantage of, or at least explore, an opportunity. As a handler, you have an obligation to look toward the completion of the play, be it a swing, a throw to the middle for a look at both alleys, or a dump backward to create an opportunity for a free throw deep. (An offense might be more sophisticated, say by creating a false expectation among the defense that it will continue the obvious play, then run an unexpected sequence—but generally a rogue handler who controverts the intentions of his offense will only introduce disunity and disloyalty.) If option A is unavailable, there are always secondary options B and C. In the case of a swing, a quick antiswing (back toward the direction the disc came from) can catch the defense off its feet as it runs in anticipation of a swing. Or, as a result of the throw and catch, you might have a sudden strike opportunity, such as a pinpoint throw to an offender who has become open as his defender misreacts. Of course, if the best intended option is unavailable, and secondary options are too risky or are covered, then the repositioning pass did not have the desired effect, in which case a reset pass is most appropriate.

Reset Pass

If as handler you receive a reset pass or dump from trouble, then you might not receive the disc in a position of advantage to you—the purpose of the pass was merely to maintain possession. (We'll discuss later how to set up to receive the disc in a way that gives you an advantage.) You do have the disc with a low stall count, however, and it's up to you to look for ways of creating offensive progress.

In the best of circumstances, you simply watch as a cut develops downfield—say, on one of the alleys or even deep—and then complete the throw to the now-open receiver. This is what a healthy, well-oiled offense looks like. Handling becomes a breeze. If, however, the machinery is not working on its own, it might need some grease. As a handler, you drive the offense and must know what you want to do. What's the priority of your offense? Is it the long game, leading cuts away from the disc, hardscrabble or squirrelly short cuts, comeback cuts, crossfield play, up-the-middle play, or a weave? You should know the goals and strengths of your offense and ensure that the seven on-field offenders are working together to achieve them.

To get the offensive movements you want, you might need to shout commands to the offense, signal with your hands or eyes, call an audible, or even call time-out to discuss the situation or construct a play. Here communication is paramount—if everyone understands what you (as offensive spokesman) want, they'll be able to work with each other to achieve it. If you're near the end zone and your team has an end-zone play, it's up to you (with or without the disc) to cue your team's shift to red-zone play. If there's a prevailing wind to the right, you might have to yell to teammates that the offense wants to progress down the left side of the field—otherwise, there's a natural tendency to flow right, and you'll get stuck there. If you're playing against a zone, make sure your offense recognizes this and takes appropriate positions. Communicate to your teammates by yelling out, "Who's popping?" If you have a long forehand with a backhand force, you might yell, "Free forehand!" to drop a hint for a long cut.

The situations in which you will receive reset passes are too many to name, but the pattern is the same. You must first know what the ideals of your offense should be, based on a combination of the circumstances and what you've practiced as a team. Second, you must see what the offense is doing. Third, you must communicate to the offense how to change in order to accomplish what you want to do. Sometimes this is as simple as yelling "Cut!" to a lagging squad.

After four or five seconds, you realize that the cut you envisioned might not be in the works and begin thinking about getting rid of the disc. (You might have done so even sooner, say, if another handler was wide open after a poach by a defender.) Right now, there's probably another handler trying to get free for a dump, break-mark, or inside-out throw up the middle. Such passes in the middle of a stall count can lead to downfield continuations. Even if your fellow handler is free enough, though, getting past your defender might involve a break-mark throw. It is up to you to judge the risk. An offense can't survive without ever making a gaining throw, so if there's a pattern of stagnation, don't be too conservative. Bear in mind that you need only one string of throws to score—or sometimes just one throw.

If all efforts at progress have been exhausted, you should make a reset pass to another handler who might be in a better position or has a lower stall count. If this pass is covered, you must avoid getting stalled. Listed in increasing order of risk and reward, your last-chance options include

1. calling a time-out,
2. making a leading throw to a covered dump,
3. making a pinpoint throw to a covered offender, or
4. making a hospital ("Hail Mary") throw deep.

In most cases, the risk of a hospital pass outweighs the reward. Considering that an offense can score most of the time (and for some teams the percentage in which they score is quite high), possession is the number one concern in a crisis. Thus, option 2, the leading throw, is the easiest to complete and the best choice, absent other factors that make successful completion of a pinpoint throw or hail Mary more probable. The keys to completing a throw to a covered dump cut are eye contact and placement. You should toss the dump cut lightly, over the defender's head if necessary, into a region of open space from which the defender is blocked (by the receiver). There's typically enough open space, even if your marker is harassing you late in the count (this is sometimes more difficult on the sideline, but even then you should have enough space). Note how the principles of possession and space combine here with rules 1, 3, and 4 of throwing (see chapter 2).

Fakes

Throwing fakes is an important part of handling but is wasted if not used purposefully. If you see a developing or existing cut you want to hit, you might need to misdirect the marker in order to achieve a viable throwing lane. In this case, throwing a fake is useful. Gross, exaggerated motions are unnecessary or even counterproductive—you want to make the marker, and not yourself, shift weight to the wrong direction. If you want to throw a break-mark inside-out forehand against a force forehand, say, and the marker is too straight up, you'll need to push her left. Taking a long step left to fake a backhand with a huge backswing will induce the marker to shift to cover your throw, but now your weight is also committed to this throw. You might not be able to get back to the business of throwing the intended forehand before the marker recovers. Many players chant "Pivot, fake!" as though this mantra alone will dissolve the mark, missing the distinction between making these motions and employing them toward a specific goal. You need only move enough to induce the marker to shift her weight or move her arms out of the way, and if you can do this without shifting—with eye fakes, head fakes, slight shifts of the hip or motions of the arm—then you'll be able to get back to your forehand while she's still out of position. Slight pump fakes can gain a few inches on the mark, and this alone might be enough insurance for you to release a throw comfortably.

If you don't see a developing or existing cut and are holding the disc, waiting for the offense to act, you're wasting your energy if you blithely pivot back and forth—a serious violation of the principle of efficiency. Further, there's no guarantee that in doing so you'll be in the right position when a cut does appear. Instead, be patient and wait in a balanced stance, so you can shift quickly when necessary. In general, pare down your faking routine to the essentials. Act purposefully. Be efficient and intelligent.

It might help to consider break-mark attempts, and the fakes that go with them, as either quick or slow (a concept further discussed in chapter 5 on cutting.) On a quick break-mark, you throw the disc before the defender has a chance to block it. Usually, this results from a positioning error by the marker overplaying the mark in one direction. (In fairness to the defender, this counts as an error only because you're quick, talented, and opportunistic enough to exploit the small gap. If you were a slow faker, the positioning might be correct.) Perhaps she is playing nearly straight up instead of force backhand, and you can throw a forehand around her without faking at all, or maybe she's marking you tightly with her arms high and you can throw it quickly under her. A type-A personality who brushes his teeth while reading the paper should probably employ quick fakes. Deliberate, cautious players will generally want to use slow fakes, a series of moves that wait for a reaction from the marker before the final throwing motion. A step to the forehand side, drawing the marker over, before stepping around for a backhand huck would be a slow fake. An example of something in between quick and slow would be if you faked a hammer and immediately went to a forehand, making sure before you released the disc that the marker reacted to the hammer fake. If she instead covers the forehand, you're prepared to try something else like a step to the backhand or even a repeat of the same fake. Whatever fake you employ, it must be believable—that is, similar to a movement you'd make during your actual throwing motion. If you fake with a big backhand windup and get the marker to bite on it, she might look like a fool that time. However, you really haven't accomplished anything, and you'll be the one who looks like a fool the next time, when the marker doesn't respond to the fake.

© Marshall Goff

With or without the disc, players must focus on their responsibilities in the game.

Without-the-Disc Play

As mentioned, handlers cycle between with-the-disc and without-the-disc play. Away from the disc, the handler has several responsibilities on which to focus. In fact, only one of the main responsibilities of a handler requires control of the disc. In general, the primary responsibilities of a handler are as follows:

1. To feed good throws to good cuts
2. To reposition the disc for downfield play
3. To help maintain possession
4. To reorganize the offensive structure when necessary
5. To receive yard-gaining passes when opportunities arise

At its most basic, handling involves throwing good, easy throws to good, open cuts, but this is the only responsibility that requires control of the disc. When without the disc, a handler has the other priorities in mind. We'll start with repositioning the disc for downfield play. To reposition the disc effectively—say, by receiving a swing, an up-line short pass, or a low-count strategic dump—you must seize the opportunity. For example, when playing against a trapping defense (one marking toward the sideline), a quick swing is a potent threat. You should be able to read the coverage. Sometimes a defender will cover the backward or lateral swing pass in anticipation of a swing, leaving a cut up the line free. Seize this chance (without cutting off a freer, longer sideline opportunity) because sideline throws are easy against a sideline trap. Conversely, if a without-disc handler's defender is too worried about the up-line play, there's likely to be enough time and space available to catch and complete a swing play to the break-mark side without trouble from the defender (who is focusing on the up-line). Sometimes the tension between offender and defender playing for the backfield and up-line cuts becomes a cat-and-mouse game that repeats itself every few passes.

At times, there might be two handlers without the disc. If so, they need to coordinate among themselves who will be cutting. For example, one might cut up-line and the other cut for the swing. Or the second might cut to complete the swing off of the first. One might play closer to the disc, and the other can respond to the first. These setups can change from throw to throw or remain in effect the entire game. Either way, coordination is crucial. Having two cutters for the same cut is almost as bad as having none. Two defenders in the neighborhood make completion unlikely. When the disc is in the middle of the field, if both handlers are on opposite sides, coordination is more difficult. Communication (verbal and nonverbal) and coordination among handlers is a must.

Some offenses will play with a "cag" or "dump handler," who remains in the backfield as a dump option for every pass. Dumps that occur early in the count can create unmarked throwing opportunities because many defenders fail to cover the dump closely until the stall count begins to creep up. Of course, this scenario also arises for offenses that play without regular cags.

Be vigilant. Opportunities abound at every turn. Your defender glances away, and suddenly you're free. Or you notice the marker has shifted, allowing you to receive a quick, break-mark backhand. A handler's without-disc play overlaps with that of other offensive positions (which we discuss in the next chapter).

The next primary responsibility of the handler is to maintain possession. As a handler, you must be there when needed. A dump must always be available to a thrower, especially in the face of a rising stall count. If you leave the backfield, make sure another handler remains for the dump—or else appoint a new player to take over the vacated role ("Joe, stay behind the disc!"). To abandon a thrower is to fail in your duties. To be sure, the defense will sometimes overplay the dump, forcing you to go up-line or clear away from the backfield. If you don't get the disc as a result, then you or another handler must cycle back to fill the backfield vacancy.

Maintaining possession might also mean cutting for, or throwing, short passes up the middle or slight break-marks. Such throws become available when, for instance, the backfield defender and marker have overcommitted to stopping the dump. The thrower turns downfield again and is rescued by an alert handler (or other player), who takes a quick step away from his defender and catches the short throw.

Apart from your own cuts, you help your offense by remaining alert. If you see an opportunity for the player with the disc or if you find an easy option for a downfield cutter, simply speak up. You fail your team if you withhold valuable information.

Perhaps the most difficult part of a handler's game, and requiring the most experience, is the responsibility to reorganize the offensive structure. We've already seen how a handler can use his knowledge of the offense to communicate to teammates, and this applies to away-from-disc play as well. The task of organizing the offense includes everything from calling an end-zone play, to aborting the play called on the line, to calling "Zone!" or "Junk!" at first recognition of a defensive set other than one on one. Add this to the other handler responsibilities, and compound it with the possibility that a team has not seen a force-middle mark all season, and it becomes clear that poise and presence of mind are vital qualities of good handlers.

How to Get What You Want

As a handler, you know what you're looking for on offense. Sometimes the cutters don't comply. If the offense is still running smoothly, don't sweat it. But if the offense is not running smoothly, it's your responsibility to get them to move the way you (and the team) want them to. There are several ways to get what you want. You might simply ask for the cut that you want when you have the disc. You can make this request by establishing eye contact with a receiver and subtly motioning. You can direct traffic either via hand signals or by speaking, even before you get the disc. (This might mean motioning to a teammate to cut to the break-mark side as you're cutting for the swing cut, for example.) If the stack is dragging, you can direct the offense to "Keep moving!" or "Push forward!" During a fatiguing point, you might whisper to your best sprinter, "Go long next time!" This sets up a plan and ensures special focus on a high-reward play, diminishing the risk involved.

We'll discuss various offensive and defensive structures later, along with their advantages and disadvantages. For now it's enough to say that as a handler you must have a clear vision of your team's offensive priorities and philosophy. You should know what you want to see in your offense and recognize the pitfalls your team tends to fall into. Organizing the flow of the disc demands that you recognize the defense, too. Whenever you're not focused on the mechanics of a play, cast your attention to the flow of cutters and defenders, making specific suggestions, cataloguing observations, and gaining an overall feel of the offense.

Finally, we should mention that handlers, just as anyone else, can catch goals should the opportunity arise. If a handler, without forsaking his dump responsibilities, decides to go downfield, he contributes to his offense's versatility. Many defenders won't be prepared for a handler's sudden burst downfield. Also, consider that many defenses put an agile, but not necessarily tall, defender against a handler. If you find a mismatch on offense—in height or in speed—then by all means exploit it.

Handler Talk

A handler should be in constant communication with his cutters, on and off the field. After a point, a cutter might want to know why he was "looked off" (not thrown to) by the handler. Perhaps the handler thought the cut was too late or that the cutter was not at full speed, or maybe he simply didn't see the cut. Sometimes a handler wonders why there's no cut at an advantageous moment. Discussion might reveal that the would-be cutter didn't have the energy or momentum to make the cut. Or maybe he was preparing for a cut off a swing that the handler looked off. Whatever the case, these kinds of off-the-field discussions about choices made on the field help your team achieve harmony.

As a warning, not everyone sees these discussions in a neutral light. Many exploit the chance to get in a snide comment or rebuke. Sometimes the situation is just too heated for dispassionate discourse, and a handler should just let things be. As a kind of "field marshal," a handler should exercise diplomacy. Complimenting and encouraging cutters fosters the kind of good will that allows for frank discussion of offensive difficulties.

Handling is a multifaceted skill, and good throws are just the beginning. Like all team members, handlers must be ready and able to cut and throw. Moreover, because they get the disc many times during a point, poise with the disc, the ability to create and recognize throwing opportunities, and consistency in throwing (and catching) are paramount. Handlers are also responsible for maintaining the structure of the offense. They must develop a thorough understanding of the offensive philosophy, real-time recognition of field situations and the proper responses, and the ability to communicate effectively with on-field teammates. A handler's skill in all these areas usually results in team success.

How to See Everything at Once

Field vision is an important mark of a good handler. Here are some tricks for being able to "see the field."

1. Remember where teammates were before you lost sight of them. When you turn your head away from a situation, remember who was where. You might have to turn your head back later in the stall count, so be prepared for what you're likely to see.

2. If a teammate was moving, he probably continued to do so. If you turn away while someone is running, when you turn back to him, he'll have progressed to a new position. Of course, he also might have changed directions. This is why you never want to throw completely "blind."

3. Figure out why things happen. Say you see an extra defender or one who's on the ground. This means a receiver must be open. Find that player or ask where he is. You might hear a defender yell "Strike!" This call can alert you to an easy pass you would have otherwise missed. Clues are all around—learn to look for them and find them.

Catching

FOUR

© Marshall Goff

Perhaps more than any other skill in ultimate, catching is a mental skill. Of course, good mechanics are the foundation, but less quantifiable attributes such as focus, intensity, and aggression play significant roles in determining whether a disc is caught.

There are four phases to the catching process: recognition of the disc, approach to the disc (or point of reception), execution of the catch, and aftermath (landing or preparation for the next throw). One phase should transition smoothly to the next. As you see the disc being released, you shift your weight to gain maneuverability. You adjust your path based on the disc flight and nearby defenders. You catch the disc and begin turning downfield. You are now in position to release the next pass.

Recognition

You should recognize when you're open and the disc is coming your way. Normally, you'll be in the middle of the cut with some separation from your defender—unless perhaps you're being thrown to in desperation at stall nine. At this point, you might make eye contact with the thrower, who communicates that he's ready to throw to you. When you see the disc released, you need to shift slightly from all-out mode to one in which you'll be able to alter your path. The change in speed is almost imperceptible, but you'll be more in balance with less weight leaning forward.

Approach

Your approach to the disc often makes the difference between an easy catch and a tough one. A poor approach might lead to the disc being blocked without your ever touching it. Consider a cut to the sideline slightly back to the disc (figure 4.1). The pass is neither too fast nor too slow, with a small amount of outside-in curve. If you continue in a straight line, you'll catch the disc more or less in stride at point B. However, a better option would be to flare out to point C. The catch itself will be a little easier, as the relative speed between you and the disc is reduced. You'll also gain a few more yards, but more important, you'll be well-positioned to deliver a yardage-gaining pass, as your defender won't be in marking position yet. (Some throwers deliberately flare the receiver to keep the defender away and keep the cutter moving—especially if the cutter is inexperienced and tends to stop prior to catching.) This plan of attack won't work if the disc is underthrown, in which case it will be moving too slowly to make it to point C or point B before the defender does. In such a case, or in any situation with the defender in hot pursuit, you need to be aggressive and catch the disc as soon as possible at point A. This is not the time to be timid or to squeeze a few extra yards out of the pass. That pass was thrown to you, so go and get it! You have to believe that it's yours, that you have a right to it. Turn in to the disc as soon as you realize it's coming up short, planting off your outside leg for a sharp change in direction. You might even need to reach forward with your inside hand to catch the disc before the defender knocks it away.

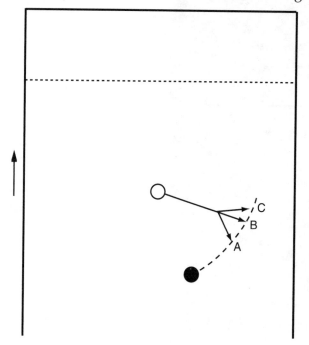

Figure 4.1 The receiver can catch a comeback cut at several locations. Point C is the most advantageous, but it might be necessary to go to point A or B.

One of the goals of the approach is to position your body so that the disc is immediately in front of you when you catch it. Reaching to the side introduces asymmetry and makes it tougher to catch the disc cleanly or recover from a mistake. This goal can conflict sometimes with another goal, which is to keep the defender away from the disc. On block attempts, your defender will usually be on your inside, so you need to keep the disc on your outside until just before the catch. The flare described above does this. Another way is to keep the disc on your outside shoulder. Then you can either reach with your outside hand for a one-handed catch (figure 4.2) or turn your upper body toward the disc so it's in front of you again. Neither way is perfectly reliable, but both are preferable to letting the defender block it. This goal also comes into play when boxing out on a floating disc, as we'll see later in the chapter. A third goal of the approach is to create a better angle to the disc. It's easier to catch a slow-moving disc than a fast-moving one. If you're cutting straight back to the throw, your velocity adds to the velocity of the disc, giving you less time to react and clamp your hands around it. At the other extreme, if

Figure 4.2 Sometimes a one-handed catch is best to keep the defender away.

you're running alongside the disc, it's as if the disc is not moving forward at all, and the catch is just a matter of grabbing it.

Execution

Almost every pass is caught by either the pancake catch or the one- or two-handed rim catch. The best catching technique for you is one that's reliable, repeatable, adaptable, and comfortable. No single technique is perfect for all situations, so you need to be able to choose the best one. There's some controversy on this topic, to be sure.

Established players who don't have a problem with drops should probably continue using the same basic technique even after reading this. Let's consider these methods in turn.

The most commonly used method is the two-handed pancake catch—also called a clap catch (figure 4.3). This method is the best for beginners because it requires little feel or timing, doesn't hurt the hands, is easy to learn, is robust, and can use the torso for backup.

In the pancake catch, you clap your hands together on the flat part of the disc. During the catch, the disc should be between the waist and the chest, which might require you to jump for the higher ones and slide or bend at the knees for the lower ones.

Your hands should be perpendicular to each other about a foot directly in front of your chest and 6 to 12 inches apart. Until they improve at judging the height of incoming passes, newer players might place their hands farther apart and exaggerate the clapping motion, but this is inefficient and might lead to misalignment when the hands are brought together and could cause a drop. If the hands are

Figure 4.3 The pancake catch. Hands are 6 to 12 inches apart and elbows bent.

parallel to each other instead of perpendicular, this too can lead to misalignment, especially if you have to adjust your hands to the side. If the disc is fast moving, you can use your chest or stomach to cushion the catch, which is called "curling your body around the catch," but your hands need to make first contact so that the disc doesn't bounce off your chest. Watch the disc all the way into your hands, and let your hands move with the disc toward your body while you're catching it. This reduces deceleration and makes it less likely for the disc to bounce out. The very best catchers with soft hands close their hands so smoothly that you can't even hear the contact.

The pancake is unequivocally the preferred method for catching while stationary, such as when playing zone offense. You have time to adjust your body so that the disc is directly in front of you, and you can cradle the disc against your body, if necessary. For routine catches under no defensive pressure, the simplicity of the pancake makes it the catch of choice. In windy conditions, too, the pancake catch is best able to handle last-second vertical motion of the disc.

The two-handed rim catch has its advantages, too. With this method, you grab the rim of the disc with your fingers just as it comes into the crook of your hands, which act as a backup (figure 4.4a-b). If the disc is moving slowly, it's okay for your hands to be on the side of the disc instead. If the disc is above your chest, your thumbs should be below the disc, two to four inches apart. If the disc is below your chest, your thumbs should be above the disc, with your little fingers two to four inches apart. In both cases, spread your fingers wide for a maximum catching area.

Your arms can be fully extended with the rim catch, giving you a foot more of reach than you get with the pancake method. Another advantage of the rim catch is that it requires fewer body adjustments for high or low passes. You can simply reach up for passes at eye level instead of jumping, or reach down, bending at the waist if necessary, for thigh-level passes, all without breaking stride or slowing down. In addition

A   B

Figure 4.4 The two-handed rim catch. Keep your thumbs up for *(a)* low passes and *(b)* thumbs down for high passes.

to catching the disc sooner, you can begin adjusting your feet and body for the next pass. More on this in the Aftermath section.

Use the two-handed rim catch (with thumbs up) for all layout catches where you can get both hands on the disc. With the pancake catch, you don't have a firm grasp on the disc, so the ground can easily dislodge it.

Use the one-handed rim catch (figure 4.5) for leaping catches and those too far away to reach with both hands. The technique is the same as for the two-handed rim catch, except there's a small adjustment based on the spin. When the disc comes in contact with your hand, it will continue spinning about the point of contact because of the friction. Consequently, you'll need to adjust your hand position slightly toward the spin. Most passes will be thrown with outside-in spin, and you'll catch the disc with the hand farther away from the direction the disc is coming from. For example, for a right-handed forehand, you'll be running from left to right, so you'll use your left hand. The disc is spinning counterclockwise (as viewed from above). It will tend to spin out of your hand on contact, so you need to reach farther around the disc (to the left) and adjust the point of contact a little bit toward the little finger so that the disc spins into your hand. With a backhand spin (still using your left hand), the disc will spin the other way, toward your body, so you wouldn't reach around the disc as far.

Figure 4.5 Use the rim catch when diving because ground contact can dislodge a pancake catch.

You can easily practice by yourself to get familiar with the spin. Stand and toss the disc directly in front of you with a lot of spin so that it goes up flat a couple of feet into the air and then floats slowly down. First, simply catch the disc a few times using the two-handed rim catch, concentrating on the feeling in your hands when you grab the disc. Next, put your hands in the same position but allow the disc to spin in your hands for a second or two before grabbing it. On successive throws, use the left, right, and both hands to grasp the disc and note the difference in how the disc spins off your hand. Visualize a pass coming in with that spin. Reverse the spin and go through the whole process again. Experiment with where on your hand and on the disc the contact is made. Continue until you're comfortable with how the disc reacts.

In rare circumstances, you might need to do a trailing-edge catch if the disc is moving by you too rapidly to catch it another way. With the trailing-edge catch, you grab the back edge of the disc as it goes by you by swinging your arm in the same direction. Ideally, your hand will be moving at the same speed as the outer edge of the disc at the point of contact (this will be the speed of the disc plus the rotational speed). If done correctly, the disc will not spin in your hand at all and will be relatively easy to grab.

Catching in a Game

Keep in mind when you're developing your catching techniques that you will be in motion for almost all catches during a game. Learn to adjust your path so that your arms are directly in front of you as you catch. If the disc is even six inches off-center, one arm will have farther to reach, possibly resulting in a misalignment (on a pancake) or nonsimultaneous contact (on a rim catch) (figure 4.6a-b).

A   B

Figure 4.6 Adjust your path to catch the disc in front of you. Reaching to the side can cause *(a)* misalignment or *(b)* nonsimultaneous contact.

In practice, expose yourself to as many combinations of incoming direction, speed, and disc angle as time allows. Then when a difficult pass comes at you in a game you'll be able to identify your best technique immediately, allowing you to focus on the disc's flight, the sideline, and nearby defenders. Needing to think about or reconsider how to catch the disc diverts your attention and leads to drops.

Most drops in a game are probably caused by lack of focus, which becomes a factor when you're fatigued. It's a good idea to practice catching, throwing, and focusing while tired. We recommend the Drill From Hell.

Drill From Hell

One thrower and one receiver stand about 10 yards apart. The receiver cuts quickly from side to side while the thrower throws a variety of passes at different speeds, heights, and angles. The receiver must focus on catching as well as making good return throws. Continue for 90 hard seconds, then switch roles. Do three sets of 90 seconds each.

Aftermath

Proper foot and body positioning during the catch prevents turnovers and improves field position. Proper positioning after the catch improves your chance of landing inbounds or in the end zone. Especially in closely contested games or in other disc games that have small end zones, such as goaltimate or hot box, many catches must be made near a boundary line and require a special effort to stay inside the line.

Let's begin by examining the footwork for a typical pass between waist- and head-height, neglecting for the moment concerns about staying inbounds or preparing to throw. The receiver needs to get to the disc before the defender, keep his head stable for good hand–eye coordination, and minimize the chance of jarring the disc loose. There are three basic techniques for passes between waist- and head-height:

1. Short hop (skip)
2. Jump through
3. Run through

Short Hop (Skip)

This technique is used primarily when coming back to (running straight at) the disc without a defender close behind (figure 4.7a-c). For the technique to work, the disc must be at least belly high. Just as the disc is about to arrive, you take a short step, slowing down a little in the process, and hop into the air as if skipping. Keep hands close to the chest with bent elbows. Keep the hopping leg down and land on that same foot after catching the pass. The hop can steady the head and body prior to the catch, reduce the jarring on the ground after impact, and allow you to use your body to cushion the catch, if necessary. The short hop is especially well-suited for passes coming in at shoulder- or neck-height, since the few inches gained on the hop allow the disc to be caught at a more comfortable level.

A   B   C

Figure 4.7 As the disc is coming in, the receiver *(a)* takes a short hop, *(b)* catches the disc in mid-air, and *(c)* lands on his hopping leg.

Figure 4.8 The jump-through catch. For a full-speed catch, note how the receiver's weight is forward and he can land in stride.

Figure 4.9 Use a run-through catch on a leading pass while pancaking or at any time with a rim catch.

Jump Through

This is really a faster version of the short hop, with the hop replaced by a full-step forward jump (figure 4.8). As with the hop, the basic idea is to catch the disc while at your peak in the air. Extend the arms away from the body and allow the trailing leg to move naturally, landing in stride after the catch. This generally requires a couple of steps after landing to stop. The jump through is probably the most common way to catch a pass.

Run Through

The receiver simply catches the disc without breaking stride (figure 4.9). This is the preferred way to catch a leading pass but is also becoming the preferred catching style of good receivers on comeback cuts. The main benefits are that the receiver maintains mobility and is immediately in position to pivot and throw. He doesn't have to slow down to make the catch as he would while jumping or hopping. In addition to making a diving block less likely, the run-through catch reduces the chance that the receiver will be injured by the defender. The downside to this technique is that the jarring from running causes a slight decrease in hand–eye coordination, making the catch less secure. It's also a more difficult technique to perfect.

There are also several techniques available for passes below the waist, including the crouch, bend, slide, and dive (figure 4.10a-c). Keep in mind that any body-to-ground contact increases the likelihood of a drop.

• **Crouch.** Similar to the hop, the crouch is generally a good technique for comeback cuts when the defender is not in position to make a diving block, provided that the disc is not too close to the ground. The receiver should slow down on the final step before the catch and bend at the knees, usually pancaking the disc and using the chest as a cushion, if necessary. This catch can also be used when the receiver is stationary, such as in a zone offense.

- **Bend.** While keeping stride, the receiver bends at the waist and reaches down for the disc, usually trying a rim catch (two-handed if the disc is in front of the receiver, one-handed if the disc is on the side). The advantages and disadvantages are the same as with the run-through catch described previously.

- **Slide.** If the disc is very low to the ground, and the receiver can slow down (either because the defender is not close or because the disc is behind the receiver), he can slide feet first.

A

B

C

Figure 4.10 *(a)* Crouch, *(b)* bend, *(c)* slide.

Figure 4.11 Keep your weight back to drag the trailing foot in bounds.

Figure 4.12 The scissor technique allows for greater extension and keeps your back foot down. With the traditional two-foot drag, you might be pulled off the ground.

• **Dive.** A rim catch is more secure than a pancake because you're gripping the disc during the postcatch slide. Often, taking an extra step and running through the disc yields a better chance for success than diving, and it's certainly less dangerous for you and your opponents.

Now let's move on to special situations. For high passes near the sideline, the best technique is a combination of a short hop and jump through, which takes advantage of the rule requiring only one point of contact inbounds. Approach the disc as with the jump-through technique, but after pushing off, keep your weight back and your jumping leg behind and lower than the leading leg. Extending your toe back, allow your foot to touch the ground lightly, placing no weight on it, and come down with full weight on the leading leg (out of bounds) (figure 4.11).

For passes near the sideline that don't require jumping, two variations of a scissor technique yield good results. The conventional technique is to drag both feet just inside the line and reach out while falling over. However, this often results in both feet coming off the ground with your momentum. The scissor technique leaves just one foot on the ground, while the other is used for leverage or extension. This technique also lets you extend your reach a bit (figure 4.12).

For passes low to the ground, make a hard plant with one foot while lifting the other, twisting your hips and shoulders toward the disc at the same time. This accomplishes three things. First, the lifting of one leg throws the other leg down and puts more weight on it, making it less likely that it will come up during the catch. Second, you'll be able to reach a little bit farther because your upper body can twist to face the disc. Third, your impact with the ground won't be hard and won't be on your chest, reducing the risk of a drop. For full-speed layouts, you'll need to modify this technique to eliminate the twisting motion because of the injury risk involved. Simply lift one leg slightly while lowering the other, dragging the lower foot on the ground lightly. Your upper body will still bear the weight of your landing, but your first point of contact will be inbounds.

For higher passes (anything up to head-height), the technique can be done at a full sprint and does not result in ground contact with the body. After making a hard plant just inside the line with the back foot, allow the other leg to come forward while keeping the back foot on the ground. Reach forward with the front arm (or both, if possible), bending at the waist if necessary, and grab the disc to prepare for the continuation pass. If you're near top speed, your foot will roll over onto the toes (which is why the plant should be a few inches inside the line); otherwise, the sole of the foot remains in contact with the ground throughout. This technique can also be used on the goal line, reaching out to the playing field while keeping the back foot planted in the end zone.

Positioning to Throw

You can also use good footwork to position yourself for the next throw. Whatever method you can use to get your hips and shoulders aligned properly most quickly is the best method. Generally, this means turning to the outside, momentarily turning your back to the flow. (This contrasts our recommendation for pivoting, during which it's seldom a good idea to turn your back to the flow because it's difficult to reorient yourself.)

In some situations, however, an inside turn is recommended. If you're behind the disc and already facing downfield, or if you have to twist your shoulders toward the disc to catch it, it's simpler and quicker to continue turning that way. Another technique can be used on comeback cuts when there's no threat of a block. Slow down before the catch and jump off the inside leg, twisting your hips inside at least 45 degrees while keeping your shoulders square (see figure 4.13a-b). In effect, you're beginning your pivot before catching the disc. As you land, complete your hip turn so that you're facing downfield, and your shoulders will naturally follow your hips. For a forehand, your landing leg is your pivot, while for a backhand, your other leg is the pivot. In either case, continue naturally with the nonpivot leg and throw the continuation pass. This technique can be readily modified for swing passes where you're stationary. Face the thrower with hips and shoulders square. As the disc is coming in, lift up the forward foot and pull it back, turning your hips toward the downfield area while keeping your shoulders and upper body facing the thrower. After the catch, complete the hip turn and let your shoulders follow so that you're facing downfield.

Putting It All Together

Good receivers are aware of many things while making a catch, weighing all factors to maximize the chance of scoring. As the disc approaches, consider the following in this order:

1. Is there anything about the throw (wobbly, fast, high, low) that will make it difficult to catch?

A   B

Figure 4.13   Twist your body before the catch *(a)* to be able to deliver a quick continuation pass *(b)*.

2. Is anyone in position to make a block?

3. Do I have to worry about staying inbounds?

4. Do I have to worry about staying in the end zone?

5. Will I have a continuation cut waiting?

If the circumstances make you question whether you'll be able to make the catch, then forget about everything else until you have the disc in your hands. But if there's nothing that indicates potential trouble, begin planning your footwork and body positioning.

A Word on Percentages

Since no offense is perfect, it's worth some amount of risk to gain additional yardage, especially if the yardage results in a goal. A good rule of thumb for an average team is that 10 yards of field position increases the scoring percentage by 10 percent, as does being in the end zone instead of on the goal line (for better teams, use a percentage increase of 5 percent). What if you can use a specific tactic or technique to stay in the end zone on a pass near the goal line that results in a drop one time in 50 but in goals the other 49 times? Comparatively, your team would be ahead of a plan that results in a catch outside the goal all 50 times, because on average that would lead to a subsequent turnover on 5 occasions.

Boxing Out and Skying

Let's look at special techniques you might use to catch in front of a defender, primarily on long, floating passes. Skills include reading the flight of the disc, establishing and maintaining possession, and getting the most out of your jump ("sky").

It is the thrower's responsibility to make passes as catchable as possible, but poor throws and shifting winds can make the disc float out there, just waiting for you to take it. The rules for doing so are simple:

1. Keep the disc in front of you.
2. Don't let the defender inside or in front of you.
3. Keep moving, speeding up the last two steps.
4. Jump off your inside leg, driving upward with your other knee and arm.
5. Grab the disc with one hand at your highest point.

The rules of ultimate say that when the disc is in the air, you have to play the disc and not the opponent. This means that basketball-style boxing out (pushing out with your butt while backing up and spreading your arms wide) is illegal. However, it does not mean that you have to step aside to let your defender past or that you need to keep running at full speed until you're directly under the disc. You're allowed to keep a defender at bay while running to the disc, as long as you're making an honest effort to catch the disc. If the defender gets by you, you've lost. On the other hand, keeping the defender away from the disc doesn't do you any good if you can't catch it. Thus, slight alterations in your path that give you a positional advantage are acceptable provided that the path leads you to a viable point of reception. Keep the disc in front of you the whole way. If the disc has any curve to it, it will curve more as it slows down. Beginners often make the mistake of running to where the disc would come down if it kept on the same trajectory, neglecting the additional curve. (Teammates on the sideline often have a better perspective on the flight and should be yelling "Back!" or "Left!" or "Right!" to the receiver.)

Early in the deep cut, you'll be sprinting to get separation from your defender and be able to chase down overthrown passes. Once the disc is up and in front of you, keep your eye on it, taking occasional glances to see where the goal line, sideline, and defender(s) are. Given the constant feedback, your brain will do a fairly good job of estimating where the disc is. If you can get to the disc in plenty of time, ease up a little so you'll be able to keep on running to the disc. If you go too far and the disc floats too much, your defender will be able to get a running start and have a better line at the disc. Give yourself enough room so that you can go all-out toward the disc in your final two steps. (Many players will stutter-step just before the jump to get their timing down. You'll get better results if you can keep stride.) Suppose you're tracking down an outside-in backhand huck so that the disc will be coming in from your left. You'll be jumping off your inside (left) leg. (If on defense, jump off whichever leg is more comfortable because you don't have to worry about making the catch.) As you approach the disc, take a very slight hop off your left leg while swinging your right hand back. Then, keeping your hips low, step quickly from your right leg to your left as you jump. Your right hand, which was trailing, swings forward and up into the air, along with your knee. Think "low-high" (figure 4.14a-b). This drive gives you your height. Strive to catch the disc at the peak of your jump, when you're at your highest point and are momentarily stationary. Try not to think about unavoidable contact

A   B

Figure 4.14 *(a)* Get low and swing your arm back. *(b)* Drive upward with your knee and arm.

with other players or the ground while catching. Catch the disc first, then adjust for what follows.

Occasionally, you'll be unable to take a running jump off one leg. Perhaps you'll be standing for a swing and the disc will soar, or you'll cut deep but the disc will float for so long that you'll have no chance but to wait for it. Whatever the pass, you'll have to jump straight up off both legs. The technique is similar: Get low, swing your arms, and push off. If there's an opportunity, take a modified two-step run-up, as a spiker does in volleyball. Step with one leg, swing both arms back, step with the other leg and crouch, and spring up, pushing with both arms to the sky. Usually, you'll try to catch the disc with only one hand, but still use the other to push up. Get low, go high.

You can become a better and more trusted receiver by focusing on the whole process of catching. Great hands are only part of the story. Good receivers make the catch as smooth and easy as possible by beginning to position themselves the instant the pass is released, then executing the catch when it's time. They also have in their repertoire a package of nimble moves that allow them to come down with the disc in tight circumstances. They recognize the situation, decide what needs to be done, and they do it.

Cutting

FIVE

Photo courtesy of Jackie Bourgeois

Though the handler position might appear to be the most glamorous, cutters are the lifeblood of an offense, keeping things flowing. Good cutters provide wide-open targets and lead to uncontested goals. Poor cutting leads to forced throws to covered targets and a clunky, slow-moving offense. To become a good cutter, you first learn the general principles of cutting during flow, understanding *what* and *where* before moving on to *how*. Learning specific techniques will give you several ways to outmaneuver defenders. In this chapter we also include tips for special types of cuts (deep and dump cuts) and details on how to move without the disc.

Each throw of the disc should accomplish at least one of the following three things: gaining yardage, improving position on the field, and maintaining possession. Down-field cutters generally focus on gaining yardage. A secondary although still important consideration is getting the disc into position to deliver another yardage-gaining pass. Handler cuts should generally focus on moving the disc to a more threatening position on the field. Late in the stall count (or earlier for poor throwers in tough situations), maintaining possession becomes the primary concern. Such a focus usually results in dump cuts or short reset cuts from a handler, although bailout cuts occasionally come from a downfield receiver.

For any type of cut, speed, agility, and quickness are necessary, but these raw skills take you only so far. Beginning cutters try simply to outrun their opponents, perhaps after throwing a nominal fake. If they're athletic enough, or if the defenders don't know how to play, the cutters can still get open, but they'll never get out of this pit and will struggle against good competition. Proper cutting relies primarily on "timing," which really comes down to three separate skills:

1. recognizing that a cut should be made,
2. knowing who should go where, and
3. knowing when to go.

In a more general sense, "timing" is similar to the principle of space. As we'll see later, being in the right place to capitalize on this timing also requires communication and focus.

To some extent, all aspects of cutting are team-dependent. A team with great long throws has a different offensive structure than one with many quick handlers. A newly formed team of somewhat experienced players might establish the cutting hierarchy based on positions called before the point, whereas a veteran team might have an uncalled but real hierarchy based on individual players' skills. Most teams also have plays where the cuts come from specified positions in the stack. To determine the right action to take, you need to know the basic structure of your team's offense and how you fit into that structure.

Recognizing That a Cut Should Be Made

One of the biggest offensive flow-killers is when a good thrower gets the disc in a good position without a mark but doesn't get a cut. This occurs when receivers don't recognize the situation. So what are the situations for cutters to watch for?

- Good flow or fast break. A series of short passes gets the disc moving, and the defense must play catch-up. The cutter who's not yet involved in the play needs to get active and stay active until the goal is scored or the flow is stopped. In typical flow, as you'll see later, setting up a cut often involves walking or slow jogging, but fast-break mode requires steady running or even sprinting.

- Break-mark pass that gains yardage. The defensive players will all be on the wrong side of the offense, and the marker is behind the thrower. The offense should be off to the races.

- Leading "away" pass with the force. This is the best opportunity for a huck during regular flow offense.

- Swing pass beyond the stack. The stack is out of the way, there's a lot of open space to cut to, and no defender is in position to poach.

- Unmarked throw after a turnover (especially in your own end zone) or when a turnover is imminent, such as when an obvious throwaway is flying.

- Dump pass to an unmarked handler. A dump to an uncovered handler in the backfield—particularly, early in the stall count—often sets up an opportunity for an easy long throw.

- Marker out of position. A marker might have abandoned the force because of an overcommitment or late-count shift.

What all these situations have in common is that the thrower has an unmarked throw available—sometimes for a split second and other times for several seconds—and can deliver a yardage-gaining pass. Receivers must read the situation and make their cut so the thrower can hit them with a pass.

Knowing Who Should Go Where

Another major flow-killer is when receivers recognize that a yardage-gaining situation exists, but the proper player doesn't cut to the proper position. This occurs usually when there are no cuts or too many cuts.

Having no cuts can result from players being out of position, tired, timid, or confused about the hierarchy. This is, of course, bad. Generally, more than one player is in position to make a good cut (although there's usually one player in a clearly preferred position), and if two players start cutting at the same time, one of them can usually see this and stop the cut almost immediately. Typically, this will be the player farther downfield. If this player chooses not to stop, he can yell at the other player to stop or clear. Generally speaking and all else being equal, the player farther downfield should have the right of way because his cut stands to gain more yardage. Some teams might have a different cutting policy. Whatever the policy, it must be well known to all team players. If neither player breaks off the cut, though, the thrower has to decide whether to throw to the less desirable cut, try a more difficult throw to the better cut, or, most likely, look off both cutters.

So why does this happen? Being tired or timid isn't a valid excuse. At the very least, if you know you're not going to cut, get out of the way by moving to the opposite direction from the flow. Consider also that if you're tired, it takes less energy to make one hard cut and score than it does to do nothing and then play defense after a turnover. Being out of position is usually caused by a lack of focus, failing to follow the changing position of the disc and the other players. If it should be your cut, but you're out of position, communicate this by shouting ("You go!") to a better-positioned teammate that he's now the preferred cut. If no one else is in position, then just apologize so that the others know that you recognized the opportunity and will make the right cut next time.

So how do you determine who should cut? It's impossible to give a fixed set of rules that absolutely determine the hierarchy, but there are some guidelines. First priority goes to the players called on the line before the point. Good offenses usually specify the order of the first few passes at the start of a point, after a stoppage during flow (pick, foul, and so on), or after a turnover. Next, if there's a stoppage, the cutters in a called play are determined by their position in the stack. This also occurs during basic regenerative offense. For instance, a typical basic end-zone offense is to throw a swing pass to the first player in the stack, who then throws a strike to the last player in the stack cutting to the front corner of the end zone. As different players rotate into these positions, they cut.

However, you can't come up with a rule for every situation, so sometimes priority goes to the player with the best position on the field. This is where ultimate playing judgment comes into play. At its most basic level, whoever can most easily get open should cut. To determine which player is in the best position, weigh several factors, including proximity and angle to the open spot, proximity and relative position of the defender, current speed, knowing what the thrower expects, and the usefulness of the cut.

Let's determine the preferred cutter on some variations on a common situation, a swing pass from the sideline to the middle of the field. The goal is to continue the flow for one or two more passes. Only a complete analysis of the situation will reveal the preferred cutter; hard-and-fast rules (such as "last in stack cuts") will lead to a less-than-optimal play.

Scenario 1: The pass isn't very long and it's backward; the handler is not in position to deliver a big strike because the cutter is too far away. Thus, the next handler in the stack should cut for another comeback cut, and if this pass is successful, the last player in the stack should cut for the following pass (figure 5.1).

Scenario 2: The pass is a little bit more leading but still not far enough to provide an immediate strike opportunity. The next handler has already begun to cut in the other direction for the original thrower so is out of position for the first handler. Thus, the third player in the stack (now the first player in the new stack) cuts for the continuation (figure 5.2).

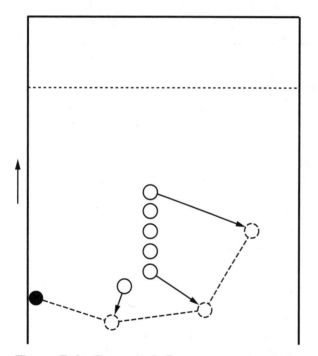 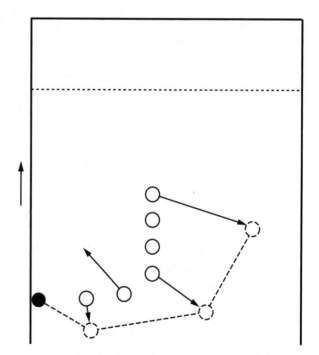

Figure 5.1 Scenario 1: From a normal stack in a trap situation, the first handler cuts for a dump, the second handler cuts for a swing, and the last player in the stack cuts for the continuation.

Figure 5.2 Scenario 2: The second handler is out of position, so the third player in the stack cuts for the swing.

Scenario 3: The first pass is a leading pass that takes the handler beyond the original stack, so he has a clear field in front of him. The last player in the stack should cut for the continuation. This is the most efficient of the options (figure 5.3).

Scenario 4: Same first pass, but the stack is too deep, so one of the players in the middle but toward the back (in this figure, the fourth player) cuts. (figure 5.4)

Scenario 5: Same first pass, the stack is the proper length, but the last player in the stack is on the wrong side of the stack by a couple yards or the next-to-last player in the stack is a couple yards on the continuation side. This could happen if the last player is also attempting to set himself up for a cut toward the disc on the original side. Another way this could happen is if the next-to-last player is still in the process of

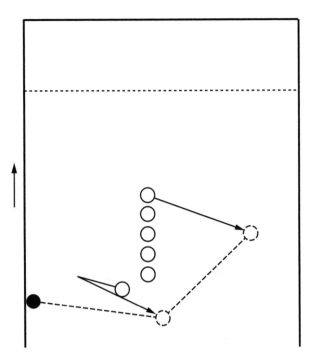

Figure 5.3 Scenario 3: For a leading pass beyond the stack, bypass the swing to the second handler and go directly to the last player in the stack.

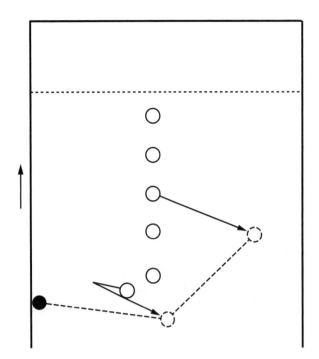

Figure 5.4 Scenario 4: If the stack is too deep or long, someone in the middle of the stack cuts for the continuation.

clearing from the original side, and his defender is lazily trailing. In this situation, both players need to realize that the default rule "last player cuts" doesn't apply, and the next-to-last player should cut (figure 5.5).

Scenario 6: The first handler has cut up the line unsuccessfully, so the second handler cuts back for the swing. It's unlikely that this handler will be in position to deliver a big yardage gainer because usually his defender will be in the way. Thus, the next player in the stack (third in the original stack) cuts for another swing, followed once more by the last player in the stack (figure 5.6).

Scenario 7: Very similar to the above case, except that the timing of the handler cuts is different. Here, the defender covering the first handler is well positioned, but the defender covering the second handler is cheating well off his man, leaving him wide open for the swing pass (which might require a break-mark pass if the thrower is being forced toward the line). The second handler needs to tell the first handler not to cut ("Don't cut!" or "Clear!" or "I go!"). Once this happens, the rest of the play continues as before (figure 5.7).

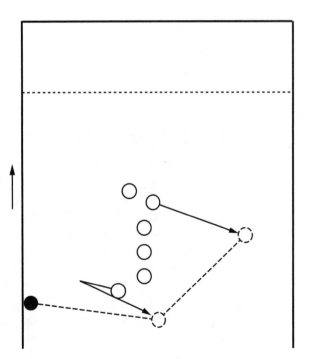

Figure 5.5 Scenario 5: The stack is in the correct position, but the last player in the stack is out of position, so the next-to-last player cuts for the continuation.

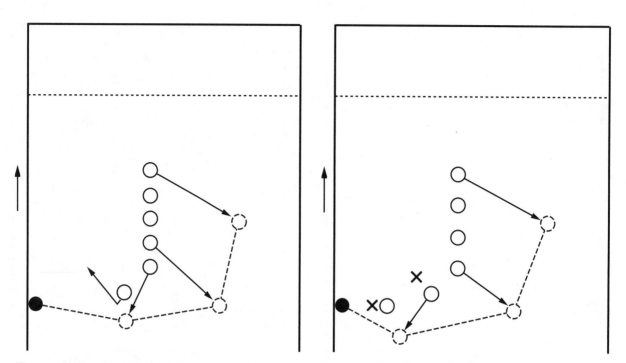

Figure 5.6 Scenario 6: The second handler receives the dump but is not in position for a continuation strike, so the third player in the stack cuts for the swing.

Figure 5.7 Scenario 7: In a trap situation, if the second handler sees that he's being given the dump cut, he communicates this to the first handler and cuts for the dump, then play continues as before.

The same hierarchy shown in these examples applies to less structured situations during flow. Positioning is much more of a dynamic process during flow, and the current speed of the cutters and relative position of the defenders are more important.

Make Your Own Cut

Sometimes cutters alter their cuts to give the thrower an easier throw. They might curl into the middle of the field to avoid necessitating a break-mark alley throw, though this means less space and more potential poachers. They might avoid the curl-out crossfield hammer cut because the throw seems too hard. They might suddenly abort a deep cut because they thought the throw would have to be too far. These maneuvers can lead to turnovers if the thrower was expecting the correct cut. Plus, a nonoptimal cut is often more likely to cause an incomplete pass. Although it's noble to try to appease your teammates, it's more noble to play good ultimate and trust them to do the same. Make your own cut—the best cut—and trust the thrower to make the right throw.

Knowing When to Cut

A well-timed offense is a joy to watch, and even more fun to be part of. The disc just glides down the field, never resting in anyone's hands for more than a couple of seconds. Often, the player who makes the first pass never catches up to the disc.

Cuts should be timed so that the receiver is breaking open in full stride at the exact moment the thrower is in position to start his throwing motion. The thrower knows that the receiver is committed to the cut, but there's still plenty of room to complete the cut. The right time to start the cut depends on the following factors:

- The speed and acceleration of the player making the cut
- The distance to the open space
- How quickly the thrower can catch and throw

Slower downfield receivers need to start their cuts earlier. In mixed play, or in recreational play in which there's a great disparity in speed between teammates, this can lead to a dysfunctional offense because the timing for different cutters is so different. Longer cuts also require cutters to start earlier. If the cutter has a longer cut, he should start the cut as soon as it's clear that the disc is going to be caught, typically when the disc is still at least 10 yards away from the thrower. But if the cutter needs to take only a couple of steps to get into an open area, as is typical for a handler cut, he can wait until just before (or just as) the thrower catches the disc.

After some practice, figuring out when to cut becomes fairly straightforward. Assessing how quickly the thrower can catch and throw, however, is more difficult and is what really determines how smooth an offense is. As a receiver, you need to assess if the marker will be in the way, if it will be a quick catch, how quick the particular thrower is, how good the thrower is at breaking the mark, and if the thrower will be expecting your cut.

Although it seems that you'd have to be watching the marker to determine whether she'll be in the way and able to stop the immediate pass, you can generally tell just from the angle of the cut. If the receiver is cutting away from the disc at all or straight across the field, he will almost always have an immediate throw available because the marker will be far enough behind the throwing lane. This is also true if the receiver is coming back to the disc but still going mainly across the field (less than about 30 degrees), and the angle between the disc path and the cutter path is less than 90 degrees (figure 5.8). In less mathematical terms, if the receiver is running in more or less the same direction that the disc is flying, he won't have a marker right away because his defender will be behind him.

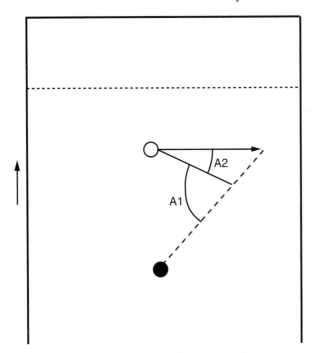

Figure 5.8 If the angle between the cutter and the disc path (A1) is less than 90 degrees, and the cutter is moving almost laterally across the field (A2 < 30 degrees), the marker will usually be unable to mark right away.

Unless the receiver can make a quick catch in stride without jumping, the timing of the next cut will be delayed by at least a second if not destroyed completely. The extra time needed to set after the catch allows the marker to set up and could also allow the downfield defender time to reposition herself and take away the open cut.

If the thrower has poor break-mark throws or is slow at getting around the mark, the cut needs to start later and from farther away. If the thrower is less skilled on all throws, the cut needs even more margin and should probably be a comeback cut to the open side. A cut for a good, quick, precise thrower, on the other hand, might allow only about a yard of extra space for margin.

Whether the thrower expects a cut is a function of the thrower, the team, and the situation. Experienced offensive players consciously and unconsciously apply the described guidelines and know whether a good immediate cut is likely. Less experienced players need to rely on a well-defined and well-known (but more predictable and less flexible) offensive structure. In the scenarios shown earlier, such an offense might always have the first handler cut up the line, the second handler cut for the dump or swing, and the third player in the stack cut for the second pass, even if the defensive positioning screams for something else.

If you have begun your cut too late, flow might be hindered or the pass become unavailable. If you have begun your cut too early, you might be able to throw in a juke to delay your cut while remaining open, but slowing down is not the answer because this allows your defender to catch up.

Cutting Techniques: The Four Rules of Cutting

Of course, knowing what to do or where to go isn't that useful if you can't get by your defender to do it. A continuous, ever-changing battle between cutter and defender takes place on the field, and the winner is generally the one who gets to dictate the playing conditions. An alert cutter has the advantage of knowing when and where his next cut should go, whereas the defender needs to split his attention between the cutter and the disc, because good defense requires frequent repositioning based on the changing flow.

Getting open requires a combination of misdirecting (convincing the defender that you're going to a place other than where you truly want to go) and positioning yourself so that you can simply run to an open space. The best cutters recognize the exact moment at which no more fakes are necessary—although they'll occasionally continue faking to get more open or to save energy. Poor cutters won't recognize when they're open and will continue faking when the defender is beaten. Good cutters understand the following rules of cutting:

1. Take what they give you.
2. If you really want something they're not giving you, fake them into giving it to you.
3. If you're not sure exactly what you want, fake until they give you something, then take it.
4. Actively get out of the way when someone else has a better cut.

Take What They Give You

Sometimes a defensive player will choose not to defend a particular cut. Say, for example, the receiver is much faster, in which case the defender might stand several yards behind him to reduce the risk of getting beat deep for an easy goal. More often, the defender makes a positioning mistake or fails to adjust to the flow, and nothing stands between the receiver and the open space. In either case, a cut that's freely available requires little or no faking. If this happens, don't be content simply with getting the disc. Maximize the yardage gained or get into position to deliver a big pass. Take advantage of the opportunity.

A surprisingly common example illustrates both types of defensive "giving." The offense is stacked off a stoppage, and the defense is in one-on-one defense. Often, each defender will match up in front of the player he's guarding, except for the last defender, who might stand at the very back as a last line of defense (figure 5.9). As the disc is put into play, the last offensive player in the stack suddenly sprints in on the force side. If none of the defenders flare out to help, the cutter will be open for a 20-yard pass or longer. While this cut is happening, the next-to-last player in the stack begins edging in slowly, as if he's getting ready to spring back to the disc, causing his defender to shift in with him. As the first cutter catches the disc, this second cutter makes a hard fake back to the disc, plants, and sprints deep for the easy goal. Neither cutter had to do anything more than take one step and begin sprinting when the defender was not expecting it.

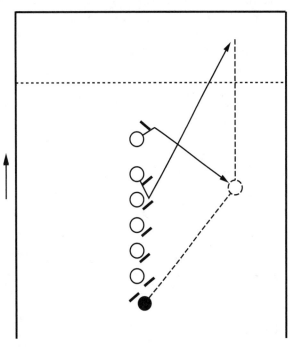

Figure 5.9 In a stagnant stack, the defense fronts each offensive player except the last. This player cuts in for the first pass, then delivers a long pass to the next-to-last player cutting away. Both players decided to "take what they give you."

This exact scenario is unlikely to occur against a good defense, but there are many times during flow when the disc changes position significantly without the defender realizing it, and a receiver simply has to run to the open space.

Make Them Give You What You Want

In some situations, there's only one place a receiver can cut, and the defender can commit to preventing that cut. But in most situations, a receiver can cut to two or more places (with various degrees of likelihood for success), and the defender tries to figure out which place the receiver wants to go.

If you know where you want to go (perhaps on a called play), you need to appear to fully commit to a cut to a different area. You can deliberately allow the defender to see subtle but "clumsy" clues (e.g., moving your eyes, shifting weight forward onto your toes, walking to create space) that you're preparing to cut to that fake area. You'll also probably need to take a few full strides in that direction, giving the appearance of moving at full acceleration while still being able to shift to another direction. Cutters must master the principle of weight as well as space.

Make Them Give You Something

In some situations where multiple areas are open, it's not critical that you get to a particular area but that you get to one of them relatively quickly. In this case, employ a succession of moves within which at any point you're ready to change directions or shift to top acceleration, knowing that the defender can't keep up. Begin each move expecting that the defender won't react quickly enough to prevent you from getting open. Commit to that move for as long as it takes to decide whether the defender has not committed (in which case you'll be open if you simply continue), has reacted perfectly (you aren't open and probably won't be on your next fake either), or has overcommitted (you aren't open, but you definitely will be if you cut to another open area). Quick or experienced players might be able to have three or four such shots in a single cut without clogging, but slower or less experienced players might have time for only one or two.

Actively Get Out of the Way

If you recognize that you don't have the best cut, do as much as you can to make your teammate's cut successful. Often this means quickly vacating some space and ensuring that your defender is in no position to disrupt the offense. In other situations, you can do more. It's one thing to avoid getting in the way of a teammate's cut but another thing entirely to create a cutting opportunity for a teammate by pointedly repositioning yourself and your defender. Suppose, for example, that you're on the break-mark side of the field in a sideline trap just as a dump-swing play has begun toward your side. If your defender is nearby to prevent you from completing the swing or receiving a continuation pass but hasn't seen the start of the dump-swing combination, make a hard motion to the strong side away from the play. If you bring your defender with you, you'll leave in your wake a large alleyway for one of your teammates (figure 5.10). Such a maneuver is even more effective if you can start it before the dump swing begins.

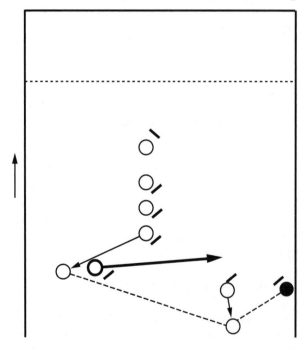

Figure 5.10 Actively get out of the way to allow others to cut. The cutter in bold recognizes the play developing but is clogging, so he clears away from the play as if cutting.

Clearing

No matter how good you are, sometimes one of your teammates will have a better cut as long as you can get out of the way. When that's the case, your job of clearing is just as important as the job of cutting. Move quickly, in a manner similar to the way you cut so that your defender goes with you. Move away from the open space; if there are multiple open spaces, determine which one the cutter is going to and head to another. In some instances, such as when you're still in the process of setting up your cut, simply stopping in your tracks can be enough.

The difficult part is recognizing the situation. One sure-fire way is for a teammate behind you to yell to you to clear or to stop. He probably sees the same opening as you do, but his defender is out of position. Another situation is when you feel you're almost in good position but you're too close to the disc. Someone behind you and in better position probably also recognizes the situation and will cut, especially if you clear the way and call out, "You go!" or "I'm out!" Another situation in which you need to get out of the way quickly is when you thought you had timed a cut perfectly but there was a delay with the catch (bobble, layout, foul, momentum carrying the receiver out of bounds). The sooner you recognize your cut was too early, the easier it is for someone else to get open.

Recognizing That You're Open

So, you make a fake, you cut to the thrower, the defender reacts, and . . . are you open? This is easy enough to answer at the moment the thrower must decide whether to throw to you, although the thrower's skill (we hope) also affects the decision. It's much more difficult to assess how open you are early in the cut because you have to project ahead a few seconds and consider several factors. The most important of these factors are

- relative position of you, your defender, and open space;
- relative speeds at that moment; and
- your defender's body position.

Your size and top speed also come into play if there's a large difference either way between you and the defender, but in general the match-up doesn't significantly affect the degree to which you're open.

A receiver could simply be standing still and yet be open if the defender is at least a couple of yards away, and the thrower is able to throw the disc to a space on the opposite side of the receiver from the defender. In the middle of the cut, if the receiver is closer to the open space than the defender is, the receiver will be open.

Relative speed can become important when there's a sudden start or change in direction. Often, the defender is late to react, so the cutter gets moving first. Thus, even though the receiver is even with or behind the defender, his higher speed soon puts him in front and lengthens his lead. It's important that the receiver continue with the cut at this point. If he gets moving first, he can run by a faster defender.

The defender's body position becomes the key factor when both players are moving, and body position can be the hardest to read. Obviously, if the defender is clearly off balance, she won't be able to react quickly. More likely, though, you'll need to look for subtle signs to know that she's off balance. One such defensive error is if her weight is on her heels, which occurs if you can get her to move backward. Another clue is if her legs cross over completely while she's running along with you. Probably the best

A   B

Figure 5.11 Defensive errors to recognize (defender in white): *(a)* weight on heels; *(b)* legs crossing over while running.

way to tell, though, is to look at her upper body, particularly her shoulders. A defender in good position can usually see your front, which requires her to be both in front of you and facing you. ("Facing" is a bit of a misnomer because it's not the alignment of the face but of the shoulders and hips that determines whether she can react to your moves.) If you change directions sharply during a cut, she must be able to turn her hips and shoulders to block you from that path. She might be in front of you (you're facing her still), but she's no longer facing you. You won't be able to see both her shoulders, so you can stop and cut behind her. One common scenario is if she's running along with you, and her shoulders are square to her path instead of turned a little toward you. Another example is if during the faking process she turns her upper body too much when trying to go with one of your motions (figure 5.11a-d).

One-on-One Cutting Techniques

Let's look at some considerations for cutting against a one-on-one defense, including tips on juking, running at the defender, and an elaboration of the previous section as it pertains to one-on-one defense.

Players in virtually every field or court sport need to be able to cut using a combination of faking with the body, planting the foot, and running hard. The basic principles are the same from sport to sport, but exact techniques depend on an athlete's quickness, amount of available space on the field, how quickly the object (disc, ball, puck) can get there, and the amount of contact permitted by the rules. Whatever technique you employ, you need to keep control of your weight and balance until you reach the point where you can just turn and run (or skate or ride) in a straight line to where you want to go, knowing you'll be open when you get there. This last point is particularly important for less physically gifted players who can't simply run by defenders but must instead rely on timing.

C   D

Figure 5.11 *(continued)*   Defensive errors to recognize (defender in white): *(c & d)* shoulders in front. The plane of the defender's shoulders is in front of the receiver, allowing her to stop and cut behind.

Many a beginning player relies heavily on physical skills to get open. This works as long as the defender is less physically skilled or is reactive, waiting for the cut to occur before shifting to defend it. An exceptionally athletic player might even spend most of his career in this trap because it works against most opponents. Faced with a tough defender, though, he gets looked off by anxious throwers or bumps into the defender who anticipates the cut, and he attributes the failure to a bad day, poor teammates, or a cheating opponent. In reality, he failed because he has not learned how to cut properly.

Reading a defender's reactions is crucial to good cutting. Any time a defender is unable to stop or change direction quickly, she's vulnerable, and that's the moment to make the final push. Capitalize quickly! There are several signs to look for:

- The defender's weight is on her heels or she's walking backward. She simply can't get moving fast enough to stay with a sudden movement.
- The defender is bent at the waist or is lunging or her weight is otherwise not over her hips. She has fully committed to preventing a particular cut. Because you have alertly kept the ability to change direction, you can just cut behind her (that is, toward her, but on the side opposite of where her weight is).
- The defender's legs cross over. While she's shuffling or taking small steps, she can easily stop, but if her legs cross over, she's in a poor position to react.
- The defender is working hard to accelerate or is already at high speed.
- The defender is slow to react and doesn't stay with you.
- The defender is no longer facing you. Her shoulders have turned so much that you can see her back. This can happen either while running or when nearly stationary.

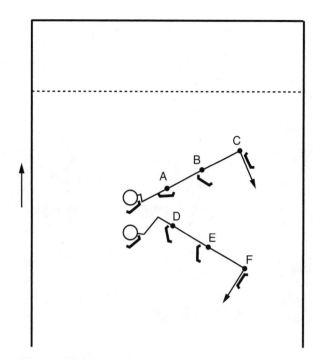

Figure 5.12 The defender can overcommit for an away cut (A-B-C) and a comeback cut (D-E-F). At points C and F, the defender's shoulders are in front of the cutter, who then cuts behind her.

Many of the defender's errors will be revealed in her shoulders, and this is something you can learn to read at a glance. Figure 5.12 illustrates this point for an away cut (A-B-C) and a comeback cut (D-E-F). After a fake (A and D), the cutter cuts (away in A, toward the disc in D). After a few steps (B and E), he has some momentum, and the defender can no longer just shuffle and must begin turning her shoulders toward her direction of travel. The defender doesn't want to allow the cutter to just run by, so after a few more steps (C and F), she's more or less at a full run, and her shoulders are perpendicular to the direction in which she's running. The extension of the plane of her shoulders is now in front of where the cutter is going, so the cutter can stop and cut behind the defender.

There are really just two major categories of fakes, ignoring those that require contact, which is of course forbidden under the rules of ultimate. The first are slow fakes, which involve convincing the defender you're going somewhere else. The second are quick fakes, which might involve a diversion. Both of these fakes rely on beginning with a small positional advantage and expanding the advantage through immediate and direct movement to the desired open area. Here, "slow" doesn't mean that you move slowly or that you don't work hard but rather that the cut requires several movements, a few seconds, and an evaluation of the defender's position.

The simplest slow fake is the juke. Although also a generic term for "fake," the term "juke" is used here quite specifically to mean a series of one- or two-step moves beginning from a nonsprinting position, intended to get the defender off balance or otherwise overcommitted to one of the moves. After each short move, the cutter is looking for one of the signs listed above. If instead the defender reacts to each move, a redirection immediately ensues. This series of jukes can be done about a single point (as for a dump cut) or combined with forward motion (as for a downfield cut).

A variant of the juke extends the length of each move, thus limiting the number of options to two or three, much as in the shoulder-extension example above. Make a real cut in a direction, and after some number of steps (anywhere from 3 to 10), evaluate whether you'll be open if you continue. If not, immediately plant and turn 90 degrees to cut behind the defender. It's possible to start a cut with no intent of turning back, but when the defender goes too far to prevent the cut, you cut back.

Some slow fakes work on a slightly different principle. The cutter takes an action, waits for a particular expected reaction from the defender, then executes a planned response. In both the stutter-step and the foot drag, the cutter starts to slow down as if to change direction (with the stutter-step by taking small and rapid steps; with the foot drag, by taking long, deliberate steps), then immediately speeds up as soon as the defender gives an indication of slowing down.

Some techniques require you to let the defender's reaction dictate your next move. Running directly at the defender often provokes an incorrect reaction. (One warning: You shouldn't plan on running into the defender if she holds her ground, but there will occasionally be contact when the defender does something unexpected, and it's usually not a foul on her unless she uses her arms to impede you, either deliberately or as a panicked reaction.) A typical defensive miscue is to back up furiously, in which case you can make a sharp cut in another direction (a good technique for dump cuts to the backfield). Another mistake is to freeze on the spot, in which case you can take a halfstep to either side and run right by her. Finally, the defender might step to one side, forcing or inviting you to run by on the other side of her.

The eye fake can be used as either a slow fake or a quick fake. As a slow fake, the cutter can watch an imaginary flow opposite the actual flow, repositioning himself all the while as if to cut off this flow. A last hard, sudden step convinces the defender a cut is in process, and as soon as she moves with the step, the cutter reverses direction and is wide open.

The eye fake can also be used as a diversion for a quick fake. Immediately before a cut, quickly cast your eyes just over the defender's shoulder, as if the disc is about to float over it. Accompany this with some body movement to indicate that you're reaching to catch the disc. This will cause many defenders to turn toward the "incoming" disc, and you'll already have begun to run away. (You can use a related technique when the disc is actually coming over the defender's shoulder, in which case you have to pretend that nothing is going on until the disc is safely past her.)

The swim, a move borrowed from football, is another diversion technique that expects but does not wait for a particular defender reaction. Begin in a stationary position, facing the defender a few yards away, as a wide receiver faces a cornerback. Take a hard step forward to one side as if you're trying to run by the defender on that side. The defender usually leans or steps out to prevent this, but you won't really have time to evaluate whether this is so. You'll immediately plant hard and step to the other side, throwing the arm that's closer to the defender high and around her as if doing a freestyle stroke in swimming (figure 5.13a-b). You can also use the swim with the "run at" fake or any time there's not a lot of room to get around the defender. This move can be particularly effective against a defender who likes to play physically by using her body and even her arms to halt your momentum.

The head fake actually involves most of the body, but the head movements are exaggerated to give the impression that motion in a particular direction is imminent. Once again, you hope the defender reacts to that immediate movement, but you can't wait around to find out. Indeed, practically any motion can be used as a diversion, as long as it mimics a move possibly used for a real cut. If it's believable, even a good defender will react to it and begin shifting her weight just as you're shifting yours in the opposite direction. Ironically, sometimes a poor defender who doesn't know enough to see this cut won't be taken in by the fake.

You can't always be cutting or about to cut, but you still need to be moving, even if it's only walking or stutter-stepping. Your two main tasks are to keep your defender's attention focused on you to prevent poaches and to reposition yourself in the stack or the backfield. Prevent the defender from getting in a comfortable position in which she can keep an eye on you and on the disc without compromising her defense. If you're in the stack, move sideways, up, or back a couple yards to change the angles. But make sure you don't create a pick and that you don't get in your teammates'

A   B

Figure 5.13 *(a)* In the swim, fake a hard step to one side, then *(b)* step to the other and swing your arm over your head and the defender's head and go by.

way when they're cutting. Keep on your toes. Move to a spot where your defender is directly between you and the disc. Start cutting and then stop after a step. All of these strategies give the defender a reason to watch you and to make her reposition. The more she has to do, the more likely she'll make a mistake.

In addition to forcing your defender to shift her weight, if you can keep her busy watching you while you watch the movement of the disc, she'll be slow to respond when you're ready to cut.

Deep Cuts

A good deep cut can devastate your opponents. It can lead to a quick and easy goal, deprive their offense of rest, and put pressure on them to match with a huck of their own.

Some tips for making a deep cut:

1. Be close to the disc (typically no more than 20 yards downfield) when you make your final move.
2. Convince the defender you're going back to the disc.
3. Allow at least 10 yards, preferably more, between you and the sideline that the disc will be coming from.
4. Sprint from the first step.
5. The disc should be in a "power position"—that is, the thrower has a clear passing lane and an open (either unmarked or with-force) throw. Often, this happens when a thrower catches the disc running laterally across the field or downfield and his defender is behind him (or on the ground after a failed diving bid).

6. Start the cut earlier than you do for a comeback cut. Keep in mind, though, that because the cut often must start before the thrower even gets the disc, sometimes an unexpected event breaks the timing and the cut isn't rewarded with the throw.

A long cut needs a lot of space to develop. If you start it from too far downfield, the thrower won't be able to throw the disc far enough or fast enough to get it past the defense. You also need the space to allow for a greater margin of error for the longer throw. Finally, as the disc comes within range, you need to allow for a misread or a change in the flight caused by the wind.

You can set up the long cut in several ways. One method is simply to sprint deep right after throwing a pass, especially if your defender has put herself out of position by lunging for a point block. Even without that miscue, the defender often won't pay attention to you in the seconds after you release the disc, giving you the opportunity to open up a few yards. A second method can work off the principle of "make them give you something." Consider the scenario earlier in this chapter in which the dump swing was successful and you as the last player in the stack cut for the continuation. However, this time the defender sees the pass coming and overcommits to the comeback cut. You make a last hard move back toward the disc, then break for the deep area (figure 5.14). Note that unlike on short cuts where you might change direction completely in one step, you have to change direction more gradually here to keep your speed up. A previous example under Take What They Give You illustrates a third method. Occasionally, the position of the disc

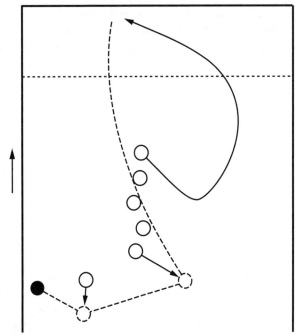

Figure 5.14 After a dump swing, the last player in the stack cuts in but then cuts long for the huck.

and the other players changes rapidly enough that all of the rules are satisfied without much effort required other than keeping the defender occupied. When that happens, make a simple fake in and then sprint deep for the easy goal.

Good deep cuts go unrewarded more often than good shorter cuts do, but that shouldn't discourage you from making them. Frequently, you'll draw a poach without your own defender switching, freeing one of your teammates for a wide-open underneath cut. When this happens, continue your cut, although you can slow down a little from a full sprint. There will often be confusion between the two defenders now covering you, so there's a good chance you'll be able to break free again if you just keep moving. Another reason to make the deep cut is the effect it has on the defender, both at the time and later in the game. At the time, she'll have to go all-out to catch up and might be too tired to stay with your next cut. Later in the game, she'll be reluctant to get beat deep again and might allow you a lot of space for shorter cuts. Also, make sure to clear out of the deep area after an unsuccessful deep cut to open it up for others.

The optimal cutting path for a deep pass is determined by several factors. Generally, it's *not* a straight line between where you are and where you want to be unless that's the only way you can get there in time. Rather, the best path is a gently curving path straight downfield for the first 15 yards or so before arcing toward the disc. This path leaves open space for the thrower and affords you more room away from the stack and potential poachers waiting. If you keep away from the stack, you might not get picked up because the poachers might not even see you, or else they'll hesitate to pop out for fear of leaving their own offenders wide open. And if they do come out, they might miscalculate where you're heading if they just go to the spot along your original straight-line path.

It's crucial in the first few steps of a deep cut that you go all-out, without looking back for the disc until you've achieved separation from your defender. Then you can glance back to reassess the situation, but don't continue to run with your head and shoulders turned because this slows you down. Once you have broken free from your defender and the stack, begin tracking the disc, adjusting your path to lead to the likely point of reception. Keep the disc in front of you because it's easier to adjust toward the disc to catch it than it is to move back away from the disc. Furthermore, the defender is usually behind you and isn't just going to let you force her back.

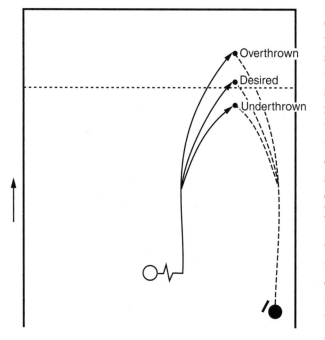

Figure 5.15 For a long cut up the line, keep at least 10 yards from the sideline to give the thrower some room and allow you to adjust to poor passes (dotted lines).

Finally, the strategies of your offense and the opponent's defense will have some effect on your cutting path. Most deep passes should have some crossfield component to them, so that if the pass is underthrown or overthrown, you can adjust your path to head it off sooner or later, as needed. This opportunity won't exist if both the throw and the cut are straight down the field so that pass must be nearly perfectly thrown to be caught. Let's look at three examples of deep cuts and the path the receiver takes. There's really no conceptual difference among these cuts, but each has a different start point and end point.

In the first example, the defense is forcing one way (say, forehand), so the deep pass stays on the same side of the field it is released on. The cut then starts from near the middle of the field (figure 5.15). Also, as shown, this cut allows you to adjust to underthrown or overthrown passes. A common flaw in this cut is pushing too close to the sideline before the final cut.

If the defense is forcing middle, a different long cut might be called for (figure 5.16). Again, the thrower gets the disc in a power position on the sideline but can't huck it down the line because of the mark, although a shorter break-mark pass is available. The receiver pushes to within 5 or 10 yards of the sideline before turning downfield. Eventually, the receiver ends up at or slightly past the middle of the field.

The final example is from a set play. The deep thrower gets the disc in the middle of the field. The other offensive players downfield from the deep cutter (positioned fourth in the stack) cut in at the same time. After a one- or two-second delay, the deep cutter heads straight downfield and then flares to whichever side the thrower can get his throw off to (figure 5.17).

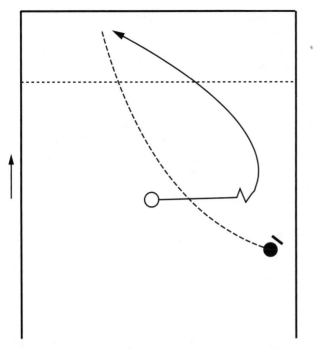

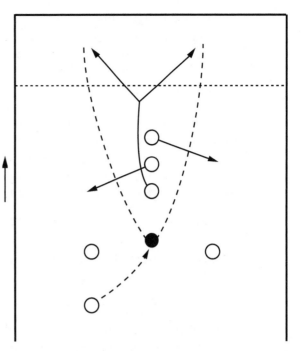

Figure 5.16 In a force middle, the cutter fakes a cut to the break-mark side, then turns and runs long.

Figure 5.17 A reverse split play lets the called cutter sprint deep down the center of the field. The huck can then be made to either side of the field.

Drill: Cutting for the Huck

You can run this drill at different levels of defensive activity and intensity. In the most basic version, four players (three offense, one defense) are involved at a time. One player has the disc on the goal line in the middle of the field. About 10 yards away, a player fakes and cuts to the backhand side. Another 10 yards away, the defender covers the long cutter, who fakes in and then cuts deep for a backhand. Other than being required to front the long cutter initially, the defender plays honest defense. If the cut is not open, the thrower shouldn't throw the disc. Give each player three to five long backhand throws, then switch to the forehand side. Common errors in this drill are starting from too deep and pushing too close to the sideline. Make the drill more gamelike by adding a defender to cover the long thrower or by removing the "fronting" requirement.

Dump Cuts

Thus far we've focused on mainly downfield cuts—the big, yardage-gaining cuts that are the most exciting to make and watch. However, short handler cuts at a high stall count present a high-percentage way to maintain possession of the disc. Technically, a dump cut is a short pass to the backfield a thrower resorts to when no other good pass is available, but for convenience we'll use the term here to include reset cuts, which sometimes gain a few yards. With these short passes, quickness, agility, timing, and eye contact are more important than speed.

The primary goal of the dump cut is to maintain possession, especially when the thrower is not particularly skilled. The cut itself is based on the principle "take what they give you," with "they" in this case including not just your defender but also the marker. These cuts are often not guarded as heavily. In most cases, they are used to reset the stall count but can sometimes be made early in the count for positional reasons. Whatever your reason for using them, the methods described here apply to all dump cuts.

Timing is the key to most successful dump cuts, assuming that the cutter has enough quickness to chase down a pass from a stopped position. Most downfield cuts in a typical offense are "receiver-directed," meaning that the receiver chooses where to go and expects the thrower to deliver the disc there at the proper time. Dump cuts, on the other hand, need to be "thrower-directed," with the thrower having a say in when the cut should be made, where it goes, or both. The basic rules for dump cutting are as follows:

1. Set up about five yards from the thrower for throws with the force and a little farther away for break-mark throws.
2. Give yourself an equal amount of space to cut into.
3. Wait until the thrower has turned to face you and has made eye contact.
4. Cut at about the time the disc is being released.

The optimal play depends on the stall count and the position of the defenders. The simplest and best case is when you're facing the thrower, and your defender is to one side (figure 5.18). Simply move away from the defender at the same instant the thrower begins his throwing motion. If you cut first instead, and the thrower has to react to your cut, you'll often run out of space.

Another situation in which you let the thrower dictate what to do is in a high stall count when the defender is directly between you and the thrower and she can't see the thrower (figure 5.19). Be on your toes, and after the thrower floats a pass beyond the defender to one side, run to it, keeping the defender at bay with your body, if necessary.

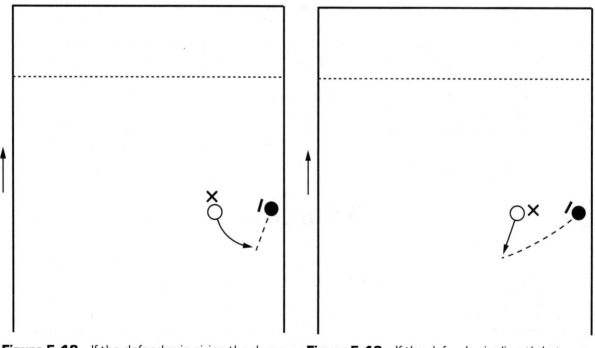

Figure 5.18 If the defender is giving the dump cut, take it as the thrower starts his motion.

Figure 5.19 If the defender is directly between you and the thrower, wait for the thrower to pass the disc to space before running it down.

You can sometimes get the defender off balance by taking a hard step at her (as if going past her and down the line), then moving back.

In some circumstances, you need to lead the way, such as when the thrower is on the line being trapped at a low to medium stall count, you're 10 yards off the line and even with the disc, and the defender isn't favoring either way (figure 5.20). Make eye contact with the thrower, then fake, cut toward the dump, and be ready to turn and cut down the line if the defender overcommits to the dump cut.

Always be ready to react to the circumstances at hand. Sometimes the defender will guess that a pass is coming and turn to face the thrower. In this event, just cut somewhere else, and the defender won't be able to follow. Take care not to get too close to the thrower, especially for

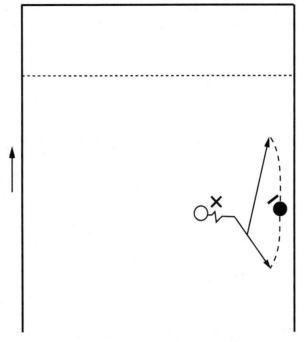

Figure 5.20 Early in the count, fake and cut for the dump. If the defender overcommits, cut up the line (dotted line).

forehand throws, as short throws are difficult to throw softly, and you'll have little chance to adjust to an errant throw.

In many offenses, the dump-cutter starts behind the disc. Other offenses don't like to position players back there, so all dump cuts start from in front of the disc, which means the cutters need to be more active in setting up the cut. As usual, a flexible plan is best. Don't always set up camp behind the disc (because this might take away throwing lanes), but if you find yourself back there after a failed cut or if you're trailing the play and in position for the dump cut, use your positioning effectively.

Although most dump passes lose yardage, they also change the position of the disc and can lead to quick continuation passes, especially if the defender lunges or dives for the block attempt. The first look after catching the dump is typically to keep the disc moving across the field as soon as possible. As described in chapter 4 on catching, you can position your feet and body before the catch to set up the pivot. Usually, the thrower's target is one of the first players in the stack, but occasionally he'll cut straight across the field for a give and go. Other options after the dump are discussed in chapter 3 on handling.

Keep in mind that the defense might change position over the course of a stall count, so a space that appears open at stall five might not be open a few seconds later.

■ Drill: Dump Passes

Use two offensive players and two defensive players. Set up a square with 15 yards on either side. All play occurs within the square. Begin with the disc on the line about two yards from one of the corners, with the thrower facing the corner. The marker is always between the thrower and the corner, pretending to take away the downfield pass. The other offensive player begins in the center.

His defender can position wherever she wants. The thrower has five seconds to complete the pass. After each pass, the cutter becomes the thrower, and the others should take one or two seconds to reposition. Continue play for 90 seconds, then switch offense and defense. As a variation, play nonstop with no restrictions on positioning and with incomplete passes resulting in changes of possession. Five completions in a row count as a point, and 10 points wins the drill.

Moving Without the Disc

Moving without the disc is another important but often overlooked part of good offense. This includes not just clearing after a failed or aborted cut, mentioned earlier, but also preemptively clearing to set up someone else's cut, avoiding or reacting to poaches and switches, and trailing a play. At most, a couple of players at a time are involved in active cuts, so the others need to be creating space and positioning themselves for later cuts. In fact, if you look at a high-level game, you might see so much downfield action that you don't even recognize a stack formation. All seven players are probably working to set up cuts down the alleys.

Clearing After a Failed Cut or to Create Space

The general rule is to move away from the open area while keeping your defender from poaching. After a failed cut to the sideline, this usually means clearing up the line before returning to the stack. It's better still to realize the cut is not viable (be sure of this) and break it off before reaching the sideline. Make sure to do this quickly to allow others a chance to cut in.

You'll be on the move for the entire point, so you must always be ready to cut or get out of the way. The principles for knowing when to clear are very similar to the ones for knowing when to cut, as discussed earlier under Knowing Who Should Go Where. Clear when you recognize that a cut should be made, but you're not in the right position—perhaps because you're too close to the disc or already next to the sideline. Plant hard with your foot and move quickly away from the open space, taking care not to run toward someone else running into that space. Even if you're in the stack, it pays to do something to keep your defender's attention on you, such as pretending to set up a comeback cut. You must act immediately to prevent the poach.

Anticipating and Reacting to Poaches and Switches

If not handled properly, good defensive switching and poaching can lead to easy blocks and broken offense. Responsibility for throwing into a poach ultimately rests with the thrower, but cutters should do everything they can to prevent poaches and punish them when prevention isn't possible.

The opportunity for poaching arises from laziness, a lack of focus, or poor spacing by the offense. You're poachable in these cases:

- You're standing flat-footed.
- Your defender can watch you and another potential cutter at the same time.
- You clear out too slowly.
- You are nowhere near a viable cutting position.

- You get too close to the cutting lane without actually cutting.
- You watch the play without being prepared to get involved.

You're *not* poachable in these cases:

- You're a threat to cut.
- You move whenever the defender looks away.
- You keep your defender repositioning herself so she can't get comfortable and watch for other cutters.
- You're not so close to your teammates that you allow a two-man defensive clam to set up.
- You clear out quickly.

The same principles for timing cuts apply to avoiding poaches, although the motions might be displaced by a second or two. However, the immediate direction of motion is opposite that you take for a cut. If you recognize a cutting situation but are too close to the disc to make it worthwhile, move away from the flow and then head downfield when you've passed the stack. If you're near the back of the stack but another player has begun to cut where you want to go, cut to the other side. If you see someone cutting long and you're near the back, cut in. But don't run at the other cutter because this facilitates a switch.

Sometimes you can't prevent a poach from occurring. In such a case, your job is to punish the poacher so she won't do it again. When you're poached, immediately move away from the poacher and the offender being covered, usually across the field but sometimes up or down the field. You probably won't get the first pass if you head downfield, but you might get the second or third pass and then throw or catch the goal. If you're at the front of the stack, the poach will usually be a quick flare to the force side. Move sideways to the breakside right away, alerting the thrower that you're poached—yell "Poach!" or wave an arm above your head—and expect to receive a "through" break pass right away. If that pass doesn't come, continue for an "around" break pass. For more information, see chapter 8 on switching and poaching.

Drill: Cutting

This drill is good for practicing the timing of cuts and defensive positioning. One thrower, one retriever, and two lines are 10 and 20 yards from the thrower in the center of the field. The thrower completes a short pass to a player from line 1 cutting toward the sideline. A player from line 2 cuts for the continuation, while the defender (who positions herself at the start of the play) defends. Lines recycle, except for the thrower, who is occasionally replaced.

As an alternative, add another cutter and another defender to the succession. Additionally, you can treat the two cuts equally, so the defense is unsure of the order.

Trailing the Play

Even when you're not involved in the play, remain focused and position yourself properly in case what's happening doesn't go perfectly. On a long pass to a teammate (or during his cut), for example, the hustling player has several options. If you see the cut and the upcoming throw developing and your defender doesn't, cut toward the thrower to draw your defender out of the way (keeping out of the throwing lane). More likely, though, the pass will go up, everyone realizes it, and at least one teammate has much better position to try to catch it. Sometimes (say, you're much taller than a teammate and his defenders) it's best to get in there and try to make the catch yourself, but typically you'll help the team most by being a backup. Determine where the disc will land if it floats over everyone's heads, and position yourself to get to that spot while also being able to chase down a barely tipped disc that floats quickly toward the back of the end zone. If many players are involved already, then get on the side the disc is coming from because it's more likely the defense will hit the disc first and smack it away from the receiver. Another option, especially when it's clear the disc won't make it to the end zone, is to stay well clear of the mass so that the thrower has

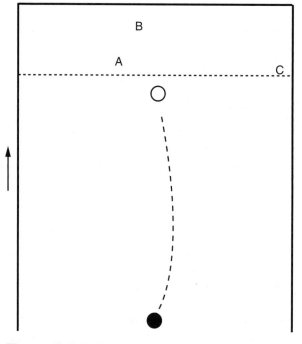

Figure 5.21 There are several backup positions to cover on a huck to a teammate. Be ready if the disc goes over everyone's head (A) or is tipped (B). Also be prepared to catch an easy goal if the disc is caught outside the end zone (C).

an easy goal pass if he does come down with the disc (figure 5.21).

During the flow, a player who has just released a downfield pass will find himself trailing the play. If the flow goes smoothly, he might never catch up to the disc again, which is acceptable in most offenses. After throwing a pass, stay clear of the expected throwing lanes for the next pass. In most circumstances, you'll probably want to jog quickly toward the front or middle of the stack if you're a handler and the middle or back of the stack otherwise. If your defender is not paying attention, sprint straight downfield in hopes of catching the second or third pass for a goal. Another option for a handler on downfield passes is to jog slowly downfield to keep his defender out of the play and make himself available for a possible dump.

Only one of seven offensive players has the disc at any time. The others have the important job of cutting. Cutters need to internalize the four rules of cutting—take what they give you, make them give you what you want, make them give you something, and actively get out of the way. There are many techniques and fakes to employ during your cut, but the physical act of cutting is only part of the equation. First you must recognize the situation and determine where to go. Then time your cut perfectly to receive the pass.

SIX

Guarding

The basic goal of one-on-one defense is to prevent your offender from receiving easy, dangerous throws. Doing this means getting between the receiver and the disc he wants to catch. As his position changes continually, so must yours. You must constantly readjust, keeping in mind this basic and simple objective (well, simply stated but less simply accomplished). In this chapter, we'll focus on the individual aspects of one-on-one defensive coverage. Please see chapter 9 for information on the team issues inherent to one-on-one defense.

How to Defend

Before you can decide the best way to play defense, you must decide what kind of defense you're playing. This means knowing what was called on the line and deciding how to play a certain force. Do you want to protect the deep threat at any cost? Or do you want to focus on preventing the comeback cut, say in a wind where deep throws are difficult? Is your offender a potent thrower? Is he aggressive or easily intimidated by physical defending? Are you guarding a novice, an old timer, a slow poke, or a speedster? How will you capitalize on this knowledge?

Decide how you're going to play your offender and take charge. When you set the tone of the offense/defense struggle, you have already gained the upper hand. For example, you and your team might decide to front the offense. You give them the long cut because you have decided it's less important than what you take away. What you give them might change dynamically over the course of a game. If you know your priorities, you'll find your optimal position quickly.

Once on your offender with a clear mindset, you must train your mind to the task. The principle of focus is crucial in one-on-one defense. Specifically, focus is on ensuring proper positioning (space) and balance (weight). Individual defense requires intense concentration because the proper position to be in changes with every step your offender takes, every movement of the disc, and every tick of the clock. A half-second delay by any defender can lead to an easy score for the offense. As a one-on-one defender, you must constantly assess and reassess risks and possibilities in real time and constantly readjust to your changing environment. We'll call these adjustments dynamic positioning. Most players have a solid grasp of static positioning—the initial setup before anyone is cutting—but many fail to make the proper adjustments during flow.

Okay, so you have to remain focused on maintaining proper position and balance—but how is that done? Basically, you want to be between where your offender is and where he'll receive the disc—that way, you'll be able to get there first. Achieving this usually, though not always, means being between your offender and the thrower. You also want to be able to remain between your offender and the place he'll receive the pass, despite his various maneuvers, and this requires that you keep him in sight. (Getting caught with your back to your offender is an easily exploited blunder.) You would also like to be able to see the throw as it's released so that you can react quickly and appropriately. Maintaining good position and a clear sight of the offender and thrower involves a concept known as "triangulation."

Triangulation refers to keeping three points (figure 6.1) under control. The three points are (1) where your offender is, (2) where the thrower is, and (3) where the pass you're guarding is likely to be thrown. Most of our discussion involves the case where the force is to one of the sidelines and the disc is anywhere on the field but the opposite sideline (this special case will be treated separately). We'll assume (as in the figure) that your offender is "in play," meaning on the strong side or in the center of the field, able to receive a with-mark pass. Note that positions A, B, and C in the diagram all are places at which you can get to the point of reception before your offender. Position A gives you the best view of your offender and the thrower at the same time. Position C protects best against the easy short throw but is a more difficult vantage point for viewing the thrower. Position B has several drawbacks. First, it's not easy to keep everything in view. Second, if your offender does cut toward the point of the reception **x**, you'll have to turn a full 180 degrees to beat him. Such a change of direction requires a full weight shift and turn of the hips. (A quick note to offensive players—sprinting right at, and past, a defender who's improperly positioned in this way gets you open.) Plus, even if the shift is accomplished, as both of you are running toward **x**, you'll have your back to your offender. It's much better to pick A or C. Even if your offender is significantly faster than you, you can find these points where you can beat him to the point of reception. Typically, you want to be as close to your offender as you can while still able to react to his moves and beat him to the reception. A slower defender will need more distance than a quicker defender, but even slow defenders should be able to prevent any single chosen pass from being completed.

The scenario just discussed illustrates that there's typically an optimal position on the inside (C) or the outside (A) of your offender. Which is better? As a rule, get inside if you can. If you're inside your defender (position C), the pass to the receiver at **x** will have to go through you. Plus, you'll be able to block a majority of imperfect throws to **x**. On the contrary, at position A you're closer to **x** but farther from most other likely points of reception. You only want to be at A if your team has put a premium on stopping the long throw. Otherwise, get inside!

One drawback to position C, the inside, is that the view of the thrower is not as good. Position A is a risk, but a known risk, in that the whole scene occurs in front of your eyes, so you won't be surprised. If you're faster than your offender, you might be able to play at A and still be effective against shorter throws, depending on your closing speed. All things being equal, though, being inside your offender (position C), shading the force properly, and getting infor-

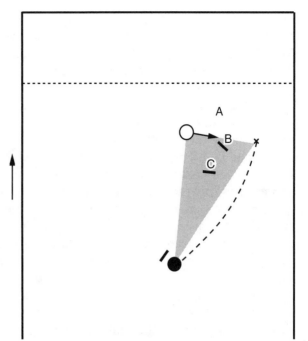

Figure 6.1 Defensive triangulation. A cutter on the strong side creates the triangle formed by his position, the thrower's position, and the likely point of reception. Position A guards against the long throw and allows full view of the triangle. Position B is poor because the defender must shift her weight a full 180 degrees. Position C guards against the intended short throw as well as any others while keeping the cutter and thrower in view. Note that the defender in position C also is in the way of the flight path of a long throw.

mation about the throw from your periphery (and your ears) offers the best package for reliable one-on-one coverage.

Note that the shape of this triangle changes as your offender or the disc moves about the field, but the qualitative features of our discussion remain the same. Remaining balanced on your feet with your hips square to your offender allows you to keep your advantageous position as he moves around. At some point, however, your offender will completely commit to his cut and sprint at full speed. Of course, if he's cutting back to the disc, you won't be able to continue to face him indefinitely no matter how good you are at back pedaling. So you, too, have to turn and sprint in the same direction, and timing is crucial. If you commit before he does, he turns and beats you in the other direction. If you wait too long to start sprinting, he gets open. The key is to commit your weight in response to his commitment. To see when this happens, you must have him in sight (look at his torso, not his eyes or head, to see how his weight is shifting). To shift your weight effectively, you must be balanced. To prevent the throw, you must be in the correct position. Our discussion has prepared you for the sprint when it happens.

Two limiting cases should be mentioned. If the disc is on the sideline and so is your defender, the difference between fronting (the inside) and playing behind your offender becomes dramatic. Being between your offender and the disc makes a long throw (which has to go around you) rather difficult, especially because keeping the throw in bounds is more difficult in this situation. Another thing to point out here is that to get a better view, without compromising your position, you'll want to be a few steps in from the sideline. While this seems counterintuitive, this perspective allows you to see your offender and the thrower, and it lets you get in the way of a throw up the sideline. It also prevents any inside-out throws or other attempts toward the middle of the field. In essence, because a throw from the sideline toward the middle of the field is still basically a with-force throw, being a few steps toward the middle is what "getting inside" means in this situation. (Playing behind your offender in this situation simply means you have chosen to give him the comeback cut.)

Another degenerate triangle is formed when your offender is lateral to the disc. Again, in this situation you don't want to be along the straight line between offender and thrower. Instead, you want to shift (or "shade") slightly downfield. In this case, the backfield throw loses yards and puts the disc closer to the forced side—both good for the defense. You want to be close enough to make the dump disadvantageous by being able to put the mark on quickly. (Take note—if the count is at nine, there's no time for an offender to run around you, so you might commit to covering the given side. Of course you might get beaten if he goes downfield just as you go backfield. There are no guarantees.)

When your offender is on the break-mark side, your mindset should still be on the defensive priorities: Cover the major threats on the force side. This means you must position yourself to prevent dangerous cuts from the weak to the force side. (The responsibility of covering the break-mark throw is secondary. If you overplay it, you expose a strong-side weakness that an alert offender will readily exploit.) It's easy to catch a deep throw to the strong side with a run starting from the weak side. The reason is that long throws hang in the air longer, and the diagonal path from the weak side is not all that much longer than the straight path up the line. This means that just being inside your offender offers you little protection against the long throw. (In this case, the throw doesn't have to go around you. It goes down the sideline, and then you and your offender race to get under it.) Thus, on the weak side, you want to drop downfield of your offender while keeping the strong-side shade. (The marker covers the short cut on the breakside.) You should stay close enough that you don't give him an easy strong-side cut. In this way, you're protecting the long throw and can still beat the offender to the sideline side (figure 6.2).

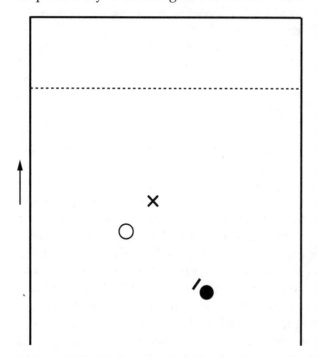

Figure 6.2 Defensive position on the break-side. The short option is covered by the marker, so the defender plays in back. The defender will have to "get inside" and return to fronting as the offender crosses the stack to come to the strong side.

Get Inside!

You might have noticed what seems like an inconsistency in our discussion. On the weak side you should be downfield of your offender, whereas on the strong side you should be fronting. What hap-pens when your offender moves in a continuous path from the weak to the strong side? At some point there's a sharp transition because, as we've mentioned, being lateral with your defender inadequately addresses either short or long threats (figure 6.3). The turning point comes at the point where, if your offender decided to sprint in for a short cut, you wouldn't be able to cover him. While he was on the weak side, you could still play downfield of him while shading in enough to beat him to a short, strong-side cut. When he comes toward the strong side, you can no longer shade as much, and you eventually have to play in front of your offender, and to do so, you must get inside. Because you'll have to go from one side of him to the other, you will have to burst past him, and this takes an extra effort. You want to cross his path on his strong side because if you go behind him he's open the entire time

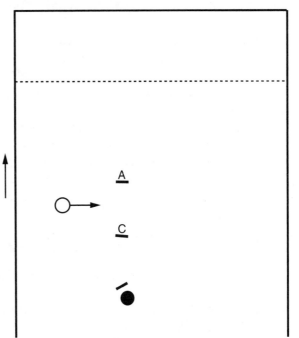

Figure 6.3 Getting inside. On the weak side, position A is favorable. On the strong side, posi-tion C is favorable. As the offender moves across the stack, the defender must get from A to C quickly by sprinting in front of the offender and turning her hips appropriately as she does.

and you lose your whole shade. Thus, getting inside means bursting to the front side of him while keeping your strong-side shade. In addition, you have to change your stance by pivoting your hips appropriately to the fronting shade.

The timing of this maneuver is crucial; it should occur roughly as the offender crosses the stack but varies depending on position. If you wait too long, he'll already be sprinting and will be hard to overtake, or he'll already be open. If you move too soon, you might be vulnerable if he suddenly goes for a deep cut. Alternatively, if he begins his sprint too early on the weak side, then you can alter your shade slightly to force a very short pass—and because he has committed his weight, he won't be able to change directions quickly. If your offender goes from weak side to strong side farther downfield, the process is similar, though it happens more gradually and with a larger cushion between you and the cutter. You reposition but never have to sprint past your offender.

Failure to get inside is a defensive error that allows the offense to easily work the disc up the strong side. Thus, it's essential that you understand the maneuver. To practice, go through the motions with some teammates at half-speed or quarter-speed, without a disc. Repeat this until the maneuver becomes natural, then increase the speed and add a disc. Proper positioning allows you to be an effective defender on both sides of the field.

Take Charge

Defense takes considerable effort and constant vigilance. One way of easing the burden on yourself is to discourage your offender early on. Anticipate his cuts and start defending them in advance. That is, begin reacting to his cut-in just before he makes it. After some practice, you'll soon understand that defense need not be so reactive. You'll begin preparing earlier and find yourself thinking through possible scenarios ahead of time. Really, the dictum "take charge" is just a reminder to think actively on defense and not be content with reacting to your offender's next move. Preemptive defense takes more focus and short-term energy, but it's more effective and efficient overall.

It might help if you think from an offensive perspective. Good cutting is about forcing the defender into tough choices and mistakes. If a defender is in good position, you fake and reposition yourself until he's in bad position, then you make the final hard cut. If the defender remains in control and dictates the terms of your relationship, you might just decide to clear out and try again later.

Stay Balanced

Every cutting maneuver is designed to unbalance the defender. As a defender, your task is to stay balanced and ready to react and respond only to legitimate offensive motions. "Real" motion is evidenced by a movement of the waist. If you focus on guarding the waist, you won't get fooled by fakes. This concept is simple, but following the waist means unlearning what comes instinctively. It takes practice. The following drill should help.

Drill: Defensive Positioning and Cutting

This drill helps both cutting and defensive positioning and can be referred to by either name. A thrower and a marker set up 5 to 10 yards from a sideline, with a force to that sideline. A cutter sets up "in play" with a defender on him. The disc is checked in, and the cutter makes several moves to try to get open on either a comeback cut or a long cut. The defender works on staying focused and balanced throughout the stall count. Go through several repetitions at half-speed and without using the disc; focus on positioning. The cutter should run in a few circles, from weak to strong side, and from short to long, to test the defender. Then switch roles. Increase the speed for a few repetitions before adding the disc and making the situation more gamelike. Stop to discuss errors before rechecking the disc. Repeat the drill with a different force and at different field locations. (Experienced teams can begin with the gamelike situation.)

After you've shut down your defender by sprinting with him, remember to continually ask yourself if you're still in the right position. You're not done playing defense. If you slack off, he might start sprinting in another direction and find himself wide open. Stay alert. If he's clearing back through the cutting area, you should continue to shade him as if he's about to cut again (you can also flap your arms or otherwise be a nuisance to the offense while you're in the throwing alley). Once he repositions himself downfield (or in the backfield), the whole process repeats itself.

Drill: Continuation and Defending in Flow

Designate a stationary thrower and set up three lines of players 7, 20, and 25 yards away. The player at 7 yards away cuts to a chosen sideline and is thrown a leading swing pass from the stationary defender, intended to create a power position (an opportunity for an open throw short or long). The player at 25 yards is on offense, and the player at 20 yards defends. The defender sets up before the play begins. While the first player is receiving the pass, the offense begins a continuation cut, focusing on timing. Meanwhile, the defense defends. The team can put a premium on defending short or long or can leave it up to the defender. It's important to practice the situation where the offense tries to cut in the area the defense is preventing.

End-Zone Defense

We consider one-on-one forcing-forehand or forcing-backhand defense in the end zone. In this situation, when any catch is a goal, you must take away the easy throw, which is the most dangerous threat. Let's first assume that there is no wide side, that the disc itself is on the strong side of the field. In this case, you must cover the near cone on the strong side. The throw to the back cone is much harder and must go through you. Cover that front cone at all costs. You might have to sacrifice a view of the thrower or give up a pass in front of the cone. Or you might have to focus so intently that you give up your periphery and the chance to help someone else. That's all fine. If your player is not cutting, you have to stay prepared. However, you should poach to cover an open defender heading to the cone.

If the disc is on the weak side and there's a big wide side of the field, then you're at a real disadvantage because open throws on either side of you will be goals. You must cover the more dangerous of the two, meaning the easier throw. If the wide side is very large, this is probably the inside (although the presence of a stack can make this more difficult), whereas if the disc is just over the middle, you'll probably want to play tight on the outside.

Above all, ratchet up your focus near the end zone. Most players are capable of guarding the cone in theory, but they get beaten because of a momentary mental lapse.

Pitfalls

Good guarding, as we've seen, comes from a focused, straightforward application of weight and space. The problem is that there are so many variations of bad defense. A defender can fall into any number of traps. Try to avoid these pitfalls:

- Getting lured to the wrong side (violation of space). This can happen when your offender moves to the weak side, especially when he runs in a circular loop. If you follow him, you'll end up on the wrong side soon enough. It can also happen if you bite on a hard fake to the weak side.

- Turning your back to the offender (violation of weight). You might take glances at the disc, but don't turn your hips toward the disc and your back to your offender. Doing so either leaves you blind to his actions or off balance and unable to react.

- Turning your shoulders away from the offender (violation of space, weight). Unless you're at full speed, keep your shoulders turned slightly toward the cutter while you're moving. If your shoulders get ahead of your offender, he can stop and cut behind you to get open.

- Poaching to a lesser threat (violation of space, efficiency). Sometimes defenders see an open player and instinctively leave their offenders to try to help out. In doing so, they create new open players who might be more potent dangers. That's no way to play defense. One-on-one defense is primarily about guarding your own offender.

- Half-poaching (violation of space). If you're poaching, poach. If you're not poaching, don't poach. If you're halfway between, you're doubly out of position.

- Being too proud to ask for help (violation of communication). If you got beaten deep, don't try to blend into the crowd. Ask for help. You might receive it. If you're playing with a team so shortsighted that it can't appreciate your efforts to overcome a shortfall, it's time to find a better team.

- Losing the disc (violation of focus or communication). Your defense suffers when you don't know where the disc is or what the thrower is looking for. During free moments, take periodic but quick glances back at the disc—anything longer leaves an unsupervised offender free to burn you. Also, listen to the audio clues coming from your teammates on and off the field shouting "Up!"

- Losing your defender (severe but not uncommon violation of focus). If this happens, ask for help!

- Forgetting the defense (violation of focus). This pitfall is especially common in defenses that transition after a set number of passes or at some field position. You must always know the defense. If you're not sure, ask! It's better to tell the offense what the defense is than to have none. Inform sideline players of the defense at the start of the point to enlist their help.

- Giving up the cone in end-zone defense.

- Crossing your legs while shifting stance or position (violation of weight). This leaves you off balance and unable to react. You're more nimble with your legs apart.

- Walking backward (violation of weight). You'll be unable to react. Instead, reposition yourself toward the strong side and shuffle your feet to move backward.

- Giving too small a cushion against a faster offender (violation of space). You need to give yourself time to respond to your offender's moves.

As a defender, you must be vigilant. Be continually aware of where your offender is, what you're trying to prevent, where you're positioned, and how well you're balanced. Because these factors change in time, you must position yourself dynamically, which means you must be in the right place now and able to get to the right place later. In guarding an offender in play, stay balanced on both feet, with your hips to the offender, in a position that allows you to beat him to the intended point of reception—while keeping the disc in sight, if possible. This requires you to get inside your offender as he crosses to the strong side. Once your offender sprints for his cut, you'll be able to see him and respond with your own sprint. If the disc is then thrown, go get it!

Marking

In most forcing defenses, fully half the responsibility is on the marker, the person covering the thrower. As a marker, you're expected to prevent throws to one side of the field; the other defenders try to cover passes to the other side of the field. Markers should keep this simple but effective strategy in mind at all times—a lapse in marking allows an offense to progress downfield by passing to cutters on their open side. The goal of marking is not to make point blocks. Markers who lunge for point blocks neglect their priorities and get broken. Most successful defensive stands come from good team defense, not individual blocks.

In this chapter, we'll go over proper marking procedure and analyze how this procedure follows from the goals of a forcing defense. We describe how a marker must focus on her task, stay balanced, avoid unnecessary risks, avoid overcommitting, receive and process information from the field of play and her fellow players, and in return communicate the stall count and flow of the disc. A marker must also know the defensive priorities of her team—preventing inside-out versus around throws, for example. Great markers can manage all these various tasks in any situation.

Basics of Marking

Before going into the details, let's take an overview of a forcing defense. As we've mentioned, the marking strategy is simple. You stop half the field, while the downfield guarders stop the other. You must think of marking in this way, not as trying to get point blocks. First, you have to know which side of the field to cover. Then you have to get into position and initiate the stall count. Once there, you want to assume a balanced position from which you can shift side to side with the thrower's pivots and fakes. Focus on your responsibilities. Think prevention, not point block. This means simply marking, counting, and shifting with the thrower. Before you know it, the stall count is rising. As it rises, you can turn up the pressure a bit by moving in closer, raising the volume of your voice (this tells your teammates that the count's getting high and they must guard particularly well), and taking the occasional chance. If it's late in the mark, you know the throw will be released. Well-timed and unpredictable risks can be very effective. Throughout all this, you want to listen to what your teammates are telling you on the field. Likewise, pass on any information that you see. For instance, yelling, "He's looking dump!" tells your teammates the thrower has turned to the backfield for a bailout.

Finally, and we can't emphasize this enough, when the throw is made, call "Up!" loudly to your teammates. This vital call serves several purposes and is important even for small passes. The "up" call tells a defender that a throw is being made, possibly to her offender; it tells her that the stall count will be reset to zero; it tells defenders with their backs to the disc that a throw is in the air and that the disc might soon be in the hands of a more dangerous thrower. It also tells them that they have a half-second while the disc is flying to glance back to see where it is. Defenders must then reposition accordingly. Of course, the "up" call might also be an alert that the disc is hanging, free for a block. More specific calls, such as, "Broken," "Around," "Up high," and "Hammer!" convey more detailed information (in these cases, respectively, "the mark is broken," "the mark is broken with an around throw," "the disc is floating," and "a hammer has been launched").

In summary, these are the basics of marking:

1. Know the force.
2. Get into position quickly.
3. Establish your marking stance—knees bent, legs slightly more than shoulder-width apart, arms out and low (figure 7.1); remain balanced, shifting and bending with the legs, not the waist.
4. Focus on the task at hand. Don't overcommit or take reckless chances at point blocks.

Figure 7.1 Proper marking stance is low, with knees bent and legs slightly more than shoulder-width apart. Weight stays on the balls of the feet, ready to shift quickly. The strong-side arm is out and low. The weak-side arm might be higher or used for balance.

5. Communicate with your teammates.
6. Call "Up!"

Knowing and Establishing the Force

A defensive captain typically chooses a side to mark while on the line before pulling, calling out something such as, "Forcing home!" or "Forcing away!" "Home" refers to the side of the field where one team has set up camp, and "away" refers to the other side. "Forcing home" means that markers are responsible for preventing throws down the home side of the field. Sometimes a physical landmark is chosen (trees, a lake, a building) if home and away are not clear. More common calls are "Forcing forehand!" or "Forcing backhand!" These calls are more intuitive but a bit confusing—by convention, "forcing forehand" means that markers are responsible for preventing right-handed throwers from making backhand throws or, more generally, any throw to the (right-handed) backhand side; "forcing backhand" prevents right-handed forehands. The actual direction of the force doesn't depend on the handedness of the thrower, as this would be too confusing for defenders without a view of the player with the disc. Other phrases can be used to be more colloquial or to prevent the defense from gaining an advantage through eavesdropping. This choice can change at any moment during the point. Let's assume that the defense has chosen a side to force. Your first priority as a marker in a point is then simply to know the force. Knowing the force is a sine qua non of defense, and yet players often lose focus and forget.

Once you know which side you're expected to mark, you must then immediately position yourself in the proper location, which depends on the marking priorities. A marker forcing forehand can't be expected to prevent every possible throw to the backhand side. Thus, you should decide which throws are most dangerous and focus on stopping those. Once you have a good idea of what you want to prevent, you can decide where to position yourself.

The most damaging throw to a team forcing forehand is an unmarked downfield backhand. Because the defense is shading the opposite direction, one open throw on the unshaded side often leads to a cascade of throws down the line (and into the end zone) before the defense can recover. While obvious, this simple observation has real consequences. Suppose you're defending a player and are running when the catch is made on the forehand side (figure 7.2). If you then decide to dive across the forehand side to block a forehand you think is imminent, though you might have some chance of getting the block, there's a

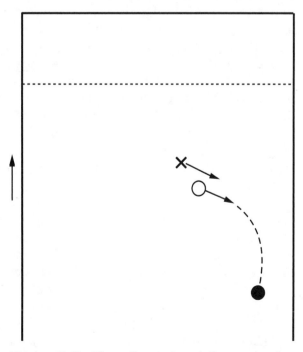

Figure 7.2 The offense has just caught the disc on the run. The defender must stop quickly, against temptation and momentum, to stay on the proper side and not give up the force.

much greater chance of ending prostrate on the ground while the thrower unleashes a free and easy backhand or inside-out forehand down the weak side. This is an obvious overcommitment error. This same error takes other forms, as well. If on the same play you overcommit to block a break-mark backhand you think is surely coming, you might leave yourself out of position for the breaking inside-out. Simply put: *Commit but don't overcommit.* You must prepare yourself for a thrower's intelligent response to your bids. Sometimes players, instead of beginning to mark, run to cut off a continuing-swing throw—a choice that might stop one threat but might weaken the defense against a host of other throws (because the marker is too far away to do anything). Sometimes the swing throw is clearly imminent, but there may be other possibilities. If you cut off the swing, you must immediately close in so you're not vulnerable to other breaking throws. (See Finer Points of Marking later in the chapter.) Short-sighted overcommitments lead to less-than-optimal defense, thus violating the principle of possession. Winning play need not be flamboyant!

Positioning

A marker's best position varies according to field position and particular thrower, and it also varies over the course of the stall count. By and large, though, if you're marking, you'll want to stand within a footstep of the thrower. Generally, being too close or too far from the thrower puts you at a disadvantage—too far, and the thrower has a greater range of angles that you can't prevent; too near, and the thrower can step around you or gain a "free" throw if contact occurs during the throwing motion (a foul on the marker means that turnovers are nullified whereas completed passes are allowed to stand).

The angle of the marking stance is also important. If you're forcing forehand, position yourself slightly to the right and facing the thrower. Your stance should be angled toward the thrower, with feet slightly more than shoulder-width apart. Knees should be bent (get low!), and your balance should be on the balls of your feet (stay on your toes!). Arms should be out and low. This ready position allows a quick response to any pivots, movements, fakes, or diversions that the thrower attempts (figure 7.1). For this reason, you should try to maintain the ready position, or not deviate too much from it. For example, if the thrower motions as if he's throwing a wide backhand around the force, you must respond by moving sideways, keeping your knees bent. If the thrower goes for a low forehand, keep your arms out and bend at the knees with the thrower. (Many throwers can throw very low forehands, so you'll want to get all the way to the ground for your block. If you're touching grass, you're doing your job.) Keeping your knees bent allows you to react further, in case the thrower's motion was just a misdirection. Lunging from the waist would leave you off balance (principle of weight). The thrower can quickly pivot back and break the mark with an around backhand against an out-of-position defender. Failure to maintain marking form while reacting is an overcommitment to the thrower's (possibly diversionary) motion. For example, jumping to block a hammer threat will leave you in the air, unable to move left or right. How sure are you that the hammer will be released? Know the risk you're taking. Always be prepared to mark for the full 10 seconds. Taking a chance, especially one that comes early in the stall count, leaves you at a disadvantage if your attempt fails.

Keep your arms out to the side and low. Most break-mark throws are thrown under, rather than over, the marker's outstretched arms. Although high-release throws are a popular way of breaking the mark, if you adopt an "arms up" philosophy you'll soon find yourself shopping for a new team.

For the most part, good marking follows a common pattern. You quickly get into a balanced "ready position," with arms out and low, and shift your stance—side to side, up and down—to prevent the thrower's backhand (for force forehand). There's more to marking, as we'll see, but all the finer points are moot if you ignore the basics.

Finer Points of Marking

Not all break-mark throws are equally damaging. A backward or lateral dump pass only becomes damaging if it leads to a downfield pass to an open thrower, especially one to the weak side. An inside-out throw is typically thrown closer to the area being covered by a defender than is a breaking, around-the-mark throw. Thus, inside-out throws don't lead to cascades of break-mark, downfield throws as often as around-the-mark throws do. For these reasons, most defenses emphasize preventing gaining, around-the-mark throws. Inside-out passes are secondary, but a team that has been beaten by a string of inside-out throws might shift priorities if the opposing handlers have around-the-mark throws in their arsenal. The different priorities lead to different stances. When preventing inside-outs, your marking stance should be closer to straight up than the standard stance described earlier.

Lateral "around" passes are generally not as damaging as gainers, but they can be if they lead to further advancement down the weak side. The recipient of a lateral pass is typically running horizontally toward the weak side and has his defender behind him, shading the strong side (as seen in figure 7.3, albeit for a gaining pass). He's in a good position to continue advancing downfield. The same can be said of many weak-side dump passes. Breaking the mark with dump swings is a common technique for foiling a force without using break-mark throws. So, if you're about to mark the recipient of a breaking pass, place a premium on preventing the "continuation" throw, especially if you see the next receiver already cutting. This is called "stopping the flow" or "cutting it off." In this case, you should prevent the continuation pass by placing yourself in the way of the "clear and present danger," running to a position (usually toward the weak side but a bit downfield) between the thrower and open receiver. Even if you're right with him as he catches the pass, be careful not to underestimate how far his momentum and pivot will take him. Many a marker will let up and

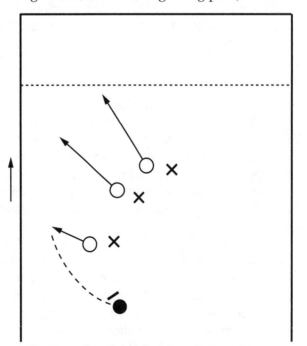

Figure 7.3 A gaining "around" pass can lead to a fast break up the weak side. Lateral around passes can also be dangerous, so defenders should be sure to establish the mark quickly.

coast into a spot near the new thrower's pivot foot, only to be beaten by an immediate step-and-throw. You might not have time to establish a marking position before the thrower releases. As soon as the continuation throw has been prevented, close in on the thrower without delay. Lazy strolls back to the mark are ineffectual; they allow the thrower several options—inside-outs and up-the-middles—for a long time. Overrunning the mark can be acceptable to prevent a continuation, but languishing several yards downfield is unsatisfactory.

Running Down on the Pull

Running down on the pull is in many ways just like establishing a mark on an offender with a continuation throw. Let's assume your offender is going to be catching a good pull (so that you're within 30 yards, say, when the catch is made). It's likely that his team has a play to run along a sideline, right off the pull. The play might run up the intended weak side (the breakside). Don't simply run straight at the player. Instead, run at him in a (gently) curving path that comes in from the weak side. This puts you in the way of the play (if it's along the break), making it more difficult to run. With luck, you'll have delayed progress enough so that all defenders are now in position.

Now continue your path in toward the thrower and establish the mark. This is the ideal situation. If you think the play will be run up the strong side, resist the temptation to come in from the strong side. This leaves you out of position in the event you were wrong (and the play was weak side) or if the offense has more than one option. Many offenses run decoys to protect themselves. If you could be sure you're preventing the only option, then changing course might be worth the risk, but the second option might come from out of sight. Weak-side flow before a mark is established is a hemorrhaging wound in the defense.

After stopping the swing, close in to the desired marking position while maintaining your ability to respond to the thrower's maneuvers. Sprinting in might leave you off balance against horizontal fakes, so weigh the competing aims of maintaining balance and restoring proper position. Bunny-hop steps back into position can be effective, though somewhat tiring. Be it hopping or stepping, your march back should be direct. Torturous routes back to position are wasteful. Don't do-si-do the thrower by running around his back. You might be tempted to run around the thrower to try to stop a strong-side throw, but resist this temptation. Preventing with-force throws is not your responsibility.

If you're forcing forehand, you might feel an urge to harass forehands as well as prevent backhands. This urge to contribute to the defense is natural, but moving too far left (to the strong side) leaves open the possibility of a very dangerous, downfield, break-mark backhand throw. Remember that your job is not to get point blocks but to prevent the break. You should only move left, thus inhibiting the forehand, if the thrower has shifted his weight toward the forehand side, thus committing to a forehand throw (often a handling error). In such a case, if you stay balanced while you shift left, you'll be able to shift back in time to prevent the breaking backhand. You'll be in better position than the thrower. Sometimes the thrower responds to such pressure by leaning even farther to the forehand side, often stretching wide and low. In this case, continue to pressure the thrower, who, now quite off balance, has a rapidly diminishing number of viable options. Always monitor the thrower's weight, taking advantage of any inadvertent weight commitments (violations of the weight principle). A similar commitment by the thrower can come from a big wind-up or other such huck preparations. On the backhand side, huck wind-ups involve a tightly curled torso and a big step. On the forehand side, hucks come more quickly but are sometimes preceded by a step backward. If you notice a huck commitment, make a *proportional* commitment toward the strong side to harass the throw. Often, it's enough just to be straight up temporarily, always remaining ready in case the thrower was faking. Remember that even if you only make the thrower alter his throw slightly, the huck will go awry. Of course, if you hear "No huck!" from your teammates on the sideline, take that into account, too.

The nature of the mark changes with the stall count. Marking risks early in the stall count (counts 1-2-3) are more dangerous because the thrower has more time calmly to recognize weaknesses and take advantage of opportunities. At 4-5-6, the danger diminishes as the thrower starts to feel some pressure to release the disc before getting stalled. A thrower who turns his torso back to look for a dump pass is unlikely to break the mark downfield without shifting his torso forward again—so as a marker, try to take advantage. Remember, though, that poise varies significantly among throwers. If you know the thrower's handling skills, you're better equipped to assess the risks of an occasional deviation from the conservative marking stance. Every thrower feels pressure to release late (7-8-9) in the stall count, and risks are more likely to pay off. One way of applying pressure without unbalancing yourself too much is to close in more tightly late in the stall count. A panicking thrower feels even greater anxiety under such pressure and is more apt to err in his throwing. Still, a great many throwers recognize that they need only about a second to find an open cutter and release a pass. If you take wanton risks late in the stall count, you might nullify nearly 10 seconds of good, team defense and incur the wrath of your hard-working teammates. For example, a marker at 8 might see the thrower turn for a dump and jump in the way. This can stop the dump, but an alert thrower will turn forward again (with the marker out of position) and hit an offender on the weak side. Even late risks can be costly.

By no means are we advocating wooden, predictable marking. On the contrary, marking risks must be anything but predictable. Good handlers can lure a marker into an overcommitment with a subtle glance of the eye and a slight shift of weight. The thrower might pretend to be all-too-willing to complete the obvious swing. So a marker's risk might not catch the thrower by surprise but rather fall into the handler's crafty ploy. This is why predictable risks are costly. The occasional sudden jab can catch the thrower off-guard, especially after a pattern of consistent marking has been established (this holds true particularly in a zone defense). If you surprise the thrower with such a risk, you might get the block or prevent an otherwise unstoppable throw—or you might make him shift his weight improperly in response, allowing you to recover before he can capitalize on your chance. For example, to capitalize on your truly out-of-the-blue stab at a forehand in a forehand force, the thrower has to recognize what you're doing, look to the backhand side for easy breaks, spot an easy break, shift his weight, then complete his throw. If he never saw you coming, this will take longer than the time it takes for you to get back into position.

You can use other clues to vary your stance effectively. Listen to the calls of your teammates. A teammate shouting "No break!" means that an offender on the break-mark side is open for a particularly damaging pass, such as into the end zone, so focus solely on the task at hand and forget about all other risks. In return, communicate to your teammates by counting the stall loudly and clearly, raising the volume as the stall nears 10. This tells your fellow defenders that a throw is definitely imminent and also adds an extra level of stress to the thrower. Of course, call it "up" when the disc is thrown.

You can also try to gain a feel for the action downfield by taking a well-timed peek. This might be difficult to do during the stall count, but immediately before the reception, you should glance back to see what the likely development of the offense will be. If you discover a completely open player in the end zone waiting for a throw, you must forsake the mark and simply prevent the score. Preventing a certain goal trumps all other defensive priorities. More typically, you'll rely on your periphery for partial information about what's happening downfield. Also, you have a good view of the backfield, so you can help a teammate who's covering the dump by alerting her when the thrower is looking to dump.

Marking is all about making a consistent effort for the entire stall count. The second you let your guard down, the thrower can break you—and there's usually a receiver available because defenders are shading based on their trust in your mark. Begin by preventing the continuation, then establish the mark quickly, get into a balanced stance in which you can shift with the thrower's pivots, and just let the stall count rise. As it does, adjust to changes in the field and in the handler's objectives. Opportunities will arise, and you can take an occasional risk, but be selective. Be aggressive without being reckless. You can't stop everything; you can only maximize your chances.

■ Marking Drill

This is a three-player drill, including two throwers and one marker. The throwers stand about 10 yards apart. The marker runs back and forth between them, with a five-second stall count. The marker sets up before the throwers try to throw. Continue for 90 seconds, then rotate markers. Usually this drill should be done with a straight-up mark, but you can also do it shading toward a side force. If so, receivers should cut slowly to the breakside. Overhead passes are not allowed. This is also a conditioning drill and helps teach marking while fatigued—when markers are more likely to get lazy and reach instead of moving their legs. To remove the conditioning aspect of this drill, rotate the marker every pass. Whoever throws the disc runs to the other player and marks. Depending on the setup, this drill can also be useful for conditioning, break-mark throws, and handler cutting.

■ Marking Drill

This is a four-player drill, including two offenders and two defenders. The cutter and defender set up about 10 yards away from the marker and thrower, as the first handler in the stack would set up. Make it clear to all whether the thrower is on the sideline or in the middle of the field and what the force is—otherwise, the throws and defense aren't gamelike. For example, pretend the thrower is on the line being trapped (it's better if you set up next to an actual field line), so the cutter lines up laterally. The defender's prime job is to stop the cut up the line, while the marker takes away the dump. Cycle through so that each player has three or five throws in that situation, then moves to another situation. There are too many variations to do them all in one drill, so vary from practice to practice. Depending on the setup, this drill can also be used for conditioning, break-mark throws, and handler cutting.

Marking Tips

1. Get low.

2. Stay on your toes.

3. Bend from your knees, not from your waist.

4. Mark with your legs, not your arms. (This does not mean going for footblocks, but that you should mark by shifting position with your legs rather than by reaching out.)

5. Use your peripheral vision.

6. Focus on the mark, not on point blocks or on preventing with-mark throws.

7. Communicate with your teammates.

8. Call it "up."

Switching and Poaching

Great defensive teams are better than the sum of their parts. One player can front her offender heavily if she knows she has a backup deep. A defender playing the middle-middle zone position can take a calculated risk, with others picking up the slack if her attempt doesn't pan out. Critical to team unity is that some players have an awareness of regions outside their immediate vicinity and are responsive to this periphery.

Switching, or swapping offenders with a defensive teammate, is a reassignment of defensive roles to take advantage of the defenders' field positions. Poaching, or leaving your offender in an attempt to thwart an offensive play, is a gamble that exploits the element of surprise and offensive confusion. Both switching and poaching allow defenders to work with each other to cover the field better, but they present considerable risks if done improperly or at the wrong time. Clear communication, whether explicit or implicit, is the key to making these maneuvers low on risk and high on reward.

Switching

You're fronting your offender, and he goes deep—no chance to cover him. What if the thrower makes a nice pass? As long as you have a fellow defender further downfield (and on the same side), you should be able to get help from her. She can come off her offender and pick up yours. In the process, you must find and cover her offender as quickly as you can. You'll be temporarily out of position, so you need to get on your new offender before the offense can find him.

You're shading sideline, and your offender cuts breakside. Just at that point, the disc is swung to the opposite side of the field, and your offender is in a position to initiate an offensive assault down the breakside. You should look for a fellow defender in the stack to pick up your offender—and you should cover hers.

You're trailing your offender on a cutback, while your teammate is trailing her offender on a cutout on the same side (figure 8.1). The two of you should lock eyes and signal, call, or simply know to do a switch. You should fade back and pick up the receiver cutting long. Your teammate should stay shallow and pick up the offender you were trailing. Do this before it's too late for you to shift your momentum.

You're getting ready to play defense as the disc is checked into play in the red zone. The offense lines up in a stack. You stand on one side of the stack, a teammate on the other (figure 8.2). You signal to her before the tap-in that you'll pick up whichever of your two offenders comes your way, and she'll pick up whoever goes her way. If they both go the same way, one of you covers the redundant two until the other defender comes. (Similar considerations apply to a front/back switch against offenders oriented vertically.)

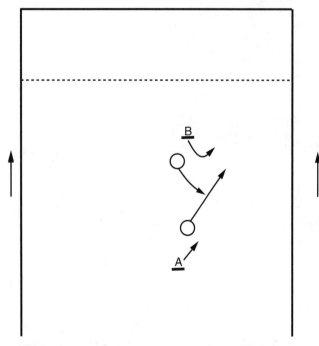

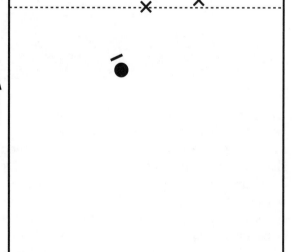

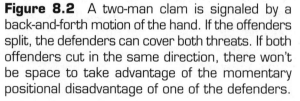

Figure 8.1 Player A is trailing her offender deep, while player B is trailing her offender coming back. A front-back switch results in good coverage of both cuts. Note that the switch must be recognized in time for player B to shift her momentum to pick up the long cut.

Figure 8.2 A two-man clam is signaled by a back-and-forth motion of the hand. If the offenders split, the defenders can cover both threats. If both offenders cut in the same direction, there won't be space to take advantage of the momentary positional disadvantage of one of the defenders.

You're near the back of the stack. Your offender begins to cut in hard, and you go in with him. He turns and heads deep immediately, and the last player in the stack switches onto him. Meanwhile, the last cutter in the stack cuts in on the breakside and is picked up by the next defender. This player's offender is now open, so you switch onto him. A multiple switch can involve more than two players.

Each of these situations turns a weakness into a strength. One player (you) is out of position on her assigned offender but finds another defender on the field who is already in position for coverage. You are then typically in a decent position to pick up the offender your teammate left (even if you're not in great position, it might take the offender a bit of time to realize the defensive lapse—long enough for you to recover). The offense watches as its hard work is matched by a quick-thinking defense.

What makes a switch possible is the synchrony between you and your fellow switcher. As you might expect, synchrony comes through communication. New teammates will probably have to rely on the spoken word—"Switch!"—as well as eye contact or pointing to ensure that the call was received. Over time, you and your teammates will come to recognize certain situations and understand each other—then you'll be ready for the "switch" call before it comes. At this point, a simple shout of "Hey!" or even just a glance might be enough to communicate that a switch should occur. The transition from spoken word to tacit understanding takes time to develop. Sometimes it's not clear what to do in a situation, or your teammate might feel she has the situation under control and doesn't want the switch. This too must be communicated. She should say, "I go!" or "I got it!" or simply "No!" Avoid the word "stay" because it could mean either "stay on your defender" (no switch) or "stay where you are" (and switch). After the point, discuss switches that were made and opportunities that were not taken. Find out what your teammates prefer. Eventually, you and your teammates might establish such a rapport that most switches occur automatically and instantaneously (as in a great clam defense), thwarting the undertakings of an unsuspecting offense.

Poaching

Certain situations require unilateral action. You might be defending in the middle of the stack when you see an open offender making a big comeback cut down the strong alley (figure 8.3). The disc is on the sideline, and you're in a trap formation. At this point, you have the opportunity to flare out to stymie the large sideline gainer. You might not have made eye contact with your teammate, and the two of you might not be in a great position to switch. Still, you have the chance to help her out and eliminate a big offensive threat. In the process, you create a minor threat—the offender you were covering is uncovered, but still in the stack, away from the strong sideline.

Another poaching opportunity can arise when you have just covered a cutter on the strong side who is returning to the stack. If you trail this offender a bit on his return, you might be able to linger in the alley, getting in the way of any strong-side developments (keep your arms out). Such a poach might last only a second or two but could be enough to discourage a throw. If your offender is not aware of his periphery, he will continue toward the stack at a slow pace and miss the opportunity to beat you.

The timing of a poach is geared to its purpose. If you're poaching to make a block, you want to hesitate as long as possible so you don't tip the offense. If your poach is to prevent a play from ever occurring, show it early to discourage the development.

Beware of "poaching by the numbers." Any defense that repeatedly makes obvious poaches will suffer the consequences—a good offense will anticipate the

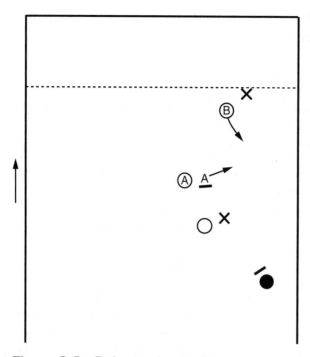

Figure 8.3 Defender A, who flares out in the alley as her player sits in the stack, poaches off offender A to prevent offender B from receiving a gaining pass with the force down the strong-side alley.

poaches and burn them, perhaps even calling a play designed to run off a poach. You should also beware of the lazy defender who uses poaches as an excuse for being off her offender. Poaching might lead to easy blocks, but these happen only occasionally. More often, you'll have to hustle back to your offender, so there's nothing lazy about a proper poach.

When you poach, do it suddenly and forcefully. Don't do half a poach. Half a poach leaves you out of position on two offenders. A forceful poach leaves you in a position to stop a play or get a block. It also leaves an offender temporarily uncovered. At this point, assuming the throw was not thrown or the block did not happen, it's up to the defense as a whole to recover from the risk. You might be able to hop back to your offender before he realizes what has happened. The defender you helped

out by poaching might find your offender and pick him up, turning the poach into a switch. Or another defender might have been in a position to leave her own and pick up the offender you abandoned, creating an even smaller threat in the process (say someone far on the weak side returning to the stack), so that you or the defender you helped have time to find the open player. In any case, a deliberate and unambiguous poach is easily read by the teammates who will help you to recover.

The cardinal rule of poaching is, don't create a bigger threat! You don't want to leave someone open on the strong side to pick up an offender who has gotten open in the middle of the field. You don't want to help out covering a dump and leave your offender free for a long gainer. You can poach to quell a threat, but don't create a bigger threat in the process.

Communication

A switch or poach that's not communicated or expected can lead to defensive confusion. By and large, switches occur in response to an offensive advantage, whereas poaches are defensive gambits initiated by a defender. Thus, switches can be called out loud—"Switch!"—without reducing their effectiveness, whereas poaches should be surreptitious. How can a defense know how to respond to a poach, then?

First of all, if the poacher is trying to cover for another defender, that defender should recognize that she was in a position to receive help—so she should in turn help the helper, if possible. You don't want two defenders on one offender, leaving someone else free. Second, if the poacher doesn't intend to make a full switch (but rather plans on taking a quick stab at a block, then returning), there may be no need for other responses from the defense—though the poacher should be prepared to find a new offender to cover in case someone else has picked up the vacated offender. Third, the defense might have a policy of allowing poaching in certain formations. For example, in a force-middle defense, the defender of a handler might choose to poach into the middle of the field and allow the dump. If this is the policy, then other defenders should be prepared for the consequences of such poaches. Finally, if you're poaching and in trouble (can't find an offender to cover), call for help! Don't put your pride above your team.

Note on Recognition

In this book, we often present a situation or create a scenario and suggest possible responses. Most of the time, the difficulty is not in making an analysis of a scenario but in recognizing the relevant aspects of a field position while playing. For example, you might be in a situation where a poach could be a good gambit, but you might be focusing on your balance or position, counting the number of passes, or trying to remember to glance back at the disc. That's why these important but routine aspects of defense must be ingrained through hours of practice, leaving you free to consider higher-order skills, such as poaching and switching, which enable the seven on-field defenders to function as a potent unit.

Offensive Players

If you're on offense and have been poached, or if you see any poach on the field, yell "Poach!" immediately and move to an advantageous position. The call signals to the thrower to be extra careful to ensure that the throwing lanes are free before making the pass. It also signals to the thrower that there's an uncovered offender on the field. If you were not the one poached, shouting "Poach!" tells your offensive teammates that they might find themselves open. Finally, the call tells your defender that you're on to her ploy. This may stop her in midpoach, which puts the defense at a double disadvantage.

While yelling "Poach," you should also immediately find an open spot on the field, far away from your poaching defender. This leaves you more open to receive the pass and makes it more difficult for the defense to recover from the poach. Many offenders seem to feel the temptation to run toward the strong side when poached. Most often, this means running right at the player who poached off of you. Avoid this, and run *away* from the poach.

If you're poached onto, continue cutting. Sometimes the poacher will abandon you after a moment, and your own defender might hesitate, leaving you briefly open. If the poach stays with you, let the thrower know not to throw it to you, either by shouting "No" or waving your hands. If possible, point toward your free teammate.

Switching and poaching are high-level maneuvers demanding an awareness of the field around you. As your one-on-one defense improves, so does your vision of the field, and these maneuvers allow you to use your vision to help your team respond to imminent threats and to receive help from your teammates. Smart play requires that you don't create bigger threats in the process. Good communication makes for smooth execution of switches and proper recovery from poaches.

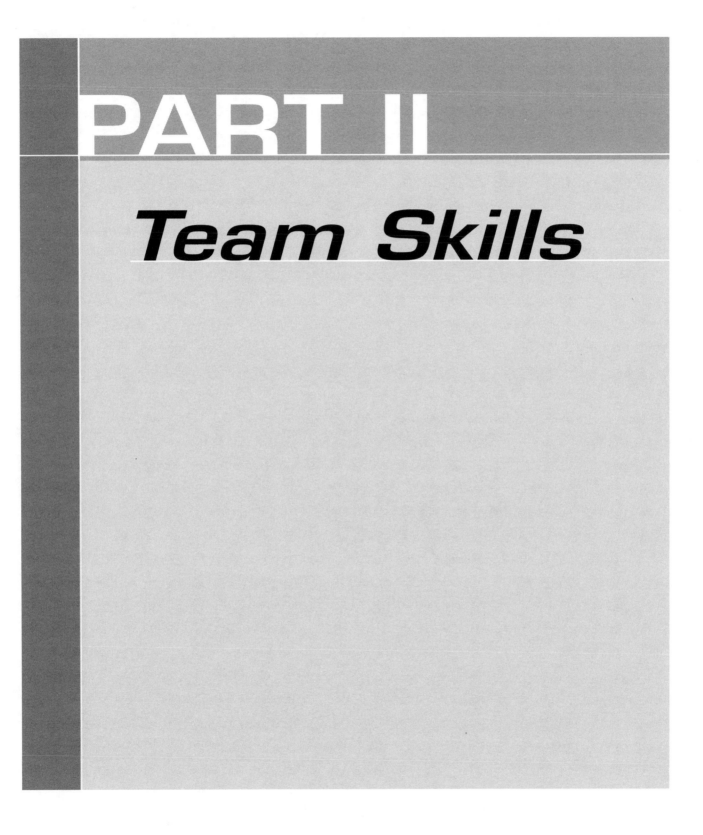

PART II

Team Skills

One-on-One Defense

NINE

© Marshall Goff

Though it sounds as if one-on-one defense would be an individual defense, there are many aspects of team play involved, many of which require field vision, coordination, and communication. All players on the field should understand and appreciate the team aspects of one-on-one coverage.

Any one-on-one defense built solely on winning seven individual match-ups all over the field is destined to fail. The field is large, and a skilled offense will find holes. A good team defense tries to shrink the effective playing area of the field so that the offense scores only with great effort, strategy, good decision-making, and proper execution. Let it be said: Defense is hard. Even against superlative defense, good offenses still score more than half the time.

Team defense begins with the force. An effective marker will do her best to prohibit all dangerous break-mark passes and to harass huck attempts with the mark. Any pass that does get past the mark should be off-line, ineffectual, or delayed enough that the downfield defender has a chance at making the block. The importance of a solid, honest mark can't be overstated. Lazy reaching with the arms and paying too much attention to the force-side throw might occasionally garner a point block, but far too often it leads to a string of passes along the breakside.

A downfield defender can trust the mark to stop or hamper break-mark throws but can't just allow her cutter to roam free on the breakside. Her job is to prevent her offender from getting open on the force side. To do this, she needs to work and constantly reposition herself according to the principles outlined in chapter 6 on guarding. If the pass is not to her offender, a safe time to do this is immediately after the marker's "Up!" call.

Both players have to do their jobs well enough that the other can get away with imperfect (although good) performance. Keep in mind that while perfect offensive execution is nearly impossible to stop, every offense makes mistakes. That mistake might be as small as taking a half-second too long to throw a pass or putting a break-mark throw on the inside shoulder of the receiver instead of the outside shoulder, but good team defense will capitalize on some of these mistakes.

Another team aspect of one-on-one defense is the underappreciated yet crucial role of sideline players, who offer communication and encouragement. Misguided players on the sideline might think they need do no more than call the force call or yell "Nice block," but there's more to it than that. They need to echo all information to the team, including the stall count after stoppages and calls of "Up!" and "Broken!" Perhaps the most important type of communication, though, and the type typically lacking in lower-level teams, is information targeted at individuals. Some players shy away from yelling to individuals because their words might be taken the wrong way, but their input is useful information sometimes required to get the job done on the field. Examples include alerting a defender that the thrower is looking at her offender, helping defenders find the uncovered offender after a poach or switch, and letting the marker and downfield defender know when a long pass is viable. Finally, a kind word about a good defensive play that does not result in a block (a switch onto an open long cutter, good shutdown defense) helps encourage solid play over heroics.

Force Middle

The force-middle (or simply FM) defense attempts to make flow difficult by taking away the sides and forcing the offense to turn back toward the (center) stack. Additionally, any huck with the force might have to travel over the stack, so the thrower must alter the flight path or risk having a low pass blocked.

In the FM, the mark and the downfield defensive side-to-side positioning can change every pass if the disc keeps crossing the center of the field. When the disc is near the sideline, the mark is almost straight up with just a shade toward blocking the line. Downfield defenders have to balance the threat of gaining an inside-out pass against the swing continuation to the far side, and this should be nearly straight up with a strong-side shade (figure 9.1). The handler defenders have a trickier job because a quick inside-out is more viable. Thus, they have to be closer to their offenders (practically touching them, in fact). When the disc is

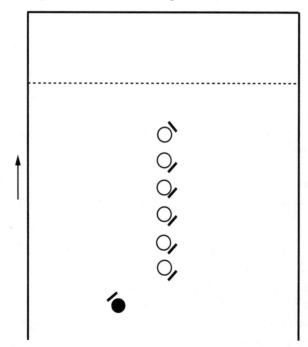

Figure 9.1 Defensive positioning for the force middle.

off the line but still clearly closer to one side, the marker is offset about half a body toward the line and angled about 30 degrees toward the thrower. Things are a little more complicated when the disc is near the center, and team emphasis is required when working on this defense. If the pass originated near the line, then the offense is probably set up to continue going across the field, so it's better for the defense to switch the force back. However, if the pass has only a small lateral component or is a dump, the rest of the defense is probably still well positioned, so it's better to keep the force in the same direction for the next pass. In either case, the marker should let her teammates know the force immediately (maybe even when the pass is still in the air), and the sidelines should loudly echo the call. In fact, it's good practice to make this call every pass. If the marker is going to switch the force, she needs to get there in time to set the mark. The receiver will often need a couple of steps to stop, and the lazy defender will jog with him to that spot, forgetting that the thrower's pivot will take him clear of the mark for a dangerous continuation. Instead, the hard-working defender runs hard to that extended spot and immediately adopts a good marking stance.

Calling a Side

The popular method for calling a side is to use "home" to designate the side where the team supplies are and "away" to mean the other side. Another option is to use "forehand" and "backhand" to indicate which way a right-handed thrower would be forced (even if the thrower is left-handed). Downfield defenders can't be expected to check in every pass to see whether a righty or a lefty has the disc. A third option is to yell out only when the mark is switched. If the team is disciplined, you can use code words so the opponent can't immediately tell what's happening. As always, though, remember that complicated calls might confuse your own team as well—it can even be easy to forget which side is "home" when you're caught up in playing.

The downfield defender must be alert when playing force middle. After an "up" call, she needs to find the disc right away to see if a force change is obvious (in which case she needs to swing around to the other side of her opponent) or likely (in which case she needs to perk up her ears for the marker's call, ready to switch). This is, of course, in addition to the normal repositioning required as the disc moves.

The FM is generally a conservative defense. Because it attempts to disrupt the flow by blocking off continuation throws at the mark, this defense forces a lot of passes. Additionally, those passes will be into an area with a lot of players around (the stack). Long passes have to travel over the stack. A careless or impatient offense will have plenty of opportunities to make mistakes. On the other hand, the FM gives a lot of room for cutters and for dumps and never creates a high-pressure trap situation. The defense also needs to make many decisions on when to change the force and to communicate those decisions quickly, so it can be easy to get the mark or the downfield positioning wrong.

One variation is to have the defender covering the dump-handler poach into the throwing alley, and together with the marker, form a two-person cup. This makes ordinary offensive progress difficult but, as the dump cut is uncovered, can lead to open break-mark passes. Still, it might take an offense quite some time to discover this key.

Force Side

The other commonly played one-on-one defenses keep the force the same way all the time. There are some differences between the force forehand and the force backhand that will be explained shortly, but they are similar enough to be described together. (Note again that the terminology is based on which way a right-handed thrower is forced. Left-handed throwers will be forced the opposite throw, such as a backhand in a force-forehand defense.)

With either force-side defense, the offense is pushed in one direction until it's trapped on the sideline. Especially when the disc is near the forced sideline, this defense can be coupled with "last back" switching to limit the deep game while providing excellent coverage against comeback cuts.

With the "last back," the deepest defender in the stack positions herself behind her opponent, facing the disc while the other defenders play in front of their cutters on the force side, facing downfield (this is also called "face-guarding"). These players are primarily concerned with cuts back to the disc. The last back needs to keep an eye out for viable deep cuts. This doesn't mean that she simply stands in the back while the others all abandon their cutters 20 yards from the disc. If the defender stays with the cutter or if the cut is just a weak clearing attempt or if the thrower can't deliver a long pass because of the wind, bad position, or a weak arm, the last back ignores the cut and changes to a faceguard position while the other defender becomes the new "last back." Even if the defense is not playing "last back," all downfield defenders, particularly ones covering idle offenders, need to be on the lookout for open deep cuts. This is one of the occasions where targeted communication from the sideline can prevent a goal. When sideline players see the deep cut and that a capable long thrower is in position to huck, they should call out to teammates.

There are a few caveats here. If her opponent cuts in, the last back needs to cut in with him, unless there is a clear switching opportunity with another defender. If that cut is off a stoppage, there usually is an opportunity, but during flow it's more likely that the others will be occupied with their own offenders. Another danger is when several cuts in a row originate from the back of the stack, either as part of a set play or through chance, and an offensive player is now the last back, and by several yards. This is one of the most advantageous positions a cutter can be in, if he recognizes it and the defender does not. This situation yields a certain goal for a quick-acting offense, so immediate action is necessary. A defender near the back of the stack needs to glance occasionally to make sure she's not the last defender back. The sideline needs to alert the new last back and can also scream "No huck!" to the marker if the receiver cuts deep. Because teams often run this as a play off a stoppage, the three deepest defenders need to be alert to the possibility. If the forward-most of the three sees the two deeper offenders cutting, she needs to recognize that the play is on and hustle to stay behind her offender. Either of the last two defenders can also act unilaterally and hang back for an extra second to prevent the long pass.

When the disc is on the far (nontrapping) sideline, the mark and the downfield positioning are similar to that of the FM (figure 9.2a-b). As the disc moves closer to the forced sideline, the mark shifts more to the breakside. When the disc is trapped on the sideline, as long as the thrower is facing downfield, the marker should be close to the thrower at a pronounced angle. As soon as the thrower turns to look for the dump, the marker shuffles over until she's facing the sideline. She also might need to increase the distance from the thrower to reduce the likelihood of a foul and make it more difficult for the thrower to get a short pass by her. Good positioning is especially important in

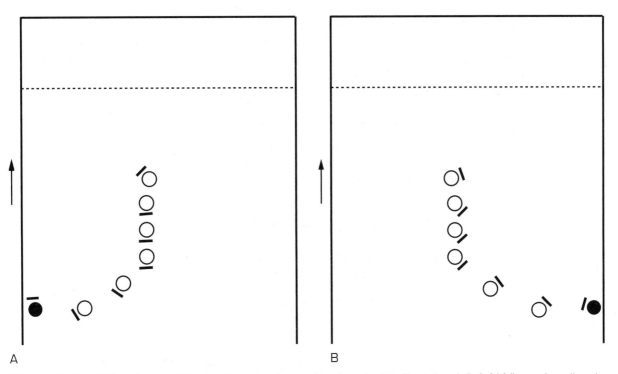

A   B

Figure 9.2 Defensive positioning for the force forehand with "last back." *(a)* When the disc is on the unforced line, the positioning is similar to that of FM. *(b)* When the disc is on the trapped sideline, the marker aggressively takes away the break-mark.

this situation. Defenders near the disc should position their bodies to prevent the cut up the line but also be ready to follow the dump cut, expecting the mark to prevent most throws or at least make them difficult. A short-break pass off the trap situation can be ruinous for this defense. Often, the offense continues moving the disc all the way across the field before defenders have a chance to catch up and set the mark. Even if just the one pass is completed, the defense has squandered an opportunity.

If a strong crosswind is blowing, it's especially useful to force the other team with the wind. In a very strong wind, just about anything will be effective. Break-mark passes then are directly into the wind, often floating over the receiver's head. Passes with the force are harder to throw with touch and will be pushed down or toward out of bounds. This defense can also be effective when the offense doesn't like to break the mark, as the offense soon finds itself playing on a narrow field. If the opponent is weaker or not used to throwing in the wind, it might be more effective to force into the wind. This way, the majority of the passes must fight the wind.

Because it's more aggressive than the FM, the side force is more susceptible to long passes. Even when the defense works well, the result is often a desperation long pass that has some chance of being caught and that eats up some yards even if uncaught. Further, some offenses have become adept at jamming the disc up the line. Offenses and defenses evolve to counteract innovations by the other side.

The force forehand (also called "force flick" or "force two-finger") is the more common of the two variations. Most players, especially at the lower skill levels, are less accurate with the forehand than with the backhand. The forehand suffers more in the wind, too, making the force forehand a viable alternative with a strong crosswind. Finally, few players (even good ones) can throw extremely long forehands well. For this reason, fronting with a last back is more likely to be effective than with the long backhand.

The force backhand might be preferable when there are players who can huck well against the force forehand (this includes left-handers who would throw backhands). The force backhand can also stymie teams with precise inside-out forehands that use this pass to start the offense or get out of jams. Finally, even if none of these reasons apply, it's a good idea to mix in the force backhand after a few points of force forehand to disrupt the rhythm of the offense. (Junk defenses also disrupt the rhythm but require more practice and can result in unfavorable match-ups.) One subtlety of the force backhand is caused by the long windup and slow release required for a backhand huck. A triangulating downfield defender who can see the thrower will know from the thrower's stance whether a soon-to-be-released pass is going long or short and play accordingly.

Straight Up

The straight-up defense, once nearly extinct, has made a comeback in recent years. This was the prevailing defense in the early years of ultimate. As the name implies, the marker plays straight up against the thrower, forcing neither forehand nor backhand, and attempts to block every downfield throw while conceding throws that are largely lateral (figure 9.3). The stack offense originated as a result of the straight-up because the defense creates a dead zone in the space that the marker is taking away and allows the receiver to cut in either direction. This puts a lot of burden on the downfield defender, who must attempt to prevent both cuts. To put it mildly, this can be difficult. However, the mark makes all long throws more difficult, which is why the defense is primarily used as a transition defense against teams with potent deep games. Additionally, there's no real break-mark or force side, and some offensive players (especially those in highly structured offenses) get confused or uncomfortable.

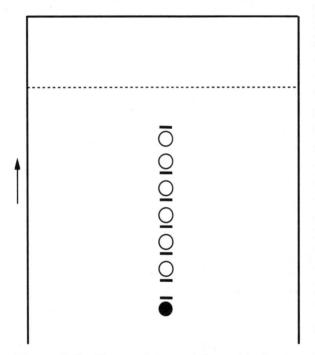

Figure 9.3 The straight-up defense blocks the downfield pass.

Choosing a Defense

Every team should pick one of these defenses as its bread-and-butter style, the one it returns to when it really needs to apply pressure in an important game. Teams should be comfortable with all the defenses, however, and mix them up throughout a game. Teams should learn which defenses work best against which offenses and recognize when it's time to abandon the default defense. Ultimately, it's the results that matter, but when making decisions during the game about what to play, you should also consider how many opportunities for blocks have arisen and how many great catches or amazing throws were necessary.

One final thought concerning all defenses: The defense's job is not just to get blocks and cause turnovers but to score. This means a defensive team needs to have some offensive ability. A defense can afford only one or two players with limited offensive skills or a tendency to turn the disc over. This also means that all turnovers are not equal. A defense that generates a lot of huck turnovers might not be as effective as one that generates only a few turnovers near the other team's goal line. Teams tend to understand this from the offensive perspective—that it can be better to try a desperation huck at a high stall count than to try a higher percentage contested dump—but few apply it defensively. If a defensive team has trouble moving the disc the length of the field (say if there's a strong wind), it should try at all times to prevent hucks. This also applies when playing against an offense unlikely to be able to move the disc. Play a less aggressive defense and force them to make a lot of passes, and just wait for the mistakes to happen. Conversely, if the other offense is unstoppable, it makes sense to encourage the huck or some other difficult pass or to play a riskier, more aggressive defense.

Whether it's force middle, a side force, or straight-up, one-on-one defense is the primary defense for most teams. Responsible marking, preventive downfield positioning, and timely sideline help deprive the offense of easy passes and make them struggle for every yard. A team might have a favorite defense but needs to be able to switch to another if circumstances dictate it.

Matching Up

Before determining assignments on the line, the defense needs to make sure they have some offensive balance and that there's a capable defender for every extremely tall or fast offensive player. If not, the person who calls the defensive substitutes must be willing to call someone off the line (or, if there's no subber, one of the players must willingly call in another more suited player). The obvious attributes to match on are height and speed, but there are additional factors to consider. It's usually best to match up by position and even style of play (squirrelly handler, burly receiver). Generally, a defender should cover the same offender over the course of a game or even a season. Ultimate players are creatures of habit, and even great players have a few moves they use all the time. Learn what your opponent does, and be ready for it.

Some unconventional match-ups can work, too. Instead of matching a strength against a strength (say, speed against speed), you can match strength against a neutralizer or offensive weakness against defensive strength. For a handler who jukes a lot, a much bigger defender might be able to hold her position and prevent the cutter from getting around her. For a good receiver who could be pressured on his throws, perhaps an outstanding marker who is only average at coverage can create some turnovers.

Zone Defense

TEN

© Marshall Goff

A zone is a style of defense in which defenders are primarily responsible for a region of the field or a throwing lane, as opposed to a particular opponent. Generally, a zone is defined by a defensive formation, and there are many different kinds of zones. In this chapter, we'll focus on zone defense in general, through the example of the 2-3-2 zone in particular. Most of what we'll say about the 2-3-2 can be applied to any zone.

The idea of a zone is to try to strategically cover the dangerous areas of the field, thus impeding offensive progress and luring the offense into taking risky throws or turning it over after many low-risk throws. The more risks taken, the more turnovers. Though individual blocks are great, they should not be the focus of a zone defense (even less so than for one on one).

Basic Positions

The 2-3-2 zone, which as the most popular zone will be taken as representative of all zones here, has three main features: a cup, the wings, and the deeps (figure 10.1). In this section, we'll describe the basic formations and positions.

The cup is a formation near the disc consisting of three defensive players. The idea of the cup is to prevent easy throws up the middle. The shape of the cup is

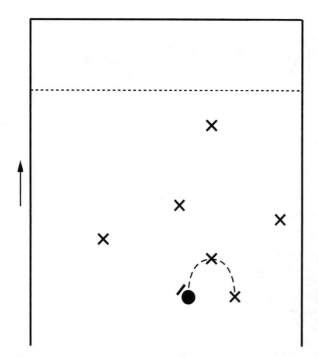

Figure 10.1 A standard formation of the 2-3-2 zone. The cup is indicated with a dotted line. This setup shows a short-deep and a deep-deep in I-formation.

an upside-down U, with two of the players at the ends of the U and the third at the middle of the curvy part. The two at the ends of the U are called "points," and they should be lateral with the disc. One of the two points—the "on-point"—will be marking the disc; the other, the "off-point," will prevent lateral crossfield throws as well as throws that are just slightly backfield or slightly downfield. When calling assignments on the line, before the start of a point, these positions are usually called "right point" and "left point," but they are differentiated in play by who's marking and who's not. The third player in the cup is called the "middle-middle" or "top of the cup" (remember that the U is envisioned upside down) and is primarily responsible for preventing throws up the middle (or "through the cup"). Thus, the cup should be thought of as an impervious shield that follows the motion of the disc. The shield can vary in shape and size, as we'll see later in the chapter.

The two wings—one on each side of the field—are responsible for preventing the offense from advancing up the alleys. They generally want to move in toward the center, to try to clog things up for the offense, but they're bound to staying near the lines whenever a defender poses a potential alley threat. The wings have no safety backups on their sides. Any offense that can get around a wing can usually proceed to the goal.

There are two deeps, primarily responsible for preventing long throws. They have no backups deep and must appreciate this priority. They can orient themselves side to side (one on the left, one on the right) or in an I-formation, or they might alternate between the two formations as necessary during the point. In an I-formation, one player will be called "deep-deep" and the other "short-deep." In this formation, the short-deep is responsible for throws over the top of the cup and for helping out the cup in general, if possible. The deep-deep in an I-formation might call on a wing to fall back to help her (say, if there are two offenders going long on opposite sides of the field) or might call the short-deep back temporarily. In a side-to-side formation, the deep on the other side of the field can be called over to assist. No position is static.

The sport of ultimate is still developing, and the current terminology is nonstandard. Our convention is explained as follows: the first and last 2s in 2-3-2 refer to the two points and the two deeps, respectively. The third member of the cup is thought of as a middle-level position. This player and the two wings—sometimes called "side-middles"—make up the middle three. Sometimes the three players in the cup are classified together, and the same zone is called 3-2-2. Also, if the two deeps are meant to play in I-formation, the zone is sometimes called 3-2-1-1. Other names exist for what is essentially the zone we describe here.

Zone Play

What does zone play look like? How's it different from one-on-one play? Starting from the pull, the cup runs down hard to assemble itself before the offense can make progress. The cup must get into formation, or else the zone begins in a weak position. On an out-of-bounds pull or a brick, the cup easily assembles itself either before the tap-in, or check, or if the zone is hidden, immediately after. The points need to decide which will be the marker, or "on-point," and which direction the force will be. This is often determined on the line before the pull. Except for during the sideline trap, which we'll discuss later, the on-point forces in the direction of the off-point, or toward the cup. The on-point wants to uphold the force, of course, but also prevent any throws straight downfield. The middle-middle's responsibility begins where the on-point's ends. At the fringe of what the on-point can prevent, the middle-middle picks up the mantle, thus preventing throws straight up the middle and those partially crossfield. The off-point's area of coverage takes over there, thus completing the U or the cup. Of course, this is not a rigid formation. It must respond to the changing positions on the field.

The cup is the primary defense against up-the-middle play. Offenses will devote one or two players ("poppers") to the task of creating throwing lanes or over through the cup. The primary holes in the cup are on both sides of the middle-middle. A tight cup, with smaller holes, might prevent these throws but leave itself vulnerable to routes that go around or over the cup. Also, given the three-meter double-cover rule (only one defender can position himself within three meters (10 feet) of a thrower, unless other offensive players are within the vicinity), a cup can't get any smaller than a minimum size (unless other offenders are present). A loose (or large) cup is hard to go around but more vulnerable through the middle. Cups try to find a balance based on preference, strengths, wind conditions, and knowledge of the opposing team. The middle-middle typically faces the thrower and tries to listen to her teammates' warnings ("Dina, left!") about who lurks where—especially those from deeper in the zone. Another threat to the middle-middle is popping, in which an offensive player crashes through one of the holes and into the cup for a one- or two-yard pass. The advantages of popping are a stall-count reset and a brief look at the cup from a different angle (there are bigger holes in the cup from the point of view of the center than from the end of the U). If possible, the middle should come in and cover the popper even if she's very close. This covers the pass and puts four people within two yards of the disc, jamming up many throwing opportunities. While in the cup, the middle-middle should make herself a hindrance to the offense. Still, if she comes in, a hole to a second popper might result. This can be filled by one of the following: the off-point, a shift from the marker, the weak-side wing, or the short-deep.

As the disc is in motion, the cup scrambles to reestablish the mark. The question of who's marking (which point) depends on the defensive priorities. A "contain" or "force-middle" zone defense looks to keep the same point on if the disc has not crossed to the other side of the field (or if it has barely moved, it might be simpler to keep the same force and allow people more comfort in their roles). A "forcing" or "pushing" defense tries to push to one particular side of the field and keep the same point on the mark, pushing the offense to the off-point (at the sideline, things change; more on this later). In going from one marking formation to another, the whole cup must be thinking on its feet. The cup in motion is not a random assortment of players running from point A to point B. The path and play chosen in transit is important because many offenses will try to take the opportunity to sneak one through while the cup is out of position. (We'll return to this point later in the chapter, as well, when we discuss cup play.)

A cup moving in response to a lateral throw wants first to prevent the swing around the cup (thereby defeating one of the aims of the swing). If the throw was to the force side, then the off-point is usually in the best position to hamper the downfield swing continuation by running in the path of the would-be throw, not immediately toward the receiver. If the throw was lateral to the breakside, the same considerations apply to the on-point, who will, however, be more out of position. If the continuation throw itself can't be prevented, then its targets must be (figure 10.2). A swing around the cup can progress downfield along the sideline or back toward the center of the field. The cup—either the off-point or middle-middle—is responsible for preventing short, downfield throws back toward the center; the wings are responsible for sideline coverage (figure 10.3). The second necessity in response to a lateral throw is to reestablish the mark. This becomes the foremost aim of a cup that has been broken by a gaining throw through, over, or around it. Such a cup is in sprint mode to stop the bleeding. If you're not to be the on-point in such a situation, resist the temptation to mark as you run past the new thrower because you'll only compromise the downfield structure. Only points should mark!

Assuming the cup does its job, the offense won't be able to go through the cup. Instead, it must go around or over the top; we'll consider the two in turn.

If the offense decides to swing around the cup, either with one pass or two, it's up to the wing to prevent yardage gains up the sideline. Repeat—the offense can get to the sideline but must not advance up the sideline. If you're playing wing, you must

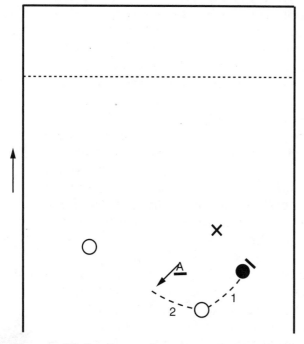

Figure 10.2 On seeing throw 1 go to the dump, the off-point A runs to block the continuation throw 2.

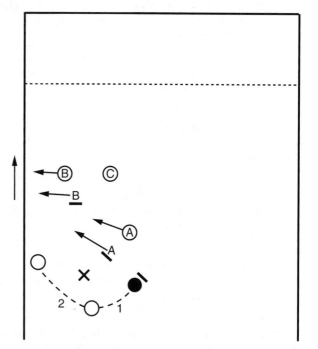

Figure 10.3 The zone responds to a swing (1-2) to the sideline. The middle-middle (defender A) moves to the side and downfield to prevent continuations (to offenders A or C) toward the middle of the field. The wing (defender B) must prevent the continuation down the sideline to offender B.

know who's threatening you most on the sideline. If there are two—say, one shorter, one longer—who's the bigger threat? The longer one typically is more of a threat, but you might be able to gain assistance from the deep and so focus your attention on the shorter one. As the wing on the strong side, you must be particularly alert. If you make a foolish play at a lateral pass and give up a downfield gainer on the line, you've probably lost the point. Against a swing, the weak-side wing wants to move in toward the middle to help out, but without forsaking her responsibility on the far sideline. The weak-side wing must be able to cover a crossfield hammer at all times. Generally speaking, the wings experience a conflict between their main job of preventing progress down the lines and their natural desire to fill space in the middle of the field. They must delicately balance these tasks without compromising their priorities (see figure 10.4).

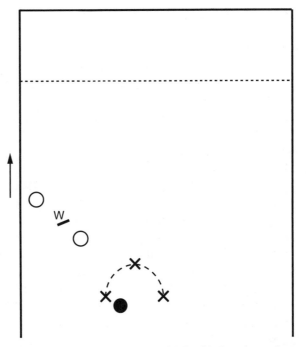

Figure 10.4 The side-middle (defensive wing W) is torn between a popper and an offensive wing. The side-middle wants to help prevent an over-the-cup throw to the popper but must remain close enough to the wing to cover the hammer. The side-middle should tell the middle-middle about the threat.

Another thing the offense will try to do is throw over the cup. In an I-formation, the short-deep should be ready to foil such an attempt. In a side-to-side deep formation, there might be space behind the cup. If the disc is on one side of the field, the wing on the same side will be busy tending the line. On the other side, the crossfield wing will try to move toward the center, as discussed earlier, and is an important preventative (along with the weak-side deep) against a hammer over the cup. (Remember that crossfield hammers take a while to alight, so the defender can afford some leeway in coverage.) If the disc is in the center of the field and the deeps are in side-to-side formation, no single player might be able to cheat toward the center. If the winds permit a hammer, the zone should respond, and a quick-thinking zone will pull the middle-middle back a bit to take away the space behind the cup. If the offense sends five people downfield for the opportunity for a hammer "over the top" (of the cup), then the cup can afford to "flex out" a bit.

The deeps in a zone are always safeguarding against the long play. They're picking up players who cut long, and handing off (usually, to the wings) players who are moving back toward the disc. They hand players off side to side, as well. In an I-formation, the deep-deep covers long cuts, and if she's saddled with two players, she asks for help. The deep-deep in a long formation must give priority to anyone behind her, as there's no backup. The deep-deep (or either deep in a side to side) has the constant task of evaluation and reevaluation. If the offense sends a player impossibly deep, the deep-deep can save energy by not following all the way. She can then help out in the middle of the field and further cramp the offense. However, the impossibly deep player, while uncovered and behind the deep-deep's back, can quickly move to a viable location—or the disc can move forward—and become a goal threat. This must always be on the mind of any deep-deep taking a chance by cheating in.

Long threats are not the only task of the deeps. With the best view of the field, the deeps must keep the other defenders informed of what's happening. Most defenders don't have a good view of their entire provenance and rely on outside information. This brings us to a central theme of the zone.

Communication and the Zone

A zone does not function without constant communication. A defender must cover the most significant threat in her region of the field, but new offenders continually enter and leave regions. Switches (changing positions with a teammate) and hand-offs (swapping offenders with a teammate) are thus essential. Further, because a defender only has so many eyes in her head, she needs her teammates on and off the field to tell her about threats she can't see. It's common practice to have seven sideline players pair up with the seven zone defenders, so that each defender is listening to just one sideline player. The sideline player stays within earshot and warns the defender about what's happening behind her back, calling her by name. Generally, talk from the sideline is meant to convey information so the on-field player can decide what to do. Only when immediate action is necessary to prevent a goal or get a block should a direct order be shouted out (often such information can't be processed in time, however). Here's a sample of some phrases commonly shouted from the sideline, and what they mean. Each should be preceded by the player's name—for example, the first entry in our list would be, "Pam, you're good!"

- "You're good." There's no imminent threat behind you. Proceed as you see fit.

- "You got one on your left." An offender is behind you to the left.

- "Cheat in." There's nothing behind you, and they need help in front of you. (This is an aggressive, nonconservative stance; hence the word "cheat.")

- "You got two." Two offenders are in your region. If you think that the handler can't hit the second offender or you're close enough to cover both, hold your ground. If the second offender is a viable threat, call a teammate over to help. (Note that if one defender is doubled up, then another one must be free somewhere. Getting the nearest defender free might require a quick succession of switches and reassignments.)

- "On your left shoulder" or simply "left shoulder." Tells a player precisely where the offender is, if out of view.

- (To a middle-middle.) "Crash!" Warns the middle-middle of a popper coming into the cup.

- (To a wing.) "Stay wide." Move to the sideline to cover your primary responsibility.

- (To a middle-middle.) "Left!" "Right!" Tells the middle-middle which of the two holes in the cup has an offender waiting for the pass. The directions must refer to the middle-middle's left and right as she stands facing the thrower. Any other convention is too complicated for real time.

- (To the on-point.) "No break!" "No dump!" "No huck!" "Strike!" Tells the marker the location of a threat (often caused by an out-of-position teammate) and reminds her to stay focused on the mark.

In addition to talk from the sideline, ongoing communication should occur among the players on the field, especially as they're constantly switching with each other. As a general rule, the deeper players warn the shallower players of what's happening behind them, and players at the same level communicate back and forth with each other. In addition, lateral hand-offs between wings and deeps (or the short-deep in an I-formation) are communicated as much as possible. Thus, even if an offense employs an "egg beater" or circulating pattern among the downfield offenders, you as a defender should be able to switch accordingly. Note that sometimes there's not a free defender to receive a hand-off (she might be busy with other matters). In such a situation, you're still responsible for the player you're currently covering. Don't leave him uncovered for a lesser threat. Stay with the threatening player and try to switch positions with someone else. For example, if you're playing wing and guarding someone in your territory who runs deep, try to pass him off to your deep behind you. If no one is there to pick him up, stay with him (or else it's a certain goal!) and look for someone to appoint as wing while you pick up the role of a deep player. If you can't find a player to switch with, simply announce "I'm deep now!" This tells your teammates on and off the field of the new vacancy, which they will help fill. This kind of flexibility is crucial. Rigid zones don't work.

Relationship Between Positions

Communication in a zone generally goes from downfield up—the deeps talk to the middles (including side-middles) who talk to the points. In addition, players at the same level can talk amongst each other—say, when deeps coordinate with each other or when the cup discusses something, such as switching formations (say, from trapping to containing after some fatigue). Beyond these rough, and by no means exclusive, rules, each position has its own communication needs, both in reception and transmission.

• Deeps. A deep must have a confidant on the sidelines warning her of the deepest offenders and those beginning to break long. Because a deep in an I-formation might move from one side of the field to the other, she might need a confidant on each sideline. Deeps talk to everyone shallower, especially wings. The short-deep talks to the middle-middle.

• Wings. A wing should direct and advise the point in front of her and tell the cup when an offender is crashing.

• Middle-middle. Middle-middles have offenders on all sides and generally do more listening than talking. Trusted and timely information from the sideline and the short-deep is essential. The information must be accurate and allow time to respond. Against a stagnant offense, a middle-middle can advise the on-point about the dump situation behind her.

• Off-point. The off-point can tell the on-point (marker) what's happening behind her head. Otherwise, she listens. The off-point coordinates (spoken or tacitly) with the wing behind her.

• On-point. An on-point can inform the rest of the zone what she sees from the thrower's vantage point. The offensive development might be revealed, as every play originates from the thrower. Communication from the sideline that demands immediate reaction might be faulty (or require an impossibly quick response), and in any case rarely demands forsaking the mark. The on-point coordinates (spoken or tacitly) with the wing behind her.

A Defensive Unit

The offense constantly shifts around to draw defenders and clear up space. If the holes are filled before the offense can find them, then the offense is helpless and hopeless. Filling the holes requires the seven defenders on the field to operate as a unit, which means communicating well. It means talking on the field, analyzing plays with teammates afterward and in your own mind after practice, and developing an unspoken "sync" with your zonemates. Don't rely on this "sync." It might not happen automatically. A cup that reviews its performance after every point might develop an identity and begin to function with more cohesion. Bonds might form between the off-point and the wing backing her up. Certain combinations of deep players might work better than others. A team that can achieve this intangible and elusive cohesion has a confident, intimidating, and effective weapon in its zone.

Cup Formations and Play

In most of our discussion of the cup we'll assume that the cup has been established around a thrower, but let us briefly discuss how the cup should form and reform itself (see also Recovery and Transition later in this chapter). The cup must establish itself at the start of the point and after any breaking throw (and even after long swings). A useful image to picture is of casting a net around the offense—getting the disc and players near it within its embrace—and then cinching it. As the net tightens, the on-point begins the stall, and the cup transforms its task from containing damage to creating a defensive advantage. Once formed, the aims of the defense direct the size and shape of the cup. A defense must choose a formation best suited to achieving its goals. We'll now describe various formations and discuss their merits as well as their weak points.

Containing and Nontrapping Zone

A containing zone or "force-middle" zone is designed to keep the offense from advancing up the sideline. It's the most efficient and most conservative zone. Generally, the point nearest the sideline assumes marking responsibilities and forces toward the middle of the field. The stance is somewhat straight up as this defense tries to force lateral play by the offense. The off-point will remain off-point until a pass is thrown to her side of the field, where she can most quickly begin the mark. By handing off the mark in this manner, the burden of chasing is minimized. For these reasons of efficiency, a containing zone can be useful for a tired or depleted squad.

Cup formation can vary somewhat in a containing zone, depending on the degree of conservatism the defense chooses. Be warned that no method is foolproof. A flat cup (figure 10.5a) is a conservative formation that protects against high-reward throws through or over the cup by pulling the off-point a little deeper and wider (reaction time is increased since the off-point is deeper, allowing some extra width) and positioning the mark slightly more upfield. This setup allows lateral throws back and forth and, due to the retracted off-point, puts less pressure in the immediate vicinity of the disc. A loose cup (figure 10.5b) is bigger in size, so it is harder to defeat around or over the top. The off-point is closer than in a flat cup, but the holes in the cup are larger, making it considerably more porous. (For example, the loose cup would leave a dump-and-swing, one-popper offense with few opportunities to advance the disc.) A tight cup is more difficult to penetrate but is more easily beaten over the top or with the dump swing. In making the call, it pays to know the preferences of the opposing handlers.

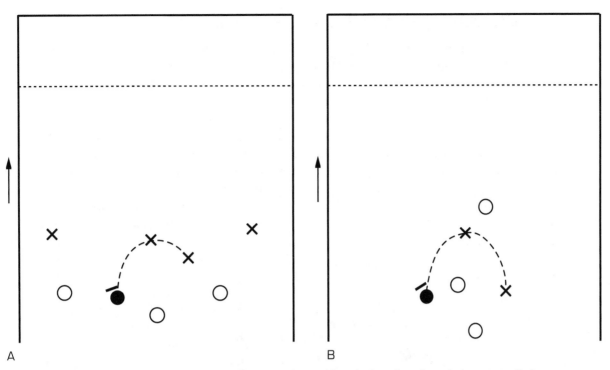

Figure 10.5 Cup formations. *(a)* A flat cup formation is hard to break but puts little pressure on the thrower. *(b)* A loose cup formation is larger, thus even more difficult to swing around or go over, yet more easily penetrated. In the figure, a short throw to the crasher will open up holes to downfield offenders.

Whatever the exact shape of the cup, the containing zone is generally conservative. With the sidelines heavily guarded, the offense has few options besides trying to penetrate through the middle of the zone, which is always risky. Thus, beating a containing zone takes patience and prudence. The problem (from the defense's point of view) is that a containing zone has no defensive "hook," no sure-fire way of pressuring the offense. Thus, the defense must also remain patient and focused to succeed in this war of attrition. Though risks are an essential part of zone play, they must be rare and well chosen in a zone that values smart, solid play.

As an example of a well-chosen risk, consider calling a trap (sideline force) in a nontrapping zone. Once the defense has established that the zone is nontrapping and the offense has been lured into complacency (robotically swinging the disc back and forth), a defensive captain can consider calling a surprise trap. A trap at this point can work only if it's used sparingly and if there's no immediate sideline threat—particularly if it's called when a weak handler receives a swing pass on one side. Often, a team has three or four players involved in swings—one swing receiver and two or three handlers. If you can identify the fourth as a poor handler, and if other conditions are ripe (e.g., no one free up the line), the sudden trap can be effective. However, a nontrapping zone that traps too often becomes a zone without a purpose, which can lead to inappropriate chances and disharmony among the defense.

A strength of the nontrapping zone is that it draws many people behind the disc, often leaving offenses with too few downfielders to be effective. Merely recognizing this as an advantage leaves the defense in the proper frame of mind to seize on opportunities.

Trap/Push Right, Trap/Push Left

In this formation, the cup is trying to force the offense to one sideline, then set up a trap. We'll discuss the forcing here. The trap formation is described below.

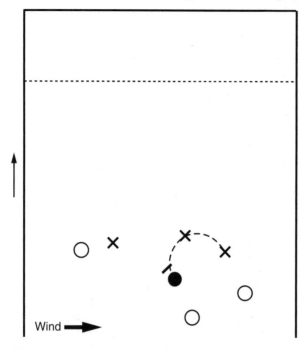

Figure 10.6. Cup pushing left. The cup pushes left (in the direction that defenders face) by employing a more angled mark, by shifting the middle-middle closer to the on-point, and by shifting the off-point slightly downfield. This opens up easy lateral throws in the direction of the push, while preventing dangerous throws around or through the cup or against the push. If the push is with the wind (as shown), then the dump swing around the on-point will be harder, and either the on-point or her corresponding wing might be able to prevent it.

The forcing cup does not want to get broken. Thus, the on-point is less straight up and assumes the stance of a forcing mark (as opposed to the containing cup). Because of the marker's regular stance, the middle-middle needs to slide a bit more toward the on-point to shore up what would be a larger hole (figure 10.6). As a result, the off-point must also shift from the standard position. In a forcing zone, the off-point is slightly downfield of the on-point. The overall effect is that the U cup is literally pointing more toward the sideline to which it's forcing. As a result, the shield will direct offensive flow to that sideline. In particular, the lateral throw to the forced sideline is free for the taking. The lateral throw against the force, however, is blocked by the on-point's regular forcing stance.

A zone that's pushing left might not have the policy of an automatic trap when the disc is on the left side of the field. A "trap left" zone should have that policy, though this distinction is often not made in play, and it's safest to call the trap on when desired, if only to alert the downfield defenders. Communication is key, and it's worth divulging the secret of the trap in order to avoid the confusion of what to do when the disc is "quite close" to the sideline, without quite being there.

The off-point must resist the temptation to mark while the zone is pushing in a direction. If she does mark, she must push back to the other point, defeating the purpose of the push. With one point always marking, this zone formation can be tiring. If play drags on, the cup might become ineffective. A change to a containing formation or transition to one-on-one might be needed.

If the on-point gets broken, the danger is greater (because the wings and deeps have been preparing for offensive flow with the force), and the cup and wing must scramble back and, while assessing the situation, quickly do damage control, and then reestablish the mark and begin the push anew. Often, however, the offense won't devote enough players to the weak side to fully avail itself of a small break-mark throw around the on-point.

Trap-As-Called Zone

The trap-as-called zone is an aggressive cup zone to be played in conditions in which no side of the field is favored. The idea is to exert pressure on the offense wherever possible, taking more chances and making more bids. This includes calling the trap when feasible on *either* side of the field. The cup can play it as a force toward whichever sideline is closer, or play it as a slight force middle that attempts to capitalize on offensive motion to the sideline. Of course, any zone should be able to put a trap on, if necessary. This zone is a way of alerting downfield defenders that the cup is looking to trap whenever it's advantageous.

Different teams play the trap formation in different ways. The most economical way—demanding a minimum of energy and motion from the cup—is as follows. A left-pushing cup eventually forces a pass to the sideline. Now the off-point (left point) is closest to the disc and can slap on the mark quickly. Her mark is toward the sideline and taking away the dump throw. The right point, now the off-point (note the right point marks every other throw, except when the trap is actually on), covers lateral throws across the field to compensate for the on-point's angled stance against the dump. The middle-middle covers 45-degree throws back to the middle of the field. Here's the hitch—the strong side wing comes in to complete a four-person cup by playing straight up the line from the thrower. This is a very aggressive cup and a potent weapon (figure 10.7a-b).

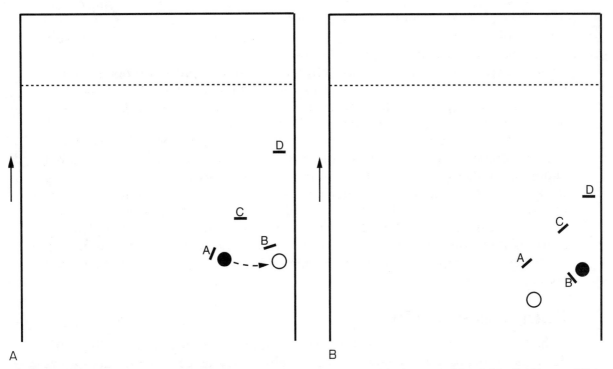

A   B

Figure 10.7 Trap on! *(a)* Defensive positioning before the trap (cup pushing left). *(b)* To establish the trap, Player B becomes the on-point and takes away the dump. Player A becomes the off-point and takes away the lateral crossfield break. Player C positions herself at 45 degrees and takes away throws in that direction, whereas D, the strong-side wing, comes in as far as she can (without forsaking the line behind her) to form the fourth member in the cup, taking away throws directly down the line. The four-person trapping cup is a very aggressive stance. Note that in going from the push to the trap, A, B, and C don't change their relative positions, and the distance they have to run to their new assignments is minimized. Other conventions lead to longer distances, thus wasting precious time—a violation of efficiency.

As with any strong position, once broken it leaves a defense particularly vulnerable. A broken trap can leave four defenders out of position and demands a quick retreat for damage control. Other defenders should back up and prevent the long cutters in hopes of delaying the offense until the cup can cast the net and reform.

The wing in the trap plays a special role; her job description takes on a new function—cup member—as soon as the trap begins. She's still responsible for line throws and must back out of the cup to cover a deeper line threat if there's no support from behind. Note that her presence on the sideline can prevent many kinds of throws to the sideline behind her, especially in certain wind conditions. Still, she must always be watching her back. The high tension of the wing in the trap should be relieved by the presence of sideline help. Deep-wing communication is, as ever, crucial.

Throws up the line are most dangerous. Closer to lateral throws are slightly less dangerous (because there are more lines of defense). Dumps straight back are the least dangerous, whereas dumps with a crossfield component are somewhat more dangerous. A player torn between two options should cover the more dangerous threat.

Trap Recovery

When the offense breaks the trap and gets past the cup, it typically has more players "in play" than the defense. The defense must recover (or transition to playing one on one—see chapter 11 on junk defenses). Recovery from a downfield gainer against a trap is much like any zone recovery (briefly discussed earlier and again in Recovery and Transition later in this chapter). Recovery against a crossfield break goes as follows: The crossfield wing and deep shift to the far side to prevent progress on this vulnerable side. The trap-side wing drops back and toward the middle to help the deep, while the cup and middle-middle head downfield and toward the middle to try to "cast the net" around the offense and reestablish itself.

Note that the trap we describe here is the most aggressive one. Other versions with just three cup players exist (e.g., with the on-point forcing sideline and not taking away the dump). This formation is more conservative because the wing remains downfield to defend longer passes. The less aggressive cup allows the offense to dump backwards. Thus, the philosophy in this trap is to "push them back" rather than to try to force a quick turnover. Note that this trap does demand more motion from the middle-middle in forming the trap, and (depending on exactly how the cup is formed) can be more vulnerable to a dump swing around the cup.

Four-Person Cup

Another variation of the zone we describe is the four-person cup, in which the short-deep comes in and plays alongside the middle-middle as part of the cup. Or the middle-middle and the short-deep can share position-dependent roles, with the player on the strong side pushing in closer and the weak-side player dropping back a bit. These roles change dynamically. Both of these formations can be played aggressively (tight cup) or conservatively (loose cup).

No single zone is best for all situations, especially if the offense changes its setup in response to what your team has played. If you find your cup doing nothing but chasing the play, consider a variation—preferably one your team has practiced!

Downfield Formations and Play

The downfield defenders in a zone (deeps and wings) must have a (switching) one-on-one philosophy. Do you ever find yourself in the middle of nowhere on defense in a one on one? No. So you shouldn't find yourself in such a position in a zone. If you're not covering anyone, your team has six covering seven. Find a way to relieve the burden on the rest. If you're alone because the downfield is flooded, pull back and help out. If not, then push in (listen to the sideline calling, "It's all in front of you!"). Often, one of the wings will be in this position because the offense has brought a lot of people back behind the disc.

That said, you don't always have to be tight on your offender. For example, an offense might station a player downfield and on the far sideline to try to stretch the defense wide and deep (leaving space in the middle). In this case, you need only remain close enough to make the play against the hammer. By staying toward the middle while covering the sideline player, you put yourself in a position to help another teammate when she needs it, essentially performing the tasks of more than one player. This is how the whole becomes greater than the sum of its parts.

The offense can circulate their downfielders all around the downfield, moving quickly between areas of the field. The deeps and wings have to hand off offenders or, if they can't, follow them and switch positions with a teammate. If there's any doubt whether you have formally switched positions with a teammate (versus temporarily occupying the other's space), you should resolve this quickly by talking to her. If the defense is better served by having the two of you at your original positions, try to switch back at the earliest opportunity.

As for the deeps, they can start in either I-formation or side to side. Either way, they must be prepared to adjust, as necessary. For example, an offense can flood the downfield by sending several long. The deep-deep must immediately recognize this and pull back a wing or the short-deep. If she pulls back a wing, then the short-deep must fill in the vacant wing position. The starting position might communicate a philosophy (for example, an I-formation means a more aggressive posture aimed at disrupting cup play), but should not prevent you from responding to the demands of the field. The downfield defenders must be able to adjust with this kind of fluidity, and communication is needed to do so.

Generally, play in the downfield follows the pattern of one-on-one, hand-off, switch, one-on-one, hand-off, and so on. Further considerations will be discussed as they pertain to the individual positions.

Which Zone?

So far in this chapter we've concentrated on different defensive stances within the 2-3-2 zone. Why choose one over the other? Or, when is an entirely different zone more appropriate? Though we don't discuss other zones (because there are a nearly infinite number of variations), we'll now describe the merits and weaknesses of different formations and zones and mention some of the factors that a defensive coordinator should attend to when setting up (and motivating) the defense. These considerations apply to whatever zone your team plays, be it the 2-3-2, some modification, or a truly unique formation.

The simplest rule is that zone works well when the offense is traveling upwind. The reason is obvious—the cup puts many people near the thrower to cover short passes, whereas longer and higher passes are considerably more difficult into the wind. In addition, a defense can adopt a more aggressive posture, such as a tight cup and an I-formation among the two-deeps, or a four-person cup. Or, in severe winds, both deeps can become "short." These formations leave spaces where they're most difficult to hit. Depending on the proficiency of the opposing handlers, or overall acumen of the offense, some of these measures of aggression can be removed. Zones can also be effective against teams that have generally poor handling skills or might be prone to errors or poor decisions in pressure situations.

In a crosswind, the defense should consider trapping. Typically, this means pushing with the wind and trapping on the sideline to which the wind is blowing (so that any in-bounds throw is made more difficult). Trapping or pushing toward the other direction leads to some difficulties (the free side is more difficult to throw to), though is generally not as beneficial as the trap in the direction of the wind. Exceptions might be made in the case of an opposing handler with a particularly strong throw from some side. If you don't know the offense, consider a variety of zones in the beginning of the game, starting with the most aggressive, to get an accurate read.

Although wind often means zone defense, zones can be played in little or no wind, or if the offense is traveling downwind. Typically, a lighter or downfield wind requires a more conservative zone because longer throws are simpler in these conditions (though downwind touch passes are difficult). In a 2-3-2, this means a nontrapping zone, and generally a looser or flatter cup. This formation allows lateral motion but doesn't give up breaking downfield passes. Passes through the zone are still possible (no defense is perfect), but any throw that has to pierce through defenders is always difficult. The conservative zone hopes to allow many easy passes that lead to little progress, thus generating errors from the sheer number of throws or by numbing the offense into taking a risky chance. Another downwind zone is the 1-3-3, which in lieu of a cup places defenders farther from the disc in a horizontal wall. It's nearly impossible to penetrate or swing around so it doesn't suffer much from the lack of wind. However, this zone offers little resistance to play near the disc and is generally unsound, though it might take an offense a while to figure it out. The advantage of surprising an offense with a novel zone formation should not be dismissed.

As is clear, sound thinking and understanding of the merits of individual zone formations, combined with a measure of unpredictability, are all that's needed to prescribe the correct zone defense.

■ Drill: Ten-Pull Set D Variation

This is a good drill for working on a particular defense. The defense plays a set D every time, which could include a clam, zone, force middle, or any other chosen defense. This ten-pull variation can also be used for offensive practice. A ten-pull set O variation means the offense plays a set O, like a horizontal stack, weave, or side stack every time.

Individual Positions

You'll be assigned a specific position in a zone defense, so you must understand the responsibilities and particular considerations of that position. We'll now review the zone positions and their various tasks.

On-Point

If you're the on-point, you should announce that you're marking if it's at all ambiguous to the other point. You can simply state your own name as the signal, or state the name of the other point if you prefer that she mark (the two of you might designate one of you to make the call). You must know which way you're forcing and call the trap if it's on (call "Trap!" or "It's on!"). Your decision must be made promptly and announced loudly. This kind of communication is more important than whether the decision was the best one. Each time a throw is made, you must call "Up!" You can occasionally take a quick step out of position to block an anticipated pass, but try to get in sync with the wing behind you. Once the two of you know each other, she'll know to cover for you when you go for a risk. If you take chances too regularly, then you become predictable to the offense and ineffectual in your force: in short, you have no zone at all.

As an on-point, you should glance around whenever you have the chance (including immediately after throws) to recalibrate the action on the field. Because zone offenses, unless in fast-break mode, are not high-speed operations, as an on-point you can get a feel for where the backfield offenders station themselves. Use this information to anticipate throws and prevent, or block, them.

Become aware of who pops and when. The pop throw is so short and easy to make that throwers sometimes let their guard down and forget that an alert marker can swing an arm around and make a decent bid. Because you'll be marking the same throwers many times during a point, take the opportunity to get to know them. You can be fooled by a no-look once, or even twice, but try to be there waiting for the block on the third attempt.

At the team level, many offenses have a limited repertoire of zone-busting maneuvers. The on-point has the best on-field vantage point for reading the offense. Once you note a pattern, communicate it to your defenders along with instructions to your teammates on how to foil the offense's schemes ("Stay wide when they swing!"). Doing this within earshot of the offenders might spook and intimidate them.

Off-Point

As an off-point you must try to stop a swing, or, if that can't be done, stop the next pass downfield. Stopping the swing doesn't necessarily mean running at the thrower. If you run at the thrower and don't get there in time to establish the force, the disc is now on the other side with the whole cup playing catch up. Often, stopping the swing means running to the midpoint between thrower and receiver. "Midpoint" is probably closer to the receiver, actually, because if you don't stop the throw, you'll have to run in that direction anyway. After cutting off the swing, close in with the mark (on a force middle) or return to your off-point position. If the swing goes around you completely, sprint to catch up and reestablish the cup.

On any dump, or whenever possible, as the off-point you should "check in," meaning look at the field positions of whomever you can. On a swing, where's the downfield threat? On a dump, where's the swing? Is there someone open long (meaning you should call to stop the huck)? Is there a crossfield hammer you might have a bid at—or can you alert the on-point?

Consider the offender setting up for the dump or dump swing. Be wary of stopping the dump. If you step back to cover the dump, you're leaving a crossfield swing through the space between you and the middle-middle. Recognize this! If you do take a stab at the dump, make sure your risks are calculated and not too frequent. You can occasionally bait the throw through this hole by creating the hole "unintentionally," and then jumping back to close it up (with luck, the handler makes his throw).

You and the on-point should also foster a relationship with the wing behind you. She should help you out, filling in holes when you take a bid. Note that the holes that the off-point creates are on the strong side and so can be particularly dangerous. The wing behind you typically has a good view of the situation, though, and can become a valuable partner to you—one who's "got your back."

Middle-Middle

This is a hard position to navigate. Basically, you just have to be in the right position at the right time. This changes instantaneously, so it pays to be quick. Of course, you need all the stamina of a cup player. You'll also have 20 people barking directions at you at all times. One solace is that you never have to mark. If you mark as middle-middle, there's no one backing you up, and the cup is a sieve. Let's say you've just crashed with someone into the cup, but he caught the disc. It's more effective to drop back as soon as possible and try to shut down the throw through the middle. If you mark, he'll step around you and find someone wide open. You can occasionally turn around to look at the action behind you, but playing with your back to the disc is not recommended. (That's not to say that in a two-deep-poppers offense with stagnant handlers that it's always bad, but the exceptions are few and far between.) Basically, you're in no position to react to or anticipate throws. You have to constantly worry about where the poppers are and when they're popping, and you must be prepared to crash the cup with them. When you crash with a popper, you can be within three meters (10 feet) of the thrower. Try to take up lots of space and be a nuisance to the offense.

It's the middle-middle who must flex out if there's a one-popper offense (weak in the middle) and who must tighten up the cup if there's too much space. Against a two-popper offense, the middle-middle must coordinate with the short-deep. When the middle-middle makes a hole, the short-deep should fill it. The short-deep should tell the middle-middle which side she's supporting. Typically, the middle-middle takes the strong side and the short-deep fills weak-side holes.

The middle-middle also has the thankless task of stopping the fall-out from a swing. Specifically, once the offense has swung to the line, they'll want to move down the line or down and back toward the center. The wing is responsible for the line, but the middle-middle must try to stop the throw back to a popper in the center. This most often requires motion back downfield and toward the sideline ("over and

Regardless of what defensive position you're in, stay alert to prevent offensive moves.

Photo courtesy of Jackie Bourgeois

back"). This is counterintuitive, as the natural instinct for the middle-middle is to run straight to the sideline. The motion backward stops the main purpose of the swing. Once that's done, the middle-middle should enter the reforming cup and resume with normal duties. (The nearest point can try to assist with this swing prevention but is usually too late.) Any talking you can do as middle-middle is valuable. You're the central, cohesive element, the linchpin. More often than transmitting information, you'll be receiving it.

Wings

Stopping the throw up the line after a swing is the primary concern of the wing. If you're doubled, stop the more dangerous—almost always the deeper—cut. Call for help when doubled. Listen to your sideline. Tell the point when you have to drop back and can no longer cover the short throw up the line ("He's left!"); the point might be able to step out and block it. Tell your deep when your offender drops back and you want to leave him for someone else. No, don't just tell her. Tell her and make sure she reacts! She might be busy. You can't just leave an uncovered offender hanging deep—that's irresponsible. If there's no one on your alley, move toward the middle to close up space and help out, ready to return in time to perform your main duty. Warn the cup when offenders crash from your side of the field. At times, you might even have to talk to the opposite wing. You could get switched with a long or the other wing (rare). Try not to, but if it happens, communicate it and adapt to the new position. Cheat in when you can, but always be mindful of the space behind you.

Deep or Deep-Deep

Deeps must talk, talk, talk! The deep (or deep-deep in an I-formation) sees the whole field and must translate this advantage to the less fortunate ones in front of her. Never stop talking when you're deep. There's always something you know from your perspective that someone else doesn't know. More information is almost always better than less. You should have a running monologue for the wing near you, listening for responses, too.

Don't do too much baiting. While baiting one player, you can lose focus or need to turn your head and then find him very far away. It's typically better just to cover the people. If everyone is just covered, the turns will surely happen. Of course, you don't need to be right next to someone who's too far away from the thrower. As with the wings, cheat in if you can do so without leaving your other deep with two. Even if those two are right next to her, they won't be for long. Be sure they'll be accounted for once they split, and be prepared to come back.

Nationals '98

In play against the Condors, Paul Greff of Death or Glory (DoG) had a game-saving layout block as the deep in a trapping zone near the end zone. To hear him describe it, he got the call from another player to drop back, and did so with complete trust in where that order was coming from. Where does a block like that come from? It comes from weeks of discussions about deep zone play. It comes from years of having played with your teammates enough to know whose barkings you can trust without a moment's hesitation. There, a momentary pause would have lost the game. Your zone only works well when you have a team of communicators, on and off the field.

Short-Deep

The short-deep must always be prepared to come back to help the deep-deep. Coming in close is always a luxury in a zone defense, as it is such a benefit to the cup. The task of the short-deep is to help out with the cup, especially filling (from a position slightly deeper in the field) the weak-side hole between the middle-middle and the off-point and communicating to the middle-middle. The presence of a short-deep can foil a two-popper offense, eliminate the threat of hammers over the top, and effectively create a powerful four-person cup (or five in a trap). The consequence of all these advantages is vulnerability in the backfield, and the short-deep must not abdicate her responsibilities back there.

How the Zone Works

We've discussed zone positions and formations extensively. Now, how does the zone actually work? Where do the offensive turnovers come from? When are blocks made? What happens when things don't unfold as planned? We'll now consider these aspects of zone play.

Where Do the Turns Come From? Turnovers in a zone come from a frustrated offense making poor choices. A turnover can result from (1) an offense finding it can no longer swing around the zone and trying unsuccessfully to jam a pass through the cup; (2) an offense that lacked confidence in itself and became predictable in its swinging; (3) throws to deeps that aren't very open; or (4) unforced errors. All of the above follow from solid zone defense. Note that even unforced errors can be forced, in a sense. If your team's defense makes an offense attempt a lot of passes, then on average even high-percentage throws will eventually yield errors. As for number 2, part of the plan of a zone is to frustrate the offense. Predictability gives the defense an edge, allowing for opportune blocks.

Chances. No blocks will happen if you don't try for them. So, when do you try? This is a difficult question, but the best answer is, "When you think you can get it." So, if you have just made your bid, say, as a wing on a swinging gainer up an alley, what then? If you got it, great. If not, the offense will often flood your vacant position and overwork the deep, then maybe score. This is not the end of the world! If you have made an honest bid on something you really could have gotten, that's a calculated risk. If an offense scores 65 percent of the time and you thought you had a 50 percent chance at the disc, that's probably a good risk. If your risk didn't pay off, get up and recover. A zone suffers when you miscalculate what is a real bid at the disc. The penalty is even greater if a deep makes a bid on a comeback cut because the offense is almost sure to score. So, deeps have to be extra cautious with their attempts. Once you leave your feet, expect to get the block because it takes a long time to recover.

Recovery and Transition. Bad things happen to good zones. If you have an injury, you want to stop the bleeding and not let it become fatal. So, when the defense has found itself out of position (failed bid, breaking hammer, throw through the middle leading to a fast break by the poppers, swing against a trap, and so on), it must recover as soon as possible. This is the time for sprinting. There are not all that many points where a real sprint should occur during zone defense, but this is where it's crucial. If you don't reestablish a defensive order, the offense will score while you're reeling.

The cup in recovery should cast its net around the breaking offense. Points should not run directly at throwers—they probably won't get there in time—but run to try to get in the way of the pass following the current one. This allows the offense one more pass, but the defense will be in better position for when that pass is caught. In contrast, if a point runs at a player about to receive the disc and doesn't get there soon enough to prevent the next throw, then the cup is in the same position as it was when it got broken, only further downfield. The principle of efficiency is at work here. All the while, the cup should maintain its shape as well as possible, so that as soon as the flow is stopped, it can tighten up and repair the damage.

The zone in general can help an individual recover from a failed bid or misstep. If only one person has been pulled out of position after a bid and leaves an open threat, then her neighbors can try to pick up the slack (never forsaking a more dangerous threat). If in the process, they are drawn away from secondary threats, then their neighbors can respond, and the threat has become ancillary. Of course, the individual carries most of the responsibility. Likewise, if you're at point and you leave your feet on a failed attempt at a block, you've got to hop up and get going. The rest of the defense will try to stave off the advantaged offense until you recover, but a one-point cup is rather porous. Be wary of leaving your feet!

Sometimes the offense breaks through the cup with a big throw and is flowing downfield with numbers against a terminally hemorrhaging defense that can't reform. At this point, a transition to one on one might be the only hope for recovery. If a single speedy cup player can catch up and nullify the number midmatch, a one-on-one defense might be established. Another time to transition to one on one might be near the end zone, where zone defense is less effective (because any pass is a score, and players are not guarded as closely as in a one on one). Transition defenses in general will be discussed in the next chapter.

A zone formation would be easy to describe and set up if the offense were static, but the offense is not static, and the zone must respond dynamically. For the seven on-field defenders to move effectively as a single body, each player must understand the responsibilities of her position and communicate as necessary to her teammates. Good communication allows smooth switching, quick recovery from chances taken or breakthrough passes by the offense, and exchanges of position. A defense that can move fluidly in formation will frustrate the offense, inducing risky passes and blocking chances. In due time, the turnovers will come.

Junk Defenses

ELEVEN

© Marshall Goff

Hybrid or "junk" defenses such as the clam are intended primarily to disrupt the offense's rhythm. They combine aspects of one-on-one defense with zone to create confusion, take the offense out of their comfort zone, and occasionally get a block during the melee. In this chapter, we'll go over zone transition defenses, the most famous junk defense (the clam), other misleading defenses, and how to use them effectively.

Zone Transition Defense

In the late 1980s, many high-level offenses had devastating set plays off the pull. Straight one-on-one defenses couldn't stop these powerful offenses, and zone defenses simply allowed them (in good weather conditions) to march down the field uncontested. As a counter, transition defenses arose. "Transition" is simply the shift from one defensive set to another during a possession. Typically, the defense is zone early in the point to stop the set play, then transitions to one on one after the flow is disrupted. However, any two (or more) defensive sets can be combined over the course of a possession to provide the most effective set for the field position.

The primary purpose of transition defense is to break the rhythm of the flow of the offense. It can also be used to break the rhythm of a zone offense. As a bonus, if the transition is disguised well, it can result in a turnover because the offense is out of position with no one to throw to.

A transition defense should be set up the same way as a regular zone defense, with players at their normal positions behaving as they do in a normal zone. If "normal" involves hiding the defense, then hide it. If "normal" means the cup sprints down while the others jog, do that. If the transition is to be early in the point, then the defense should be less aggressive than normal and content with simply having the offense see the zone and taking a few short passes until the transition. Otherwise, play the zone normally.

When transition is imminent, each defender needs to look around to identify an opponent to cover. Players away from the cup should play more of a match-up zone and can leave their areas as necessary to follow an offensive player as long as they don't leave a spot wide open. Players in or near the cup need to stay in the zone for a few more counts but can switch to man if the stall is high and no other potential receivers are in the area. If this transition is pulled off smoothly, the offensive players might not realize for a few seconds that the zone is gone and won't be in good cutting positions. With luck, this could force a turnover.

One of the downsides of transition defenses is that match-ups after the transition might be unfavorable. Thus, players should be on the lookout for switches with mismatched teammates in the first few passes or any time they're in the stack. There might also be some flexibility in choosing match-ups during the transition. Before the point, the team needs to decide when to transition to one-on-one defense and what the force will be after the transition. A good transition can catch the offense by surprise. There are several common times for transition:

• After a set number of passes (usually three to five). Some teams prefer to start counting as soon as the cup is set up. However, there's often uncertainty about whether the cup has had a chance to set up, so it's better to begin counting from the pull. Usually, the sideline counts loudly to help the players keep track. The sideline should also count during regular zone D to avoid informing the offense that a transition defense is being played. Players actually begin transitioning on the previous pass as they identify likely match-ups.

• After a stoppage (foul, pick, travel). The marker should remind the team before checking in that the transition is on.

• At a particular place on the field, such as midfield. The offense will have settled in by then and won't expect a transition.

• When a key defender calls it. One player is in charge of determining when to transition, and a predetermined call activates it. The player can call it when the zone is broken, when a particular spot has been reached and the defense has had a chance to set the cup there, when the zone no longer appears effective, or at any sign that the team agrees is a good time to transition.

Advanced Transitions

The disc world is currently showing some signs that advanced transition defenses are in development—and this represents great potential for strategic advancement. A defense that could flex instantly into a trap after a downfield pass on the sideline or one that could shift zones between a 2-3-2 and a 1-3-3 as the disc swings would have a large advantage over unprepared offenses.

The Clam

The clam is the most famous of the hybrid defenses. In the clam, the front three players play one-on-one defense against the handlers while the back four players each cover cuts from any of the downfield defenders to assigned areas. The clam, developed to stop comeback cuts from the long, spread-out offenses of the late '80s, was intended to get blocks on switches and poaches and to force high stall count desperation heaves. The clam was willing to give up occasional easy goals on great passes and could be beaten by patient throwers who had the coolness and presence of mind to seek out the third or even fourth option. These days, the clam defense is used more to disrupt an offense's rhythm (especially the set play off the pull) and prevent a quick score (with an occasional block as a bonus).

Think of the clam as a one-on-one defense with some aspects of zone responsibilities. At any given instant, most or all of the players are attempting to stop cuts rather than blocking throwing lanes. The clam differs from a conventional one-on-one in that the individual match-ups aren't determined until a cut is made, and they exist only for as long as the cutter stays in an assigned area. Furthermore, each defender has only one or two specific cuts to try to prevent instead of having to shadow a cutter over the whole field.

The clam offers an organized way to determine match-ups and intelligent switches. The simplest form is the two-man clam, in which two defenders split side-to-side or front-to-back responsibilities for two offenders. For example, if two cutters are at the back of the end zone in a goal-line defense, both defenders would be ahead of the front cutter, one on either side. The only cutting options are at an angle back to the disc on either side of the field, so when one of the cutters commits, the defender on that side goes with him, while the other defender claims the remaining cutter, repositioning herself if necessary to take into account the force. Conventional defense would have both defenders on the force side just in front of their respective offenders, relying exclusively on the marker to prevent the breaking pass for the goal.

This concept is extended to four downfield defenders and the whole field in the regular clam. The rear four defenders surround the last four players in the stack (we assume the offense is roughly in a stack), while the front three play the handlers one on one. Defensive positions in the clam are numbered 0 through 6 according to their assignments (figure 11.1), the number loosely corresponding to the position of the nearest offensive player in the stack. The marker (position 0) forces a predetermined direction, which will remain in place for the point.

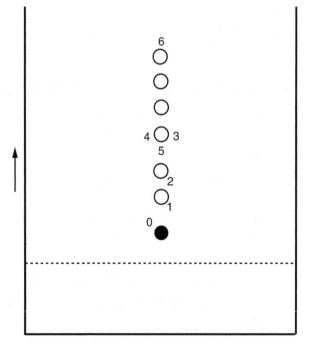

Figure 11.1 The clam. Defensive positions are numbered 0 through 6 according to their assignments.

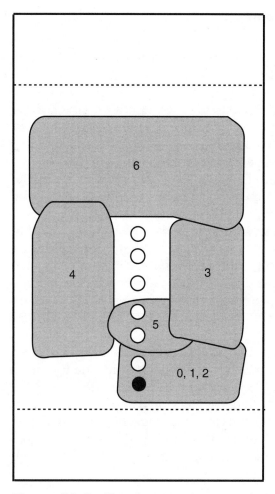

Figure 11.2 The deepest player on the field (6) covers all long passes.

Positions 1 and 2 play one on one against the first two players in the stack (usually the other handlers). The 3 (on the force side), 4 (on the break side), and 5 (in the middle but favoring the force side slightly) positions are all in front of the third player in the stack, facing the stack in anticipation of comeback cuts from any of the four deepest cutters. The 6 position is the deepest player on the field and covers all long passes (figure 11.2). In a clam for one (pass), the middle players (3, 4, and 5) pick up the first cutters in their respective areas and stay with them for the remainder of the point. Generally, "clam for N" means to transition to force forehand (or some other chosen force) after N number passes.

The clam as just described is the original one developed and modified by the Boston teams of the 1980s and 1990s. There are many existing variations and more possible. For example, the marker could play straight up, and each pair of defenders could split left-right responsibilities on a pair of cutters. The defining characteristic of all these defenses is that a group of two or more defenders covers an equal number of cutters, with match-ups being assigned dynamically depending on the cuts made.

Force Forehand or Backhand?

The clam was exclusively a force-forehand defense for many years, but there might be reasons to force backhand as well.

Why forehand?
- The break-mark forehand has less margin of error.
- Few players can throw a long forehand well.
- Short forehands (especially dumps) are tougher to throw with touch.
- That's how everyone plays it.

Why backhand?
- The hammer is effectively removed as a weapon.
- Midrange (~20 yards) break-mark backhands are more difficult to get past the mark.
- Left-handed players have the backhand huck against the force forehand.
- Some players do have better long forehands than backhands.

The team needs to decide on how to label 3 and 4 in the backhand clam, whether 3 refers to the player on the forehand side or to the player on the force side. Either way is acceptable as long as the team is clear. Here, 3 will refer to the player on the force side.

The clam is most frequently played for a set number of passes at the start of a point. It should be long enough that the defense gets a couple of opportunities to create havoc and take the offense out of their setup but not so long that the defense loses track of the count or the offense has a chance to develop a new rhythm. This means that players must be comfortable with switching and making decisions on the fly about which player to cover. One of the front three (0, 1, and 2) will always cover the thrower (though this will vary from pass to pass), with the other two picking up the two nearest offensive threats (generally these are the three players closest to the disc, but as described later, this might not be true if the offense uses a nontraditional stack). After the first pass, there's no distinction between these three players. If a handler cuts away from the disc up an alley, his defender has to pass him off to 3 or 4 and look for a cutter closer to the front of the stack. When a gaining pass is completed, one of these players has to sprint down to provide a mark (although it might be preferable for the team to transition to one-on-one defense at this point, even if the pass count hasn't been reached).

Positions 3 and 5 (and 4, to a lesser extent) are the most mentally demanding in the clam, as they are the most likely to be overloaded or to have to fill holes created by other players' coverage. Position 3 probably has the best opportunity for blocks, especially if she can slyly hide her intent. As is the case with poaching, she can wait until the last second to flare out and sprint for the interception. She can also move out as soon as she sees a cut to prevent the pass from being thrown. In this case, position 5, in addition to her regular duties, must be ready for the underneath cut to the area just vacated by 3. The regular duties for 5 are primarily cuts up the middle, especially high in the count after cuts to the sides have been stuffed.

Position 4's primary job is to prevent comeback cuts to the breakside. In a forehand clam, an important task is to be aware of the hammer over the 4's head. Consequently, 4 needs to look at the thrower a bit more often than does 3 or 5. Finally, 4 needs to be ready to drop deep in case 6 comes in on the other side in an unsuccessful block attempt. Because of the forehand force, 6 will most likely be needed to back up 3 when an offender cuts down the alley. If 6 gets pulled far to the strong side, 4 must come back to prevent the deep throw to the middle of the field (abandoning break-side responsibilities, as they are a lesser threat). Coordination among the downfield defenders in the clam is a key to its success.

Position 6 is the last line of defense. Besides long passes, the defender needs to watch for passes over or around 3 and 4. She needs a high degree of certainty that she'll get the block because a missed effort leaves the deep area unprotected, leading to an easy goal. Also, 6 has the whole field in front of her and is often the only defender facing the thrower, so she can let her teammates know about coming passes or cutters and remind the team of the transition—including calling off the clam ("We're out!") if need be. Ideally, everyone on the field should be aware of the pass count, but it's not always possible to see every pass, and sometimes players get so caught up in playing defense that they forget.

Setting It Up

On the line before the pull, players call out their positions in order, starting with 0. Generally, one of the back players should pull, as 0, 1, and 2 need to sprint down to set up. Some teams will call off the clam if the pull can be played immediately (without a check), so the defense needs to be aware of whom they're lined up across from. It's good practice to line up normally to avoid tipping off the defense. Positions 0, 1, and 2 should line up across from the likely handlers, while 6 should line up across from a deep. If the pull is out of bounds, and offensive players are moving around as the disc is being walked in, defenders can move with them until the disc is about to be put into play, or can openly say "Switch" to teammates near where the offenders are moving to give the impression that the defense is one-on-one. (Teams generally learn ways to get better and better at hiding the clam.) As the disc is being put in, 3 and 4 need to separate themselves from the stack just enough to be able to read cuts from the stack. Position 5 can delay a couple seconds if she wants because it's unlikely she'll be involved in the play right away. If the clam is being played on a "live" pull (no check), then 0, 1, and 2 should sprint down and try to disrupt the first pass. This usually means that the first one down runs between the pull catcher and the first receiver. The second one down then initiates the mark (0, 1, and 2 are interchangeable on a live clam).

Nontraditional Stacks

Occasionally an offense places a fourth handler close to the disc on the breakside. Often, the best solution is to simply ignore the player because coverage is 7 on 6 on the remaining players and it's a tough break-mark pass, anyway. Position 4 should probably not come in to cover because that just opens up too much space. If instead the offense moves one of the handlers there and doesn't move someone else up in the stack, it might be better for one of the front three to go out and cover him. If both handlers line up even with the disc or if the downfield receivers line up in a spread offense instead of a center stack, it's probably better to transition immediately to one on one, as the current incarnation of the clam is not optimized for these stacks.

For the most part, the clam is a supplemental defense, not a primary one. It can be deployed as a surprise weapon after a few points of straight one on one. It's important to get inside the offense's head, making receivers reluctant to cut and throwers hesitant to throw because they're leery of poaches. You have achieved success when you're playing your regular one on one, and the offense thinks it's a clam.

Fake Defenses

Another tool that defenses should have available is the ability to appear to set up in one defense but go immediately into another. A "zone for zero" (zero passes) would set up in a zone only long enough for the opponent to recognize it and fall into a zone offense—then the defense would transition to a one-on-one immediately before the tap-in. This generally is more effective on out-of-bounds pulls or other walkup situations. Similarly, with a fake clam (commonly called an "oyster"), the players need to appear to set up, calling out positions as the disc is about to be checked in, and 3 and 4 can flare out from the stack.

Teams should also fake transitions occasionally. The sidelines should count the passes, as usual, and scream to transition at the designated number; the defenders then flare to cover offenders briefly before returning to their zone positions. To add another layer of complexity, the defense might then transition for real on a set number of passes after the fake. As is true for all junk defenses, the hope is to garner turnovers from the confusion.

Straight one-on-one defense and zone defense might be the primary defensive schemes that most teams rely on, but junk defenses are frequently needed to confuse opposing offenses and break their rhythm. Hybrid defenses such as the clam combine elements of both one-on-one and zone defenses to shut down conventional cuts from the stack. Transition defenses attempt to slow down the offense and gather some blocks when the offense fails to recognize the defense. An offense stymied by well-played hybrid defenses is always guessing and never gets a chance to settle in.

Stack Offense

The stack is the most basic offensive structure in ultimate. After learning individual skills and positions, a newcomer to the game learns the stack. Put simply, the stack offense is keeping noncutters in the center of the field and keeping the two alleys (the space near the sidelines) free for cutting and flow. The stack offense is the natural response to the historical straight-up defense. This simple structure gives direction to the offense as a whole and to individual offenders, keeps viable parts of the field free for offensive progress, and allows the offense to exploit the swing—plus it's easy to learn and easy to teach!

The Point of the Stack

Why free up the sidelines? Because defenders won't encroach from out of bounds. This blithe response is really sage wisdom. It's easier to clear up the sideline alleys because the opponent approaches only from within the field. In contrast, poachers can thwart offensive progress up the middle by poaching from either side. Also, free sidelines mean two viable options against a straight-up defense, which is harder than a force forehand mark or a force backhand mark to break because of the more restrictive presence of the marker's body.

The benefits of the stack offense are many. Within this structure, players can rest and prepare in the middle of the field, keep the alleys open for cuts and flow, space themselves evenly downfield, be prepared to swing to the other alley, and keep defenders occupied.

Basic Stack

The basic stack is comprised of five players: seven minus the two involved in a pass at any given moment. These players are stationed in the middle of the field,

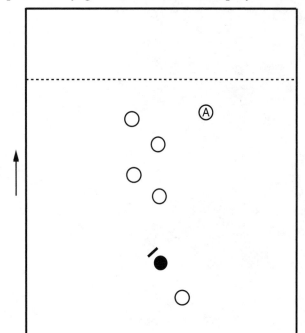

generally between 10 to 30 yards downfield from the thrower. They are arranged roughly in a line and regularly spaced from each other so they don't hinder cuts or create picks. These players are either preparing to cut, just clearing from a cut, or are occupying their defenders while resting (figure 12.1).

Consider a point in an offense where one player has caught the disc and is looking to reset the count or restart flow with a small throw to a handler (typically lateral or backward). Let's pick up the action from where the handler receives the pass. The thrower (assuming no give and go) will now be clearing out, freeing up the alley to make room for other cutters. The handler wants to find someone open and ready downfield, which means having a clear pathway from the disc to the receiver. At least one path should be available no matter the direction of the force, and this is ensured by

Figure 12.1 The basic stack is shown, with one offender (A) about to cut and one handler playing for the dump. Variations in size, shape, position, and angle of the stack have their relative merits, but all stacks share the philosophy of clustering the noncutting offenders to free up swaths of open space for flow.

the stack structure. Before the catch even occurs, one of the five players in the stack should have recognized himself as the best option to receive the next pass and begun making his cut. While this is occurring, the other four stack members should either be gearing up for the next cut, preparing another cut in case the first one fails, actively freeing up space for another cutter, resting, or making an alternative cut ("option B") on the other alley. For convenience of explanation, let's assume that while one player makes his cut, each of the four remaining stack members assumes one of these tasks. In reality, there might be more than one inactive player at any given time, but let's consider the offense at full steam. This situation is illustrated in figure 12.2. The player preparing for the next cut should move downfield to be far enough to gain significant yardage on the second cut. The player cutting for option B takes care to time his cut to be most convenient for the handler; he should keep his defender from interfering with the offensive progress. The cutter cutting to the opposite side should be mindful of any swings or hammer opportunities that might require an adjustment. This is just part of the general principle (space) that cutters should be attuned to the needs of the offense. Even the player resting must be sure to keep up with the motion of the stack.

If the pass goes to the first cutter, he should find the next one available and complete the pass. And so on. Once no pass is available, the disc should be returned to a handler and the process repeats. This regenerative, fluid structure that we've described is the stack at its best.

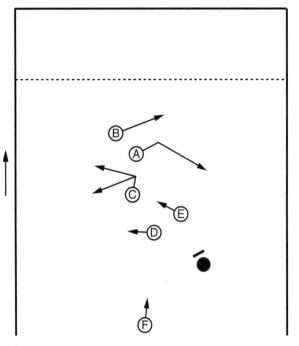

Figure 12.2 Downfield motion in an active stack. Player A is cutting for the thrower. Player B is preparing a flow cutoff of A (or as a second option if A fails). Player C is preparing to cut breakside for a hammer or swing. Player D is resting and shifting the stack slightly. Player E is clearing out and making space. Player F is keeping up with flow.

Long Stack

The long stack employs considerable spacing between stack members. In all, the stack might stretch 35 yards or more downfield from the handler. There might be a full 5 yards or more between offenders in the stack. Con-sequently, there's less congestion, fewer picks, offenders stationed along a deeper range of the field, and more clarity on who is most likely to be the preferred next cutter. For these reasons, the long stack is usually taught first. It's easier to learn and maintain. The drawbacks of the long stack are its predictability (it's obvious who's next) and diminished deep threat.

Short Stack

The short stack aims to exploit the deep space and the alleys. Stack members are squeezed into a relatively small range—from 10 to 25 yards (or less) downfield from the thrower. The extra space deep means more long-range opportunities, with fewer chances of being foiled by a poacher. This option is especially potent after a short gainer, as two or three cutters have nearly the whole downfield to play with.

Of course, the added benefits of the short stack come at a price. Players must be vigilant about keeping pace with the offensive motion. As soon as the disc flows downfield, the stack must flow with it. There's no leeway, as no one is stationed far enough downfield to keep up with flow and second cuts. Instead, the whole stack must move downfield with the disc, so that after one pass is completed, there are enough offenders moving downfield to create a viable cutting option for the continuation of the flow.

Another responsibility expected of short-stack players is the selection of the next cut. The next cut does not fall as obviously on just one player as it does in the long stack, and this ambiguity needs to be resolved—often through talking ("I'm out!" or

"Not me!"), a sense of "right of way" gained through experience, or one player simply holding back if two begin the same cut. The skills needed to resolve such difficulties are higher-order skills and might be too much to expect of beginning players. The short stack is the more advanced of the two stack formations.

Angled Stack and L-Stack

When the disc is near the sideline, only one viable sideline alley exists for the thrower, so the stack should angle away from the thrower to create more space for flow. This repositioning is dynamic, and the stack must shift back to its regular formation (short or long, say) when the disc is moved off the sideline. If the disc is stopped on the sideline and the thrower might need to reset with a dump pass, two handlers should make themselves available for a potential dump. A formation more like an L shape (with handlers forming the base) is recommended, so that the handlers' defenders can't poach into the alley and the handlers can cut down the line or to the backfield. If the disc is slightly off the line, something between an L and a straight line is preferable. Note that the angled stack and L-stack are temporary formations. In contrast, the other stacks in this section can be permanent offensive sets.

Shifted Stacks

Of course, stacks can also be shifted to the side to open up a single, larger alley. These formations can create wider spaces or free up a particular throw (or cut) for a strong player (or a team might want to take advantage of a prevailing wind), but they also have the disadvantage of having just one alley—and a poachable one at that. Because of these deficits, use shifted stack formations only occasionally. Other stack formations are discussed in chapter 15.

Flow

What is flow? Having the right cut available at the right time. A player cuts, the pass is made, and another cut appears at just the right time, over and over again. The disc flows effortlessly down the field. Such effortlessness takes effort, of course. The stack is essentially a blueprint for flow. By freeing up the sideline and placing offenders downfield, the stack offense clarifies how to proceed. In the best of cases, after a player close to the handler cuts from the stack and receives the disc close to the sideline, he looks downfield and finds a teammate cutting from the back of the stack and hits him. The combined play then leaves the offense within striking distance of the goal. At this point, if an offensive player has moved downfield fast enough, he's ready to receive a goal-scoring pass. Even if no player has moved downfield fast enough, the offense can reset to an end zone formation and score. Thus, flow can be as simple as two passes in close succession. It can also be a fluid combination of many throws—such as in a dump, swing, and continue downfield combo—or simply an offense in which players are in sync with one another, ready when needed.

Flow is achieved through practice and more practice, but this alone isn't enough. During practice, players need to talk before and after points about what they were expecting where and when; they need to listen to each other's reasons for not being there for the cut or not attempting the pass. In this way, players come to understand each other and begin to gel.

What exactly should players be talking about? Making sure an open pass is available at the right time requires preparation. In a stack offense, the alleys must be kept free. This means the offense must be on top of a number of tasks. Offenders must clear out after their cuts. This means stack occupants must angle the stack slightly toward the weak side to widen the preferred alley (without banishing closer cutters). They must move the stack downfield enough so that the cut gains substantial yardage and does not clog the offense near the disc. Offenders must signal to each other as necessary to avoid confusion about who's ready for the next cut. Proper preparation also leads to individual responsibilities, such as preparing a crossfield option if you're not involved in the main play (this can work as a second option for the thrower or simply as a way to occupy your defender). Keep your defender honest and busy by always appearing ready to cut. If you're not involved in the current play, gather your strength for the next one.

To summarize, flow is a result of the following practices, among others:

- Clear out after cutting.
- Move the stack downfield with the flow of the disc.
- Angle the stack toward the weak side to widen the strong alley.
- Resolve confusion about who is cutting.
- Occupy your defender with secondary cuts and decoys.
- Rest up for the next play.

At the team level, flow can be improved instantaneously in two ways: (1) Throwers never hold the disc past stall six, and (2) sideline players continually remind cutters with calls of "Next!" These two strategies can dramatically improve an offense whose main problem is lack of flow. For an offense in which flow is not a problem, these two strategies might do more harm than good.

Filling In

Offenders must remain alert, even while resting. The stack is not a subtle ploy; the threats are easy to predict, so the offense needs to respond quickly to poaches, switches, heavy shading, and other defensive tactics. Defenders often poach into the alleys to help out with coverage. When an offender cuts, the defender can be on only one side of him—so she might need help deep if she's fronting, or help underneath if she's protecting the deep—and this leads to poaches.

If you're in the stack and have been poached, you must immediately recognize the poach and take action. Sometimes, just yelling "Poach!" is enough to rein in your defender and free up the cutter (to chasten your defender, you might occasionally yell "Poach!" even before the poach occurs). More likely, the poach will occur and you might be free to step out of the stack and receive an open pass. If you were deep in the stack, and the poach came off to cover a deep threat, you should now cut diagonally in and toward the sideline. This keeps you away from other poachers and away from the original play. This is called "filling in underneath" and is a basic responsibility of stack members.

If a set play is called for a second cut underneath, but the initial deep cut draws a poach, the poached player should be given the right of way to fill in. "Filling in" also refers simply to cutting into the wake of space left by a deep cut, even if there's no poach, and this should occur periodically during flow.

Pairings

To minimize confusion about who is the preferred cut, many teams adopt a pairing or "buddy" system among downfielders. When one member of the pair catches the disc, that member's first look is to his buddy. This system allows pairs of cutters to work with each other, know who's likely to cut, and develop a sense of the other's preferences. The pairing system is simple and is easily taught and learned, so we won't elaborate further. Such a system is a critical part of many stack offenses. Think of the harmony achieved between a pair of basketball greats, such as Stockton and Malone, and you'll understand the kind of possibilities we're talking about.

Stack Motion and Reformation

As we mentioned previously in our discussion of flow, the stack must keep moving downfield along with the flow of the disc. The stack must also move back to stay short if a series of dump passes causes a loss of yardage, and it should angle or transform into an L-stack when the disc is near the sideline. Although you may rest in the stack, you can't remain inert. A responsive stack creates an environment in which someone is always in the right place to make the next cut.

Stacks must also create room for their cutters, which demands that they widen the alleys. If the stack is a diffuse mass of offenders—say, 10 yards wide—and sits in the middle of the field, then the alleys (both strong and weak) are only 15 yards wide and rather vulnerable to sudden poaches. If, however, the stack shifts a few steps toward the weak-side alley and has the discipline to remain tight (just a few yards wide), then the strong-side alley can be widened by 7 or 8 yards without narrowing the weak-side alley. The extra space means that a defender will have to reveal her intentions by standing out a few yards, thus thwarting her chances at a surprise poach block.

The stack must be disciplined. Keep tight, keep up, and keep out of the way!

Communication, Reassignment, and Improvisation

As we've said, stacks must react to the flow. People get tired and need help. "Not me!" signals that you're not ready to cut and directs that someone else take over. "I go!" tells your teammates that you're ready and willing to cut and can signal to a second cutter that you want the right of way. A call of "Poach!" is clear and must be made as soon as the poach is recognized. It's usually not necessary to yell if you're filling in underneath, though a yell might still help in some cases—say, if someone else is called on the line for the underneath cut. If you're in the stack and won't be ready to cut, or if you can't play your designated role as main cutter (because Speedy Gonzalez is your defender), inform a teammate by calling out, "You're it!" Don't hesitate to yell a teammate's name if you think he should be cutting (though you might hear from him after the point). If you see an opportunity to gain an advantage, take it! If you're cutting for a continuation swing pass and notice your defender overplaying you, break rank and sprint deep to the crossfield (strong side). If it works, great. If it doesn't, your stack offense should have the flexibility to bend with your improvisation. Someone else will take your cut—perhaps a bit later—and the offense will manage.

Poaching, Predictability, and Preparedness

As we mentioned previously under Filling In, stack members must be prepared for poaches and respond immediately—by calling out the poach and cutting away from it. More generally, if you're playing stack offense, you've got to be alert. The stack offense is very predictable, and what's obvious for the offense is just as apparent to a defense. If it's clear who will be the next cut, a competent defender will figure it out and take away the first-step advantage (the element of surprise)—this is particularly true in a long-stack formation.

Stack offense is not rocket science. If it's played with wooden rigidity, it's easily stymied. For the stack to be potent against high-level defenses, it must be versatile. Every downfield cut should start from a level that makes either short or deep options viable. The offense must have a plan B (and a plan C) ready and be able to implement it before the defense can respond. For example, if the defense sends someone into the alley to poach, what should the offense do? If the poach covers a deep throw, there might be an easy underneath play available. There are other types of poaches, too. In any case, the poached offender should find an open route—say, to the opposite side of the field. The offense can then break the mark in one throw or after a quick dump. (A handler who has just received the disc has a good chance of throwing a quick break.) If the defense responds and picks up the poached offender, the chain of poaches and reactions continues. At each stage, the offense has a chance to burn the defense. (This aspect of offense is not unique to the stack, of course.)

There's more to preparedness than anticipating poaches. Is your offense ready to swing to the other side at a moment's notice? Can it fake a swing by initiating a swing then returning to the same side of the field and up the line for a score? Can it take advantage of an up-the-middle pass by creating simultaneous options on both alleys? Is there always someone ready to sprint deep when a defender is out of place? Every offender must be prepared for all of these possibilities. A stack offense that is anticipating, baiting, and reacting to many of these possibilities can vary significantly from its underlying stack formation—but the basic line up the center of the field remains the foundation of the offense. Sometimes the fundamentals are obscured in high-level play, but the crux of the offense reveals itself whenever the defense has a lapse—the offense can score in a heartbeat.

Stack formations are designed to make space for cuts. The elements of good stack play—moving the stack, keeping it downfield, responding to the defense, and signaling for the next cut—are applications of the principles of space and communication, which create opportunities for offensive flow.

Zone Offense

THIRTEEN

A team can get by without a quality zone defense, but it's almost impossible to succeed without a good zone offense. Ultimate is frequently played in wind and bad weather, and with bad weather come zone defenses. Plus, a team with a reputation for having a bad zone offense is more likely to see a zone defense.

Zone offense relies on patience and calculated risk taking. Long passes are rare against the zone, though they should be used if the defense cheats in too much. Instead, a series of tactical strikes is most effective at piercing through the holes in the defense. Some of these passes, most notably those that break the cup, appear to be high-risk, and indeed they are more likely to fall incomplete. But simply completing passes is not enough if the passes don't move you closer to scoring, so an occasional risk is called for.

Traditional Approach

Although the traditional zone offense approach is not recommended here, we'll include it for comparison purposes. The traditional set (figure 13.1a-b) features three handlers, two poppers, and two deeps. This style attempts to move the disc down the sidelines by swinging it from the handler on one sideline to the handler on the other sideline (usually by going through the middle handler) and hoping

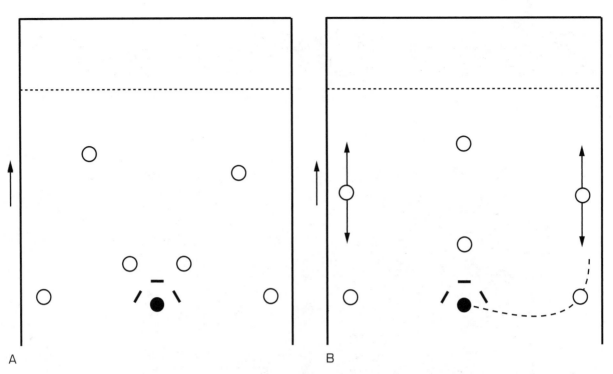

A   B

Figure 13.1 The traditional zone offense features three handlers, two poppers, and two deeps (or sometimes three handlers, two wings, one popper, and one deep). This offense looks to swing the disc around the cup and up the line to gain yards.

for a continuation pass to a popper cutting across or a deep coming in. (Alternately, the traditional set can be three handlers, two wings, one popper, and one deep, in which case the continuation pass is thrown to a wing cutting back up the line.) If the continuation pass is not available, the disc swings back around to the other side for another attempt. Ideally, every pass in this offense is high-percentage, but there will be a lot of those passes, and a lot of running as well. All this running does have the advantage of tiring out the other team, but the nonhandlers on the offense will also be running a lot and might be more prone to fatigue-related mistakes when they get the disc.

We don't recommend the traditional zone offense because no pass is truly 100 percent, especially in windy conditions, when you're more likely to face a zone. In addition to drops, turnovers can result from crossfield passes that fly over the receiver or bury themselves in the turf. Furthermore, because the disc is often on the sideline as a matter of design, a trap situation often arises, leading to low-percentage passes, particularly when a weak thrower has the disc. It's not unusual for this zone offense to take 50 or even 100 passes.

So, why is the traditional zone still played? For several reasons—some of them reasonable:

- For the sake of tradition
- In fear of making a turnover on anything but a "100-percent" pass
- Because the rules are simple and require little judgment
- When handlers have weak break-mark and overhead throws
- When downfield players have exceptionally poor throwing skills

If the traditional approach is employed, one way to improve the chance of success is for handlers to squeeze every yard they can out of the swing passes. There are several ways to do this.

- Side handlers should position themselves as far downfield for the swing as is safe.
- The middle handler should be only as far back as necessary to get the pass around the off-point.
- Swing passes should be thrown as far downfield as safety allows.
- Handlers should try to jump forward while catching the disc.

Of course, there's an element of risk in each of these tactics, particularly if repeated enough that the defense makes adjustments.

The Two-Handler Zone Offense

A better approach than the traditional zone defense is to attempt to move up the center of the field by throwing through or over the cup and then fast-breaking for as many yards as possible before resetting. This is most easily accomplished with a different set (here called "two-handler" for want of a better term) that uses two handlers, two poppers, two wings, and a deep. More important than the set, though, is the philosophy.

In this two-handler offense, handlers pass through and over the cup to the poppers, who then fast-break at full tilt with the wings and the deep, until their momentum is stopped. (If the cup is catching up or the middle of the field becomes heavily trafficked, then poppers should regroup instead of pushing the fast break too far.) While the disc is still contained by the cup, the poppers and wings move slowly, if at all, and hand-lers allow themselves at least five seconds to look for an open breaking pass. Dump passes should not lose much yardage; frequently, they'll result in an immediate give and go back to the original thrower.

The reason this offense works is that there are five offensive players behind the cup (and just four defenders) who should be able to exploit temporary two-on-one advantages to get open. The players must be aware of the defenders, sometimes attempting to draw double coverage or overload a single defender so that another receiver can get open. If the defending zone covers this rather static formation well, the poppers become more active, one crashing the cup (or approaching it) and the other cutting to receive a pass through the resulting hole.

Figure 13.2 illustrates the setup and basic principles of the two-handler

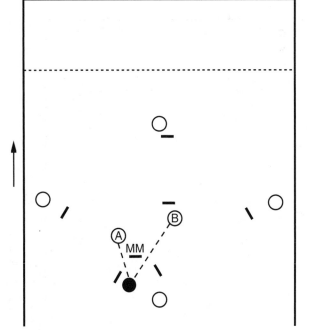

Figure 13.2 The two-handler zone offense employs two poppers, two wings, and a deep. The basic setup has five offensive players downfield behind the cup.

offense. In a stationary situation, the off-handler is positioned to avoid losing yardage on the dump but is far enough away to throw a pass around the off-point if there's a swing. If the point attempts to cover him, he can head back for a dump. This also opens up a hole behind the point. The wings are far downfield and near their respective sidelines. If the side-middles abandon them to cover the poppers, the wings should get into an open position for an overhead throw. One popper (A) is positioned in the slot three to five yards behind, between the middle-middle (MM) and the point. The other popper (B) is farther away in the other slot, about three to five yards behind the first popper. The thrower's goal is to get a pass to either of the poppers.

As an example, popper A can work the middle-middle by stepping a little closer into the gap to draw her over (while the thrower fakes that throw). Then he can begin to drift away while continuing to face the thrower to present a viable target, also drawing the attention of the side-middle wing. Popper B slides up into the now-open slot. The side-middle has to cover the offensive wing and is too far away to help out. Popper B is now in perfect position for a quick throw through the cup. Up to this point, the offensive players have been moving slowly (figure 13.3).

But as soon as it's apparent that the pass is going to B, everyone starts in motion. Popper A cuts hard to the middle at an angle so that popper B can immediately turn and throw. He can't run too far downfield or one of the deeps could alertly poach in. He can also talk to the other popper to let him know that he's in position for the quick pass. The wings both begin slanting in as well, expecting to get the next pass from A, again not going too far downfield for fear of getting blocked by a deep. Either wing is a viable target, depending on how the defense reacts. After one of the wings gets the disc, the offensive deep is the next target (figure 13.4). Occasionally, if the wings find themselves stuck on the sideline (maybe it's very windy, and they've come back toward the disc to offer an outlet for the handler), the deep will catch a pass directly from A, in which case the wings should be hustling upfield for the next pass from the deep.

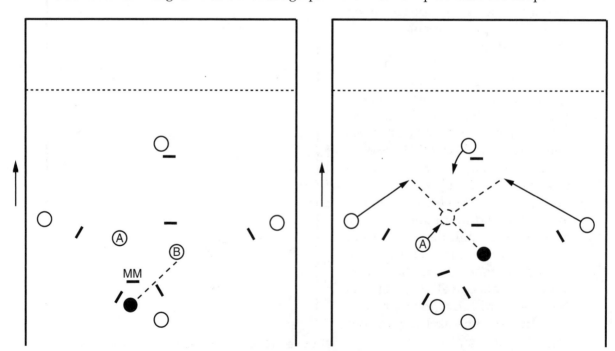

Figure 13.3 The poppers work the middle-middle to create an opening. Players are still moving slowly and deliberately.

Figure 13.4 Fast break in the zone offense. The downfield receivers are sprinting.

The Key

To work properly, this offense must be able to exploit temporary two-on-one advantages. A good defense will adjust after a few seconds to close up the holes. When the disc is stationary, any two offensive players have overloaded one defensive player (figure 13.5). Popper A and the near wing have overloaded the side-middle. The two poppers have overloaded the middle-middle. However, if those players get too close together, the defender can effectively cover both players. To create space, the wings and the deep should stretch wide and deep. In general, it's the responsibility of the front player to distract the defender and for the back player to find his way slyly into the most open spot.

Exploiting advantages moves the disc down the field, but the team also has to avoid turnovers while looking for holes. Good zone defenses often create turnovers by changing their tactics partway through a point, or even a stall count, so a player who was expected to be open is suddenly not. For instance, the off-point might leave the dump-cutter open the first few times, but on the next pass at stall six will run to cover the dump. To counter this, the players near the disc (poppers and handlers) need to be ready to sprint for the high stall count pass, while others shift to exploit late holes (figure 13.6). Handlers must remain poised during late-count maneuvers. In the above example, the popper on the side of the dump-cutter would need to run to the area vacated by the off-point, and because the middle-middle might rotate to pick up the cutting popper, the other popper needs to be ready to move into that vacated area.

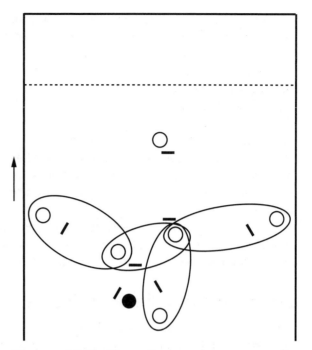

Figure 13.5 The offense uses two-on-one advantages. Any two offensive players overload the nearest defender.

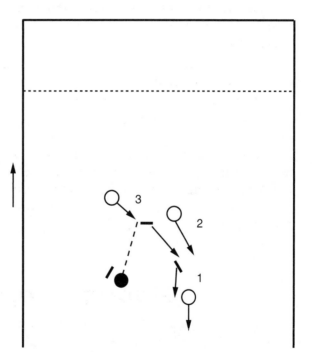

Figure 13.6 Adjusting to late-count defensive maneuvers. (1) The off-point runs to the off-handler, who then moves for a dump. (2) The popper moves into the vacated area, but the middle-middle moves with him. (3) The other popper runs to where the middle-middle was and receives the pass.

The handlers need to be in control, especially early in the point when the rest of the team might still be setting up. If the downfield players are not set in their positions, the handlers need to assign positions and make sure the others know what they should be doing. Even if the handler needs to hold the disc and yell to the wing to move downfield and stay near the line, those few seconds will pay off later in the point. Once the offense is set, the handlers need to be tactical. A handler might see a downfield pass that's open but that has a greater risk of error. His options are not simply to throw or not throw but include waiting for a few passes for a similar opportunity with a slightly larger margin of error. Pinpoint strikes by handlers to opposite-side wings are not uncommon, especially when a defense tries to trap aggressively on a sideline. In such situations, the offense relies heavily on the handlers being able to make accurate risk-reward assessments.

When all players on offense know the overall philosophy and the individual responsibilities of each position, the team functions well and can score with only one or two nontrivial throws. Stay calm, and be tactical.

Responsibilities of Each Position

• All positions: Keep the middle of the field open. Stretch the zone wide and deep. Be patient while looking for a weakness, but strike quickly after finding one.

• Handlers: Look to go through or over the cup, often to poppers but sometimes to wings. Don't lose yardage on the dump. Look to give and go into the cup after dumping to the other handler. Be ready to cut hard for the dump at a high stall count. Look for hammers to the off-wing. Ensure that your team assumes the proper zone offense formation. Stay poised and balanced with the disc. Keep all options in mind in case the defense shifts.

• Poppers: Find the holes behind the middle-middle. Coordinate motion with the other popper. Be ready to sprint for the other popper. Always be ready to receive a pass. Don't turn away from the thrower.

• Wings: Spread the defense out, leaving the middle of the field open for the poppers. Be a threat if the side-middle ignores you. Be ready to sprint for the fast break from the second popper. Be ready to cut back up the line if the side-middle is in the middle, but the deep defender prevents the deeper throw. Be ready to sprint deep if the deep defender comes in. Be a hammer threat!

• Deep: Manipulate the defensive deeps. Don't allow them to get comfortable. Finish up the fast break. Give the team a viable deep threat, just in case. Stretch the defense thin.

Recognizing a Zone

Several cues, though not foolproof, often reveal that the defense will be setting up a zone, giving the offense a few extra seconds to get into position. These cues include the following:

• The pulling team makes no effort to match up on particular offensive players.

• When the pull is in the air, an offensive player crosses from one side of the field to the other, and no defender crosses with him.

• Two or three players sprint down on the pull to set up as the points and perhaps the middle-middle.

- These same players might unscrupulously be off-side to get a head start. Don't be afraid to ask for a repull. At least remind them before the next point to hold the line.

- One or two players barely jog downfield (because as deeps they won't be involved in the first few passes).

- The puller might deliberately throw the disc out of bounds to set up the zone (although this is just as likely to be a setup for a junk defense).

- When an out-of-bounds pull is being walked in, defenders appear to be covering positions instead of players.

One cue for a transition from zone to one-on-one coverage is when defenders stay with one offensive player instead of trying to cover an area or a throwing lane.

Ideally, a player on the sideline or uninvolved in the called play should be watching for the zone or for a transition from zone to one-on-one coverage. Cues for such a transition include the following:

- One defensive player yells out a code phrase ("Let's go!") and others repeat it.

- Defenders stay with one offensive player instead of trying to cover an area or a throwing lane.

- Defenders turn their backs to the disc to find or cover an offensive player.

- The marker makes a clumsy effort to foul the thrower, with the transition coming at the first stop in play. (Fouling the thrower is illegal and a violation of the spirit of the game.)

- The players on the sideline, after initially counting each throw out loud, stop doing so.

Some Additional Concerns

Overhead throws (hammers, blades, and scoobers) can be either the salvation or the ruin of a zone offense, depending on how they're used. There exists a greater element of risk than with a flat throw. In the zone, hammers should be thrown only when the receiver is stationary and won't have to jump in a crowd to catch the disc. The throw should get there quickly but not be moving so fast that it's difficult to catch. Catchability also rules out many blades, especially in strong winds. Because of the higher risk, there should be a significant reward to justify the throw. If the side-middles and the deeps cheat in too much to cover the poppers, the wings will be wide open for a huge breaking hammer. This pass is occasionally necessary to keep defenders honest.

Leading passes are also beneficial, if employed regularly. If a breaking popper is expecting a leading pass, a pass thrown right at him might surprise him and result in a drop. A normal leading pass, though, can yield free yardage if the receiver runs alongside the disc without catching it. However, danger awaits if the pass is thrown too far ahead (especially in the middle of the field) or if the receiver isn't paying attention.

Be objective in your evaluations of the offensive scheme and of the specific passes. No team scores every time it has the disc, so some level of risk is acceptable. The best pass is the one that gives you the best chance of scoring, and that isn't necessarily the least risky pass. The team culture can't paralyze individuals so that players are afraid to do anything for fear of turning the disc over and getting benched. This natural tendency in players to want to avoid causing turnovers is why zone defenses are often effective at crucial moments in the game.

Playing Against Other Zones

The offense must adjust its positions based on where zone defenders set up. For example, if the middle-middle sets up 10 yards from the disc and won't budge, the poppers have to be willing to set up in front of him. If the whole zone is different, the first thing to assess is whether the defense is passive or aggressive. If it's passive, as for a typical 1-3-3 or for a flat 2-3-2, the offense needs to pay attention to every yard on every pass because one bad dump pass can lose 20 passes' worth of gained yardage. If the zone is aggressive, trapping or double-teaming the weaker throwers, the offense needs to be more concerned with avoiding dangerous situations. A wing would thus look to dump the disc to get it off the line early in the count rather than spending five seconds looking downfield. The whole team would also need to be more active on the fast break to get as many yards as possible before the defense resets. Players on the sideline should help assess the defense.

The strength and direction of the wind also changes the nature of the zone, even if the defense plays identically. Typically, teams play zone defense when the wind is at their backs. If the wind is exceptionally strong, the offense has to adjust because throws are more difficult, especially longer ones. The wings should not be as far downfield (though still close to the sideline), even, on occasion, coming all the way back even with the disc. The poppers also need to move a step or two closer and must be willing to cut into the cup at a high stall count to offer another option for the thrower. All players must be more disciplined with their throws, making them crisp. Sometimes strong crosswinds are blowing. Watch for throws behaving differently. Overhead throws, such as the hammer or blade, are particularly less predictable in wind.

Wind also calls for adjusted strategies. If the disc ends up on the downwind sideline, try to get it off the line as soon as you can and continue moving it to the other sideline. (Most zone defenses will trap if there's a strong crosswind.) More important, though, is to avoid letting the disc get to that sideline. For cup-breaking or yardage-gaining passes, don't worry about whether the disc is moving closer to the downwind sideline. For dumps and other reset passes, however, make every effort either not to throw the disc downwind or to regain the position with an immediate follow-up pass.

Defense After a Turnover

Inevitably, your team will turn the disc over against a zone and have to play defense. Against a one-on-one defense, players usually take the player who was covering them, but against a zone, offensive players need to identify match-ups on the fly. Most critical is to prevent the fast break and the easy long pass. Immediately after a turnover, look behind you to see if any uncovered opponents are deeper than you are. Point to the player that you're taking, and point to other players for your teammates to pick up, as necessary.

Zone offense is a game of calculated risks. A well-played possession might feature a few low-risk passes to search for a weakness, one riskier pass to exploit the weakness, and then a series of low-risk passes to gain yards. The two handlers throw through and over the cup. Downfield players patiently work two-on-one advantages to free one of them for a cup-breaking pass, and then go all-out on the fast break. All players focus on good decision making and purposeful movement to score easy goals.

Set Plays

FOURTEEN

© Marshall Goff

Special situations on the field are easier to handle if an offense has a variety of structured plays to call. Set plays are an essential—though typically not decisive—part of the game. That is, a team must have and be ready to use set plays, especially for disc stoppages, but the outcomes of games are rarely determined by them. Overall, ultimate is a free-flowing game in which passing and scoring occur in the context of unforeseen circumstances taking place on the field. Still, all good teams have some set plays to use in a pinch or when situations call for them. In this chapter, we'll present several set plays to use in common game situations.

Set plays are choreographed for key situations to ensure that a thrower, cutter, and noncutters perform complementary tasks. These plays can also be designed to employ the most dangerous players in favorable positions, such as plays off the pull. Ideally, set plays take advantage of defensive tendencies, expectations, or positional mistakes. They shouldn't be the building blocks of an offense but should work within the offense's structures to enhance the offense under special circumstances. Much effort is required to coordinate the movements of set plays, so newer teams are better off spending practice time on the fundamentals of their basic offense, using only one or two simple set plays.

A team should have a clear sense of what its set plays are for, such as breaking the mark, developing a long cut, scoring in the end zone, or simply picking up a few yards anywhere on the field. A team's set plays might even look the same as the regular offense, but just having a way to call the play so that everyone knows what to expect is useful.

Play Options

Set plays can have options built into them, where the cutter or thrower must make a decision based on how the defense reacts. For example, a cutter could choose to cut with or against the force, or a thrower could have two cutters go simultaneously and then pick one. This allows you to run a play several times against a team without the play being recognized and stopped.

Another option is to have several different ways of calling the same play. Think of a third-base coach in baseball flashing a series of signs in plain sight, with only one (or none) of them meaning anything. Play A could be called by yelling out any word that begins with the letter A. Another play might be called by shouting the name of a car. If a series of plays is called, the second (or the first, or the first one after an indicator call, such as "Red") could be the one that counts. Of course you need to remember the decoy or have a system that allows the decoy to vary. These schemes might be useful if your team plays the same team several times, or if players migrate from team to team. Audible calls hardly ever make or break a game, however, and few teams bother to figure out an opponent's calls.

As your team develops, your playbook will grow. Rather than adding totally new plays, try adding counters to existing plays. A counter begins the same way as a particular play but diverges after a key fake. You can use a counter after you've run a play once or twice. It's important that the fake is believable. Remember that if a smart defense has seen a play once, they'll be anticipating the play again. Instead, run a counter. Counters often have active stack movement.

Plays can be run to a specific player, a called position (say, primary deep), or a position in the stack. Generally, the circumstances dictate the best choice. A pull play or time-out play should name certain players. Another good time to call a specific player is after a stoppage in which one player is naturally isolated and clearly in the best position to cut. You might run a play using called positions after a stoppage when no particular play or cut stands out. A danger in this is that the designated players might be out of position or have forgotten their assignment. Plays by stack position can be called near the end zone or anywhere else where space is at a premium and clogging is likely. You can even mix and match, adding a name to a position play to indicate the named player should make the key cut instead.

There are many ways to call for a particular player. Against teams that don't know you well, you can simply call out the first or last name of the player you want to cut. Any unique identifier will work, really—the name of a pet, street, town, company, and so on. Just don't get too cute or complicated in an effort to throw off the other team, because your team might get confused, too.

Pull Plays

Most modern offenses try to run some sort of set play off the pull. The basic idea is to open up space so a single defender can't cover it all. The simplest method is the four-person play (also called a "string" or "chain"), where the play-caller specifies on the line the first four players to touch the disc. As the pull is coming down, the pull catcher (called "Catch" or simply "one") or the first pass catcher (called "Hitch" or "two") calls a side of the field to run the play down. (It's best to have the first catcher call the side because he doesn't have to concentrate on the pull and can see the defense coming down. The call must be loud so that the pull catcher and the stack know what to do. It's also fine to call the side before the play starts.) The first pass goes to the called side or to the middle. The stack should line up on or move to the other side of the field. The third player in the play (called the "Man," primary middle, or "three") is given the choice of cutting deep or faking deep and coming underneath. If the pass is underneath, the fourth player (called the "Buddy," primary deep, or "four") has the same options (figure 14.1).

The first way to improve on this play is to give jobs to the other three players. The third handler ("Seventh Man," or "X," to go along with Catch and Hitch) can act as a decoy for the first pass and as a bailout for a high count anywhere in the play. The other middle ("Short Fill," secondary middle, or "Y") should cut if the Man doesn't get open, and should fill underneath if the Man cuts deep. The other deep ("Long Fill," secondary deep, or "Z") cuts if the Buddy doesn't get open or if the Buddy catches the disc short of the goal.

The next step is to add counters and variations. For instance, as the Man cuts in, the Hitch fakes the throw, the stack shifts to that side of the field, and Short Fill cuts back to the other side, then finishes to Long Fill (figure 14.2). Or, Catch fakes the pass to Hitch and hits Seventh Man on the opposite side. A variation would be to toss in an extra pass to Seventh Man before going to the Man.

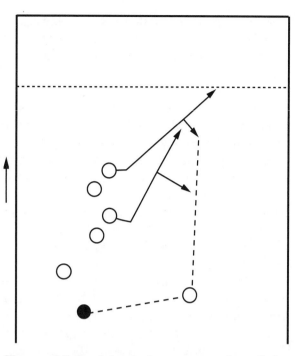

Figure 14.1 A basic four-person play off the pull gives the downfield cutters options. Either player can cut deep if open or can return underneath.

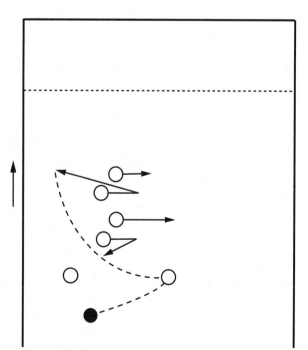

Figure 14.2 A counter to the basic four-person play begins the same way, but the stack follows a decoy cutter, and the play then runs up the other side.

An offense should tailor its basic play and alternatives to its strengths. Teams with good deep games should have huck options in their plays. Huck plays need to clear the deep area and get the disc into a power position with a throwing lane open. The actual deep cut can originate from a receiver who fakes a comeback cut or from a handler who clears deep. The following two plays illustrate this.

In the first example, the stack lines up as the pull comes down, and the first pass comes to the middle. The last player in the stack cuts in as if in a normal four-person play. Simultaneously, the next to last player in the stack cuts in on the opposite side. After a slight delay, the next player (now last in the stack) fakes in, then sprints deep straight down the field, and the thrower hucks with the force, whichever way it is. The rest of the stack has to maintain a tight formation to open up both sides for the long pass. There are many variations to this play in getting the disc to the long thrower.

Another play could be used after an out-of-bounds pull or any time there's a center stack after a stoppage. The first player in the stack cuts inside-out back to the disc, and the thrower pretends to try unsuccessfully to get the disc to him, perhaps apologizing for failing to break the mark or screaming "he's right on you." The cutter expresses disgust and appears to clear out, but actually is sprinting downfield. Meanwhile, the last player in the stack cuts in on the force side and receives the pass. By the time he catches the disc and is set, the original cutter should now be in position for a long pass. Again, the other players in the stack need to keep defenders busy and maintain a tight formation to free up the passing lanes and prevent their defenders from poaching on the long cut.

Other teams might prefer that their set plays simply gain a few yards and get the disc moving. Ideally, the disc will end up in a position from which more yard-gaining cuts will naturally flow. These plays would involve more stack movement, misdirection, and variations. From a stack or from flow, the first player in the stack cuts with the force and is thrown to if open. Each player in the stack then cuts hard for the continuation, with the last player stopping after a couple of solid steps and cutting to the other side. The next-to-last player continues for a few more steps, turns downfield, and then can cut deep or back underneath for the next pass.

Stoppages

A team should have a few plays for stopped-disc situations with only a few seconds left in the stall count. Usually, these plays are for just one pass, and the primary goal is to maintain possession. Many will have two or more cutting options going at the same time. In those plays, the thrower can take only an instant during the action to assess whether a cutter is open, but he can often tell before the disc is put in play that a particular cutter will be open based on his defender's positioning.

One simple play is the isolation (or "iso"), preferably to a dump. This play is often useful when a time-out is called at stall nine or when there's a contested call. A player with a quick first step lines up 5 to 10 yards behind the thrower, possibly to one side. The thrower decides where to throw the disc so that the receiver can run it down. The receiver moves only after the throwing motion has started. If time allows, the cutter (and possibly the thrower) can add in a fake, or the thrower can wait for the cut to start, although there's a danger of miscommunication. To reduce the danger, the cutter or thrower can indicate the direction of the cut with a head movement, a subtle point with the elbow, or a code word. The disc can be thrown to one side of the receiver (particularly if his defender is standing on the other side) or beyond both the cutter and his defender (if the defender is directly between the thrower and cutter).

The isolation play can be called for a downfielder as well, although you should have at least five seconds in the stall count to allow him to get open. An experienced team might have different calls for each of the following:

- Last player in the stack
- First player in the stack
- Specific player in the stack
- Cut to forehand or backhand side
- Cut to breakside or force side
- Cut away from the disc for a leading pass

These calls can be combined—for example, "break" might normally mean that the first player in the stack cuts to the breakside, but "break two" would mean that the second player in the stack cuts that way. (You'll want a less obvious call than "break," of course.) Numbering starts at the front of the stack and ignores players behind the disc. That's why there's a specific call for the last player in the stack, because that player could be either fifth or sixth, and the team shouldn't have to check for the presence of a handler behind the disc.

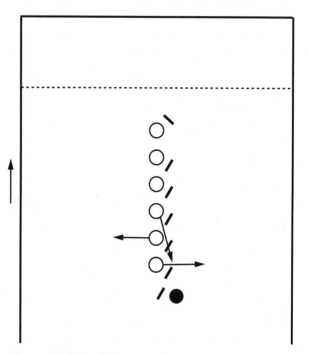

Another simple play is to run the first three cutters in different directions. The first player in the stack cuts to one side, the second player to the other, and the third player comes up the middle (figure 14.3). This is the basic split, though there are many variations. The direction of the first cut can be left up to the cutter or be specified (forehand, backhand, break, with force). If the cut is to be based on the mark, the thrower needs to call out what the force is if the mark is straight up or unclear. This play can be run equally effectively when the disc is trapped on the sideline and the first two players in the stack are even with the disc (L-stack).

Figure 14.3 A simple play off a time-out gives the thrower several options. Here a split play is shown.

For either of these plays (and many others), it's easy to add a continuation cut to the play call. For example, in the above play, the last player in the stack would go next if the first or third cutters caught the disc, whereas the next to last player would cut for the second cutter.

Flow Plays

A team should also have set plays designed just to gain yardage. Although they can be run off stoppages, these plays are ideally run during flow.

A simple flow play is the give and go. After making a swing pass toward the middle of the field, the thrower cuts across the field in front of the disc for a leading pass. He is then in good position to deliver a yard-gaining pass or even a huck. The give and go itself will also gain a few yards, especially if the second throw is milked, making it a useful play near the end zone. Sometimes this call can be made after the first throw has occurred if the thrower sees that the cut will be open. Making the call (instead of just cutting without a call) lets the downfield cutters know not to cut for the immediate continuation and also alerts the second thrower. The give and go is most effective when the force is toward the wide side of the field. It's less effective (though useful if available) when trapped on the sideline because the break-mark passes are more difficult to get off and get downfield. A counter to this play is to have the cutter go hard for several steps, then stop and turn back to the original side.

Another flow play is to go directly to the main cutters (3-4 and Man-Buddy) or the alternates (Y-Z and Short Fill-Long Fill) in the pull play. This play can be used after a stoppage or turnover or as a transition from junk defense. In cases where the stack is jumbled or the players are otherwise poorly positioned, add a "hitch" or extra pass to the call so that one of the handlers cuts for a swing pass to give the rest of the team a chance to reset.

While most passes in an ultimate game occur in free-flow contexts, there are several critical opportunities per game where structure makes a difference. Set plays can help you avoid a jam or gain some easy yards. They can begin your offense off the pull or finish your offense for a goal. Just make sure that any set plays you develop are a natural part of your offense.

Other Formations

The center stack has been the dominant offensive structure for most of ultimate's history, and for good reason. The center-stack formation helps create open space on the sides of the field while providing structure. However, in some circumstances the principles applied to the stack must be adjusted because the open space on the field has shifted, such as when the disc is on the sideline or near the end zone. Additionally, more and more offenses are spreading their offenses across the field, creating new open spaces and throwing lanes.

Trap Offense

Many defenses attempt to force an offense to one of the sidelines and then trap them on the line. The cutting area is reduced, deep help is often available, and many offensive players react poorly in this situation, especially with an aggressive mark. However, a disciplined offense will create space and options against this kind of trapping defense.

Downfield, the stack needs to maintain its normal distance from the line in the trap. There's a great tendency for downfield players to edge closer to the line, but they must stay away in order to open up an additional cutting area and be ready to continue a swing pass. The handlers need to reposition themselves to be available for a dump cut or a cut up the line. Typically, this results in an L-stack or a curved stack (figure 15.1a-b).

The first look in the trap offense is usually to a downfield cutter. Each offense needs to make it clear what its hierarchy is so that only one player cuts in this situation. This cutter needs to give himself enough space to go deep, come in, or fake in and go down the line for a leading pass. If this cut is unsuccessful, several options remain. Another of the downfield cutters can come underneath (sometimes this will happen even later in the count as a last-ditch bailout effort), which usually results in a slight inside-out pass to a point 5 to 10 yards off the line. Before the dump becomes the only option, the thrower needs to shift his focus from gaining yards to maintaining possession. This typically occurs at a stall count of about five or six (or earlier in the count if the thrower is weak or it's windy, or if the team has been having trouble working off the line). Instead of facing downfield, the thrower turns his body 90 degrees to face across the field toward the handlers (figure 15.2a-b). This makes the mark effectively more straight up instead of a force forehand or force backhand. The handlers can cut for the dump, expecting to continue swinging the disc across the field, or if the dump is overplayed, cut up the line. Typically, the handler closer to the disc chooses one way, and the second handler must be prepared to go the other way. Occasionally, a downfield defender poaches to the line, and his offender is open all the way across the field for a hammer.

Once the disc moves off the line, the offense should look to continue moving all the way across the field. The defenders will be positioned on the wrong side of the cutters. If the dump pass is successful, the dump receiver should generally not turn back toward where the throw came from but should turn the other way and look for another handler cut to the far side of the field. From here, a downfield cutter should continue the flow. Especially against a trap with a supporting crossfield wind, the offense should continue to try to move the disc down the weak side of the field.

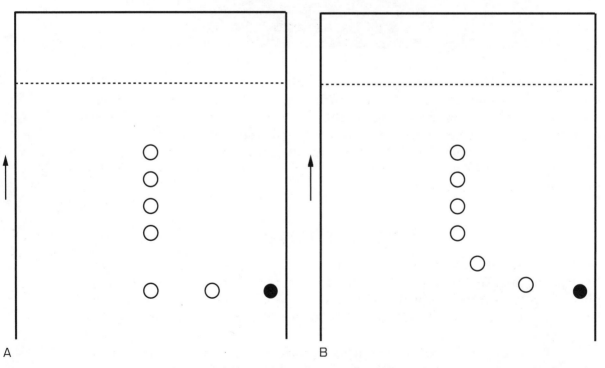

A   B

Figure 15.1 The stack repositions the handlers in a trap situation. The handlers can be *(a)* straight across, forming an L-stack or *(b)* slightly offset to give the thrower a direct look at both handlers.

Figure 15.2 *(a)* Early in the count, the thrower faces downfield and looks for cutters. *(b)* Later in the count, he turns to face the marker and looks for the dump.

Offense Against Junk Defenses

Defenses will attempt to disrupt the rhythm of the offense by playing hybrid defenses such as the clam or a zone for a few passes. The first task for the offense is to recognize the defense, communicate "Junk!" to one another, and reorganize their structure. These defenses often have several defenders near the disc, so one or more handlers must be prepared to come back all the way to help out. To tell whether the defense is playing the clam or a zone, take a look at what the marker does immediately after the throw. If she stays with the thrower, it's probably the clam. If she heads toward the thrown disc, it's probably a zone.

Patience is of the utmost importance. These defenses attempt to confuse or trick the offense into taking dangerous throws. The thrower might focus on the cutter and the defender originally lined up next to him and not realize that another defender in the clam was about to pick up the cut. The thrower must wait to confirm that the cutter is indeed open. Taking this to an extreme is good, conservative strategy for dealing with junk defenses. The offense decides to minimize the risk of a turnover and accept the disruption of the called play, taking short, conservative passes until the transition. If the defense is a clam, flood the area near the disc with three or even four players, and play catch. When the transition occurs, yell it out and fast-break or run the called play. You might end up with a favorable match-up or two—if so, exploit them.

A more aggressive approach is to try for a yardage-gaining pass beyond the first line of defense before the transition. The offense will then have more players downfield than the defense does. The handlers have to be willing to hold onto the disc deeper into the stall count to wait for the breaking cut and to keep the pass count down, relying on the other handlers to get open if necessary. Against a clam, one way to penetrate the first line is to flood the strong-side defender (position three) with two or three near-simultaneous cuts. At the level of offensive formations, horizontal or split-stack formations offer a more-ready response to a clam, which was created to defend the standard stack.

The Weave

The weave, also known as the dominator, can be an effective offensive structure if used sparingly. In the weave, the three handlers throw short passes to each other to work the disc downfield, while the downfield cutters simply stay out of the way. Begin play with the downfield players in a horizontal stack 10 to 20 yards beyond the deepest handler. This allows plenty of room for the handlers to cut nonstop for give-and-go passes. The handlers do not clear after failed cuts but rather cut back the other way immediately. This continues until one of the handlers receives a leading pass with his defender behind him. Prior to this, the downfield cutters keep in the stack, faking and repositioning to keep their defenders occupied while avoiding picks. A leading pass is the cue for the downfielders to cut. Assign the roles of first and second cutter on each side.

Because the handlers have to run so much, the weave offense shouldn't be used as a primary weapon. It can be particularly effective when employed by the defensive squad after a turnover. The other team might be tired after a turnover, and in some cases their handlers might not be that athletic and thus unable to keep up with all the cutting. If this is so, make sure that whoever those handlers are covering are involved in the weave. The same tactic can also be used to tire out the other team's most important receiver.

Defenses often have a downfield defender poach into the handling area, leaving three players to cover the four offensive players in the stack. They can time the poach to intercept a leading pass, or they can be obvious about it in order to break a play. The counter to this is for the downfield cutters to be ready to act (and for the handlers to avoid throwing into the poach). If they see this poach, they alert the rest of the team, and the designated first cutters on each side cut in on their respective sides, while the second cutter shallower in the stack cuts straight up the middle. The other second cutter remains in the stack but is ready to sprint deep if left open. Alerted to the poach, the handler with the disc looks downfield for the open receiver. If the poach returns to the downfield cutters, resume the weave.

End-Zone Offense

End-zone offense should be a subset of a team's regular offense, adjusted to reflect that less space is available. If the regular offense features several long receiver cuts, then the end-zone offense should feature cuts from the back of the stack to the corners. If the regular offense uses squirrelly handler cuts, then the end-zone offense should use the give and go and breakmark passes. If the regular offense has timing cuts thrown to empty space, so should the end-zone offense.

Players do need to change their mindsets near the end zone in some ways, however. Organization and discipline are especially important. Cuts must come one at a time from a stricter hierarchy, and clears must come immediately after. Throwers must resist the temptation to force risky throws into cramped areas to get the goal (though, as stated previously, a score is worth some additional risk).

The offense needs to have a basic, regenerative strategy as well as some set plays. It's useful to shout "End zone!" when the offense nears the goal line to remind the team to shift gears. One such strategy is to swing the disc and look for a continuation to a cutter going from the back of the stack to the front corner of the end zone (figure 15.3). Because many defenses overplay the corner, a second option is to have the next-to-last player in the stack cut at a 45-degree angle to a point about 10 yards from the corner, leaving one to two seconds after the first cut has started. If neither of these options is open, the cutters return to the stack, the thrower swings the disc back, and the new deepest players in the stack cut to the opposite corner (figure 15.4). Alternately, the goal-scoring cut could come from the first player in the stack who is in the end zone. Other variations on this offense would be to look for breaking passes to get started or to employ the give and go. A common set play in the end zone is the split (also called "Moses" or "Red Sea"), in which the stack splits to both sidelines, and a cutter comes up through the middle.

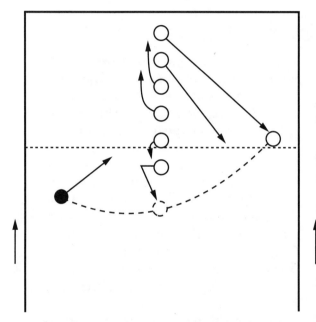

Figure 15.3 A basic regenerative end-zone offense features swing passes and cuts from the back of the end zone.

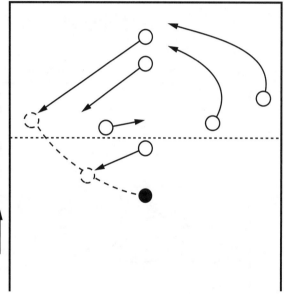

Figure 15.4 Players return to the stack after unsuccessful cuts, and the team looks to score in first one corner then the other.

Most of the full-field set plays can be adapted for end-zone use, and a team should have an assortment of misdirection and two-pass plays. However, because the yardage needed isn't great, and there's no concern about setting up the next pass, most of a team's end-zone plays should simply be isolation plays, calling for a particular player in the stack to make a particular cut. Assign names to a few of your team's favorite options (e.g., first in the stack to the breakside or last in the stack with the force).

When calling end-zone plays, also pay attention to how close the disc is to the forced sideline. If the disc is on the sideline, a give and go might work very well if the defense is force-middle but could have trouble getting started if the defense is trapping. Some plays work best from the middle of the field. Before a tournament, visualize yourself in different situations near the end zone and determine the best call.

■ Drill: End-Zone Offense

This drill gives every player the opportunity to make end-zone play calls and can also quickly indicate a team's weakness. Split into two teams and spend a few minutes discussing play options. Begin with the disc about 10 yards outside the end zone. One team then takes five opportunities to score. After each chance, the player catching the goal (or nearest to the turnover) walks the disc straight back to 10 yards outside the end zone and puts the disc into play again after a check. Some possessions will take only one pass; others might involve repeated dumping and swinging. Switch and give the other team five opportunities. After this, continue for another 10 or 20 possessions, flipping the disc after each one to see which team is on offense. Make sure to call a play every time there's a stoppage (or at least make the call reminding the team to go into end-zone offense). If players don't make calls, captains should step in and remind them to do so.

Spread Formations

The main purposes of a stack are to give structure to the offense and keep open viable cutting areas. Many offenses are now employing formations other than the traditional center stack. The structure can be radically different, and the viable areas of the field might not be the same, but alternative stacks can be effective. Part of the benefit of these spread formations lies in novelty, as defenses are still unsure how to stop them. On the other hand, these offenses are not maturely developed, and players might not have the intuitive feel for where to go in different situations. Nonetheless, spread formations are gaining in popularity and becoming more complex.

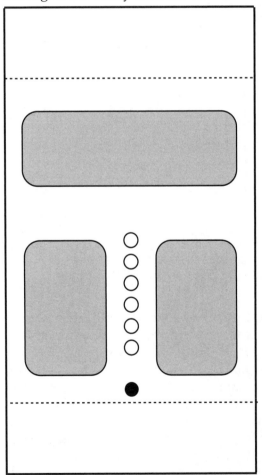

The traditional stack places all the players in a line down the center of the field, with the handlers at the front (figure 15.5). In most alternative stacks, the handlers are removed from the front of the stack, and the downfield cutters are spread out more. The handlers have little cutting responsibility other than for reset passes; instead, they have a greater role in delivering gainers. The downfield receivers have to run more as a result and have less opportunity to rest in the stack. However, having two fewer cutters downfield creates more space and leaves fewer potential poachers for deep throws.

Figure 15.5 The traditional stack, with handlers at the front.

On the other hand, because the handlers are not big cutting threats, their defenders often poach into the throwing lanes and allow the disc to be thrown laterally to the poached-off handler. The robust spread offense needs to plan for the poach. Another potential weakness is when the disc is being trapped because several offenders might be so far from the disc that they're ruled out as viable threats. End-zone offense can become difficult, too, as there's no room for a deep cut, and defenders can front the receivers.

The simplest spread formation places the handlers even with the disc and keeps the cutters in the center stack (figure 15.6). The alleys are still the primary cutting area, but the more compact stack (with only four players, it might be only 10 yards deep) opens up the deep area as well as the area in front of the thrower.

Another option is to stack two players on either sideline 10 to 15 yards downfield from the disc (figure 15.7). This creates open space in the middle of the field as well as in the deep area. Poaching and switching are difficult because cutters are so far from each other. In this formation, the stack can't stray too far downfield and must move back if there are several dumps in succession.

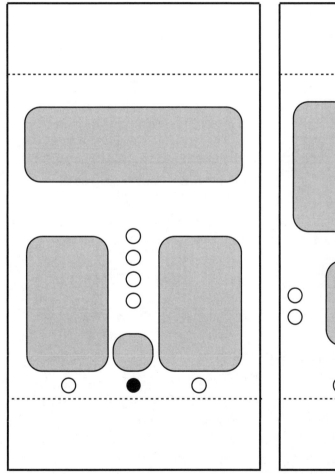 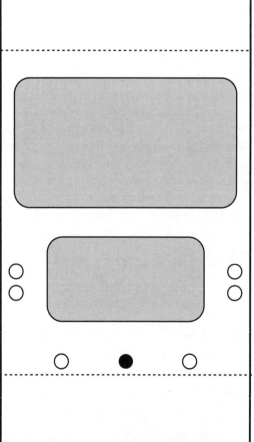

Figure 15.6 Moving the handlers even with the disc opens up the deep area.

Figure 15.7 The side-stack offense makes the center of the field the cutting alleys and also opens up the deep area. One player could also be placed in the center.

A horizontal stack spreads the four receivers laterally across the field (figure 15.8). Cuts go up and back in a straight line and also make it difficult to receive defensive help. Each player is as likely as the next to cut back or go long, so defenders have a tough time shading either way. The four players might be organized into two groups of two partners or operate independently.

The so-called "German" offense takes the concept of throwing to space normally applied to dump throws and uses it for downfield throws. A main receiver is isolated in the center of the field and is thrown a leading pass. This offense is especially popular in beach ultimate, where defensive speed is neutralized.

The general offensive philosophy for any of these stacks remains the same—create open space and allow cutters to find that space. Plays can be easily tweaked for the new formations, and new plays will suggest themselves. If you implement one of these offenses, you'll need to develop a way to reset the flow when it breaks down. Additionally, if the offense doesn't function well near the end zone because of the reduced cutting area, the center stack can

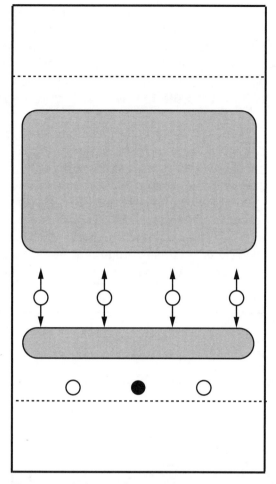

Figure 15.8 Cuts from the horizontal stack go up and back in a straight line.

be employed (but make sure to call out when the transition occurs). Every team needs to become familiar with these offenses as they grow in popularity.

Drill: Game Variations

Here are a few options for game practice that are good for focusing on a particular aspect of the game.

Zone O: no hammers, encourage hammers, narrow field, warped disc

Zone D: wide field, ask offense to try new things

Stack O: one player just clears, 'roach the poach' (cut deep after every time you throw a pass), encourage defense to poach

Junk D: make offense line up for real, even if they know junk is coming

Alternate stacks: try them, ask the defense to play honestly

Mini games: play hard, play fast

PART III

Building a Successful Team

Team Structures

Because most ultimate teams have no coach, players assume responsibility for ensuring that the team is functioning properly, that authority has been designated, that morale is high, that practices are structured, and that the many other duties typically assumed by a coach or manager are being done properly. In this chapter we discuss aspects of team identity and operation that need to be in place and provide several pointers for how individuals can contribute to building a successful team.

Team Identity

Players need to know what they're working for. Your team should have a clear sense of itself and what it wants to accomplish. Basically, when you ask yourself, "Exactly what am I doing here?" you should have a clear answer.

Say that your team, the Toughs, thinks of itself as a group of gritty warriors. Your season goal might be to gut it out against some more experienced competitors and still be in contention on the second day of regionals. Another team, the Cools, might foster a laid-back attitude, with players calling their own substitutions and generally assuming responsibility for themselves. Yet another team, the Grays, might be a reunion of grizzled veterans who want to do well together but can't make the time commitment required to become more competitive at major tournaments. Each team's identity shapes how its players contribute to the team's success.

A team identity also fosters a mindset in its players. If a militant workaholic joins up with a team that proves to be a collection of easy-going players who spend a lot of time discussing team feelings, he might soon be disappointed in the team chemistry. However, if the team's identity is apparent and even emphasized to him before he joins, he'll be prepared for the new culture and might even adopt it as his own. If the fit turns out to be a poor one, he might switch teams, but at least he knew what he was getting into and gave it a shot.

First Tournament With DoG

In my first tournament, Bill Rodriguez was called for a long cut, but when the play got underway there was a big open space and no one visible. I went to fill in and heard "Get out!" The shrill cry traumatized me, but I learned what it means to be on a team that takes a play call seriously. Sure enough, Bill was streaking long at light speed, having emerged from some hidden location on the field. I got out of the way and learned my lesson: these boys mean business.

—Zaz

Beyond its character, your team should have a well-defined goal and style of play. Having a target—making it past sectionals, for instance—motivates you to work toward your goals; having a style of play focuses the nature of your work. If your team is a run-and-gun squad, you know that you should be pushing the stack downfield at all times and that you must be attentive to the quick pass and exploit every offensive opportunity. If your team values possession of the disc above all else, you'd better lean toward more conservative play and holster those crossfield hammers in the wind. If your team is about running defenses into the ground, don't step on the field if you can't go all-out. As with writing in verse or playing in an orchestra, the defined parameters of the style or activity shape the work. Or, to use a business analogy in which we consider the team a corporation, a team's goals and aspirations are reflected in its mission statement, whereas the team's character and style are part of its corporate brand. The importance of a team adopting and maintaining goals and a style of play is difficult to overstate.

Team Operations

Your team should have a clear structure of how it will function. Early on, decisions should be made regarding operation and governance. Well before the season, if possible, players should agree on a method for determining how the following issues will be decided:

- Who determines the practice schedule?
- Who's in charge at practice?
- Who schedules fields?
- Who arranges travel and accommodations?
- Who makes tournament arrangements?

A team needs to determine who speaks during huddles.

- Who's the treasurer?
- Who calls the offensive and defensive lines?
- Who determines strategies?
- Who calls substitutions?
- Who speaks during team huddles?
- What training regimen will the team follow?
- What are the penalties for breaking the rules?

These and other operational questions arise during the course of the year. Your team should be able to address and resolve these questions respectfully and expediently, avoiding any harm to team morale.

Squads

Most teams are divided into squads. These might be formal divisions or just groups of players who share a common role on (or off) the field. The most common division of a team is into offense and defense. Because of the differing nature of offensive and defensive play, the "O" and "D" squads might have only a few players in common (if any). As a result, these squads might develop a distinct identity within the identity of the team as a whole. Other subdivisions of your team might form, as well. Generally speaking, such groupings promote commonality of cause rather than exclusion and divisiveness and should be encouraged. Squads bond in different ways. After practice one day, the D might hold a separate huddle to talk about the clam defense. Three handlers who work well together might start calling themselves a name that unites them, such as the Dreamweavers. Members of a particularly strong zone squad might shave their heads. Whatever the method, an act of unity is likely to be positive for your team as long as it doesn't alienate team members. If you see this occurring, hold a team meeting or otherwise communicate the problem before it gets out of hand. After all, no matter what subdivisions are formed, you're all on the same team in the end.

Offensive and Defensive Platoons

Most players are better on either offense or defense, sometimes extremely so. Teams take advantage of this by employing offensive and defensive platoons. Platoons also allow individual players to focus on their specialty (though, unfortunately, this is often at the expense of their all-around skills). Platooning promotes cohesion among players on the field because each player needs to be familiar with the styles of only half the team.

Many teams won't have enough quality players to divide into exclusive offensive and defensive platoons, but in such a case limited platooning is still useful. Picture a slow handler and a fast rookie. They should work on their full skill sets at practice and on their own, but in a game, the team will benefit more by playing the thrower when receiving and the speedster when pulling rather than simply alternating them. Of course, turnovers occur, and everyone has to play some offense and defense, so the platoons need to have some balance. You can't put all the handlers on the offense. The defense needs to be able to score, and the offense needs to be able to get the disc back after a turnover.

Finally, an adjustment can be made in extreme wind. Upwind goals are precious, so the team needs to be more offensively minded when going into the wind. Going downwind, throwing is easier, but it's imperative not to allow the other team to score, so the team on the field needs strong defensive skills. Just one or two players can be enough to make a difference. Players responsible for substitutions at tournaments should keep all the pertinent factors in mind. Are there enough handlers? Are players fresh? Have proven duos been given the opportunity to work together? Is the defensive squad appropriate to the defensive set (zone or one-on-one)? Do we have an answer to the opponent's tall receiver? Team coordinators should plan substitution and platooning policies well in advance of tournaments, trying to reach consensus regarding the strengths, weaknesses, and skill levels of the players on the team.

Social Structure

Often it's way off the field—at parties, bowling alleys, sports bars, or backyard barbecues—that some of the most formative team moments take place. The social life of your team is an important part of its being. Especially among newer players, these moments can be the glue that bonds them to one another and to the goal of achieving excellence as a team. Players' contributions to your team's social life should not go unappreciated. Of course, a team that wants to achieve greatness avoids excessive partying. Work hard at the track, then grab a quick burrito with teammates. It'll taste great!

Practice

Yes, you need to practice to improve, but exactly what should that practice look like? Repetition is good, but only if what you repeat is correct. It's no good to learn to execute a fake perfectly if that fake doesn't fool anyone. In this section, we'll go over how to get the most out of your time and how your team can structure practices to accomplish its goals.

What You Can Do

For you to advance to the next level, the time you spend on ultimate should be purposeful. For instance, whenever you're throwing, whether on your own or during warm-ups for practice, pretend that you have a marker on you. Pivot, fake, then fake again when your first fake doesn't get the marker off balance. Visualize your favorite receiver making a cut with a defender on him, and make the best pass for the situation. Don't just stand and chat while tossing aimlessly. The same principle applies when you're catching during warm-up. Catch the disc early, and make sure you catch with the appropriate grip. Pretend a defender is right on your hip. Try not to waste your time.

Practice with focus.

If you play recreational ultimate, say in a summer league, pick two specific skills or techniques—one offensive and one defensive, preferably with a common theme—to work on during each game. For instance, on defense, work on keeping your balance while marking. On offense, make sure you have set yourself before every throw. Don't just show up and try to impress everyone with your poaching or your hammer. Playing recreational ultimate is a great opportunity to work on fundamentals without worrying about diminishing someone else's experience.

Playing recreational ultimate can also give you the chance to develop new skills. Typically, the recreational teams you play on won't be as good as your regular team, so you'll have the chance to take on roles not normally assigned to you. As always, you'll want to be a good teammate and make responsible choices, but the acceptable level of risk for a throw might be higher because the offense isn't as good.

Team Practice

The bulk of your learning and development comes through team practices. Tournaments are great fun, give you feedback on your progress, and help your team gel, but the work is done on the practice field. To be most beneficial, practices should be structured, focused, efficient, and realistic. Simply scrimmaging for three hours with a catching drill at the beginning and a few sprints at the end doesn't do the job.

You don't need to post a minute-by-minute breakdown of the practice schedule for the day, but captains do need to set a start time and a practice plan for the day. Depending on the temperament of the team, fees, penalties (extra sprints), or assignments (collecting trash) can be assessed to latecomers. There should be one or two goals for the day (end-zone offense, stack plays, zone, marking, breaking the mark, hucking, and so on) to supplement the principles worked on at every practice. Conditioning is key for every team, but the other fundamentals you'll focus on depends on the strengths and weaknesses of your team. Beginning teams might emphasize catching and basic throwing; advanced teams might highlight marking and breaking the mark.

Each part of a practice should reinforce one of the goals of the day. Spend most practice time in situations that simulate important game situations. Although it might seem that this is best achieved through scrimmaging, in fact the barrage of stimuli that occurs in a game makes it hard to focus on a particular skill. In drills, you can clearly isolate particular areas that need work. Still, along with drills, you'll also want to improve team focus through doing gamelike activities. For instance, playing a game to three simulates a late-game scenario. Often, instead of immediately starting up another game, it's most beneficial to take a break at the end of a game to let players discuss what happened and how things could have gone differently. Sometimes, you might want to change the rules slightly to emphasize a key principle. For example, limiting each team to one turnover before pulling again makes players value possession. Forbidding the use of arms during a marking drill forces players to shuffle and use good body position. Lowering the stall count forces an offense to keep moving.

The components of practice are individual drills, team drills, and scrimmaging, although these categories can overlap. Individual drills, such as the basic marking drill (pp. 84-85), are usually done in small groups and focus on specific skills or tasks frequently necessary in games. The team can also organize a short special-skills session for the end of practice. For 10 minutes, pullers can work on their pulls, handlers on their break-mark throws, defenders on their agility, and receivers on timing their jumps.

Team drills allow players opportunities to apply individual skills within a team context. For instance, the huck drill (p. 63) gives the long thrower realistic cuts and forces him to decide whether a cut is the best for the situation. Various cutting drills work on cuts as well as flow in general. The following 10-Pull drill, along with the end-zone drill (pp. 157-158) work on particular game situations. Your team should also develop drills to address problem areas, such as moving the disc off the line, beating a trap, improving play during transitions, and so on.

Drill: 10 Pull

In the 10-Pull drill, the defensive squad pulls the disc. If the offense scores, that's one point for them. If the offense turns the disc over, the defense gets an opportunity to score a point. If the defense turns it over, neither team scores and play stops. Repeat for 10 pulls, then reverse the teams. If your team has strict offensive and defensive platoons, then in the second half of this drill, start the defense in a fast-break situation instead of pulling. You can do this by requiring all players to run and touch the back of the end zone before getting involved in the play.

You can also use the 10 Pull to focus on particular skills. For team skills, such as zone offense or defense against a horizontal stack, simply require one of the squads to play a particular set. You can also implement rules to emphasize particular skills.

- Zone offense—play on narrow field with an extra defender and no hammers.
- Zone defense—play on wide field with offense trying different styles.
- Stack offense—one player clears instead of cuts; reduce stall count to five seconds.
- Alternate stacks—play while alternating stacks; ask the defense to play honest.

- End-zone—offense-play "double score" (after a goal, team takes the disc back out to the 10-yard line and must score again for the goal to count); goal doesn't count unless preceded by a play call.
- Marking/Guarding—ban poaching; broken marks earn five push-ups for all team members.

Every practice needs to have some scrimmaging, even if time is tight. Scrimmages are fun and useful, but a team must appreciate and understand the pitfalls of scrimmaging as well. One danger of scrimmaging is that it can easily lead to undisciplined play. Teams get so wrapped up in playing to win that they neglect to focus on key principles. Sometimes play reverts to using only existing strategies and combinations, which can reinforce bad habits. Finally, intensity can sag during a scrimmage if there are few substitutions. Fortunately, there are ways to reinvigorate scrimmaging. Short, distinct games heighten the intensity of play. For longer games or for 10 Pull, one of the teams can run a particular defensive or offensive set most of the time. This can be done after a 5- to 10-minute instructional session in order to develop that set but can also be done to give the other squad some practice against a set they rarely see. Another variation is for one team to receive every point, but the pulling team starts the game with a lead, say 3 to 0 in a game to 7. To get players accustomed to the timing of a tournament, even long games to 15 or 21 are fine occasionally, if played at the beginning of practice and treated as real games. If teams can be determined prior to practice, it's a good idea to "hype" these games and generate some tournament-style intensity.

Conditioning is part of practice, too. A portion of every practice should be devoted to pure sprinting, but include other conditioning elements as well. These might take many forms. Conditioning drills can be done separately or combined with a basic skill, such as marking or throwing, to promote good fundamentals when fatigued. Group runs or races can build team unity while strengthening team legs. The same can be said for sprints and other calisthenics at the end of practice. These routines might combine push-ups, jumps, sit-ups, or any number of exercises, but sprints and calisthenics should always be a focus.

What Will Your Team Do When . . . ?

How well do you know your team's policies? You should know how your team reacts to various situations and how it expects you to react. Here are just a few questions you can ask of yourself and your team. Everyone should have the same answers. What will you or your team do when . . .

- trapped on the sideline?
- facing a force-middle defense?
- confronting a clam defense?
- facing poachers?
- the stall count is high and no one's open?
- playing zone defense near the end zone you're defending?
- you need to call for a break-mark pass?

- you intercept the disc?
- your offense has just thrown through the cup?
- your best forehand thrower has the disc?
- playing a team with a great deep game?
- playing defense against a weave?
- your offense gets scored on three times in a row?
- your defense fails to garner a turnover?
- your best handler gets injured?

A team is a group of athletes united by a common purpose and an identity. A team should know what it wants out of a season and have a philosophy of how to achieve that goal. This means developing a style of game, a strategy with clear contingencies, effective squads, and a focused approach to practices. A team is also a social unit comprised of individual personalities. If you encourage and enjoy your teammates, your team will work in unison—and you'll also have more fun.

Off-the-Field Players

How do the principles of ultimate apply when you're not on the field? In fact, of the six basic principles introduced in the first chapter, space and weight are the only ones that a sideline player is not directly involved in, and even those two principles (and situations involving them) can be analyzed while not on the field. Even on the sideline and otherwise outside of the game, communication, focus, and efficiency play an important role in how players should think about their disc season and career. In this chapter, we'll detail the ways in which players can contribute to their team's success while off the field.

Personal

During a game, the only selfish acts players should perform on the sideline are those pertaining to immediate physical needs, such as rest, hydration, nourishment, and injury care. Proper care of your body makes you more effective on the field, which adheres to the principle of efficiency. Many of these "selfish" tasks can be done alongside activities that help the team.

Helping On-Field Play

As you know, players on the field have a lot to think about, so help from the sideline is invaluable. Sideline players always have something to do, including several functions through which they can get involved on defense.

Sideline Defensive Help

The sideline must know what the planned defense is. One player from each sideline should ask the on-field players what the plan is before the pull, then communicate it to the rest. Then, as necessary, remind the defense. If individual defenders forget the force or the call on defense, all is lost. Disclosing the secret is less harmful to the team than defensive chaos. The sideline can also help by counting passes. Many defenses switch from one defense to another after a set number of passes. In such a case, sideline players should shout the number of the pass. The counting should continue beyond the switch, in hopes that the offense won't notice the switch (and then get foiled by it).

Successful Sideline Players

The job of a sideline player is integral to the success of the team. Players working just as hard on the sidelines as though they were on the field give a team an edge over the other team. Here are a few tasks players can do from the sidelines:

- Count passes.
- Help with the zone.
- Call last back.
- Call "Strike!"
- Call "Get inside!"
- Ride a player (continuously shout motivating remarks).
- Call "Keep the force!" and "No break!"
- Call "Up!"
- Alert the defense.
- Acknowledge good play away from the disc.
- Hustle downfield with the flow.
- Patrol the opposite sideline.
- Encourage cutters.
- Call poaches.
- Alert receivers.

In a zone defense, each of seven sideline players should be accountable for one on-field player. The sideline player should keep her on-field teammate informed of what's going on with the offense outside of her field of vision. To establish trust, this communication should be rehearsed at practice. Once trust has been established, the sideline player becomes a pair of eyes in the back of the head of the on-field teammate. A good sideline is absolutely vital to a good zone. Stay within earshot!

Other defensive calls from the sideline are "Last back!" and "Strike!" It's important to know which on-field defender is the farthest downfield, most able to help with deep coverage. The sideline should continually remind whoever is last back. The "strike" call alerts a marker on the sideline that a dangerous sideline threat exists that she should try to prevent at all costs. This applies even to a sideline force. The sideline players have a great perspective to alert the defense of such a situation. Sideline players need to know what the force is in determining when to yell "Strike!"

The sideline can help individual players with their defense by selectively reminding them to "Get inside!" This call encourages defenders to get inside their offenders, especially in a give-and-go scenario or if an offender cuts diagonally up the sideline from the middle of the field. Such encouragement goes a long way. Constant encouragement can also be effective, as when a sideline player "rides" an on-field player—that is, continuously shouts motivating remarks to the player. Encouragement as simple as, "Come on, Jen! You got him! You got him!" can be remarkably effective. Note that some players are motivated by positive remarks and others by negative ones, such as, "Pick it up, Jo—you're dogging it!" Know your teammates. Other words of encouragement are "Keep the force!" and "No break!" Such comments help defenders and markers alike to put maximal effort into their defense. Repeat them again and again, as necessary.

The sideline is a watchdog. When the disc is thrown, call it "up." The sideline should shout "Up!" at every pass. This reinforces the marker's call and fills in if the marker forgets. Also, alert the defense whenever you see an undefended player or if someone is grossly out of position. A vigilant sideline can call on another player to shore up the hole in the defense or at least leave a less dangerous

Sideline players should call out hidden dangers that on-field players might not see from their current position.

threat. Stay active. Hustle downfield with the flow. You have to be close enough to the on-field defenders for them to hear you. Patrol the opposite sideline, too, especially in a zone. Acknowledge good play on the field, including away from the disc. This reinforces solid play that won't show up in individual statistics.

Sideline Offensive Help

An offensive squad typically wants to maintain its composure, make a few select cuts, score, and quietly get off the field. "In-your-face" encouragement from the sideline might not be well received. Still, the sideline can play a useful role. Here are ways for sideline players to help on offense.

• Encourage the cutters. A tired team might need motivation to initiate cuts. "Who's cutting?" "Who wants to score?" "Who's next?" are reminders to put the offense in motion. Even a fatigued team can create opportunities by acting and responding to the reaction of the defense.

• Be an offensive watchdog. Alert the thrower and other offenders to poaches on the field, including those out of view of on-field players. This signals the thrower to be careful and tells the whole team that someone is open. Alerting receivers can also be helpful, though it's difficult for them to process information as the disc is arriving. Encourage receivers to attack the disc or to "come to" the disc aggressively, without slowing down. Shouts of "Man on!" and "Nobody!" quickly convey information about whether a defender is approaching quickly. The sideline can also help receivers track a floating disc.

Loud encouragement and clear communication from the sideline elicits extra effort from on-field players. Every little bit helps.

More Ways to Help

Other ways of contributing to the team from the sideline include doing any of the following:

• Bring on-field players liquids during time-outs.
• Scout the opponent's offensive and defensive patterns.
• Critique your own team's play.
• Discuss (but don't vent) any miscommunication or misunderstanding from a previous point.
• Console teammates—cheer them up.
• Take statistics.
• Mark lines.

How to Avoid Arguments

Have you ever noticed patterns in the way fouls are (or are not) successfully resolved? It seems to depend very little on actual knowledge of the rules but rather on diplomacy in handling a hostile player before invoking the rules. Here is a realistic scenario of how disc argumentation can be improved. First, the contact, foul, or event occurs and a close call is made. What follows is typically an emotional outburst by a member of the other team. The player who made the foul should take responsibility for mollifying the situation by calmly explaining his point of view and sequestering himself and the opponent from the rising tide of emotion from everyone around the play. At this point, the two should isolate the exact complaint and note which facts are being disputed. (It helps if you are the one making the call to be clear in your own head of what you are asserting. Having a vague notion that you've been wronged leads to a murky situation.) Then if the facts are still disputed, you can seek factual input from other observers. Here's how an emotional close call might go down:

Player 1: Foul! Push out.

Player 2: What? That's ridiculous! Just another stupid call!

Player 1: Dude, you pushed me out.

Player 2: You missed that disc! Anyway, you were out of bounds before you even jumped. I had the right of verticality.

Both players: It's okay, we got it under control! We can handle it.

Player 1: Dude, I jumped up to catch the goal, we collided, and I landed out of bounds because of the momentum.

Player 2: I was just going for the disc.

Player 1: No problem there.

Player 2: You would have been out of bounds anyway.

Player 1: I doubt it. Sideline? Can you tell if I would have landed out of bounds if there was no collision?

Sideline: Yes! No! It was close!

Player 1: Okay, contested call. Send it back.

Things go bad when either a chorus of voices is allowed to muddy the waters, or the point of contention is not isolated. It's silly, but the same conflict resolution techniques apply even in the trivial case of line calls. You may look silly to everyone when you mark the agreed upon spot where the foot was and go to the cone to see if it was in or out. Looking silly is okay for a bit, if it avoids a possible spirit meltdown. Allow for some emotional response, but only from the players. To yell a response from the sidelines is childish and unproductive.

You're invested in your team's success and want to do everything you can to help, even when you're not on the field. This natural desire to help might induce you to think of new ways of pitching in. Some teams take this to the extreme and bring to the sideline tents, massage therapists, trainers, music, and many coolers filled with a variety of cold drinks. This is all great, but be sure not to undercut competitiveness with comfort. Players on the field should not be distracted by what's happening on the sideline. Another warning: No matter how emotionally caught up you get in the action on a field, don't get involved with on-field disputes. Leave that to the players on the field. Encourage teammates after the dispute is over, but otherwise stay out of it.

Away From the Field

A team's success is largely due to individuals' decisions to commit themselves to something they believe in. Fostering this belief among teammates adds value to your team and makes the team a more enjoyable group to be with. You can build team unity in many ways:

- Show up on time for practice with a good attitude.
- Support your teammates at track workouts.
- Encourage attendance.
- Help organize travel arrangements and team administrative details.
- Bring extra liquids to practice.

- Design the team jersey.
- Set up the practice field.
- Throw a party.
- Maintain the team Web site.

If you're committed to improving your team, these and other ways to help will come to you naturally. Being a good teammate is part of being a good player—because good players are always working to serve the team. In this regard, your best contributions, both on and off the field, are your dedication and enthusiasm. Spread them around.

Conditioning

EIGHTEEN

You've got nothing if you're not in shape.

*—Steve Mooney, two-time ultimate world champion,
seven-time national champion*

Ultimate makes strenuous demands on the body and mind, so a rigorous training regimen is a must. Consider that national and international tournaments are four to seven days long with many hours of playing each day. Tournaments sometimes pack seven or eight 90-minute games into a grueling weekend, often requiring teams to take long, shared car rides. No other team sport—and few individual endurance sports—regularly demands such conditioning of its athletes. On top of all this, the outcome of a game can hinge on which squad is sprinting better, so endurance must be coupled with speed and strength. All said, an ultimate athlete who wants to compete with the best must be superbly conditioned.

Your conditioning needs (and regimen) should depend on which position you play and what level of team you play on. However, if you're a handler, for instance, that doesn't excuse you from running 400-meter sprints with your teammates. Likewise, if you're a seldom-used defensive specialist, you're not excused from the team's long-distance run. Although routines might vary according to players' needs, the amount of effort each player gives should be about the same.

Not every team demands a lot of its members by way of conditioning. Some teams rightfully place the emphasis on skills during practice. Many teams are just in it for the fun, and don't aspire to ever reaching "The Show." Your captain might never mention conditioning or might tell you not to worry about it. We're here to tell you otherwise. You're reading this book because you aspire to be a better, even a great, player. This takes work. The good news is that conditioning really takes no skill—everyone can do it and improve. What follows are some general strategies for conditioning; then we'll present a training regimen with detailed workouts.

When you're getting ready to go to sleep and realize that you've only completed 200 of the day's 300 sit-ups, you have only yourself to confront. With only yourself to argue with, you might use the typical rationalizations: "A few sit-ups won't make much difference, anyway"; "I don't want to be sore for tomorrow's workout"; "I'll make it up tomorrow." By now, you know the tricks you fall for.

This is your big test of grit. Grit is not tested when the whole team is watching. Grit is not present when you're running your hardest to chase down an overthrown huck. Who wouldn't run hard when the pressure is on in front of everyone? The big test comes when you don't even realize you're being tested, when you could easily give up. Going the extra mile means going the *extra* mile, not just thinking about doing it.

The workouts in this chapter are difficult. They're intended for players who come to the table with significant conditioning. That is, you can run 5 miles without too much strain and can sprint 10 field lengths and still bend without much soreness the next day. You might not be able to complete these workouts. You must decide if you're straining yourself too hard and need to take things easier. We're not doctors and have no medical training. Consult your physician to make sure these workouts are right for you.

Basics of Conditioning

Basic conditioning for ultimate focuses on endurance, speed, and strength. These are listed in order of importance, not in order of training. Generally, endurance can be improved relatively quickly and lead to marked improvement on the field. Strength can also be improved somewhat quickly, though the results on the field are not as obvious. "Speed" might refer to speed endurance—your ability to maintain high intensity for a long time—or to the top speed you're capable of running. Sprinting speed makes a huge difference on the field, but it's much harder to improve through training. Still, it's important to make the effort.

Generally speaking, a regimen for ultimate should look something like this: You begin the season (including preseason) with longer running workouts and some strength training. After you have a good cardiovascular base and some strength improvement, you train for speed endurance through track workouts. You decrease the running distances over time, gradually moving to sprints for the last eight weeks. The last four weeks should be your peak. Meanwhile, off the track, you progress from weights in the preseason to agility training throughout the season.

You should do your basic endurance and strength training before the season begins, either in the off-season or over the 12 weeks immediately before the 12-week season starts. It's best to begin with some running. The improved endurance and recovery will help out in doing plyometric strength training or in the gym lifting weights. Although running is the most gamelike for ultimate players, other cardiovascular activities, such as swimming or cycling, can also build endurance, with less impact on the body. At roughly three weeks before the start of the season, your track workout should become more focused and begin to incorporate shorter distances. Throughout the season, your week should include some of each kind of conditioning. Your team's practices should incorporate sprinting and other conditioning (such as push-ups, sit-ups, and jumping), and should be long enough to be an endurance workout. Many teams practice for three to four hours each weekend day during the season. Don't take more than two days of rest a week. Do a full-fledged track workout once a week and agility training at least once a week. Go for runs on other days.

All the while, pay careful attention to how your hamstrings are feeling. You'll know if your hamstrings feel tight when you start to run. They might feel fine at low speeds, but if a hamstring is even slightly injured, you won't be able to sprint. A pulled hamstring is impossible to sprint on and takes three to four weeks from which to recover. Running on legs unaccustomed to running can quickly lead to injury. Don't overdo it. Other common injuries are calf pulls and groin pulls. Calves heal the fastest; the groin heals the slowest.

Injury

If you're injured, you must get better before returning to the field. Many players have ended promising careers by coming back too soon from an injury. However, don't use an injury as an excuse for not working or not coming to practice. If you're hurt and your team is training, figure out something you can do. This will earn you high marks with your teammates and free you from the torture of idly watching others be physically active (we're assuming that even injured you're showing up for practice). You don't want to be seen as a slacker or let yourself develop a taste for slacking. Keep working!

See a doctor for injuries, and don't return to playing too soon. There are other ways to help your team in the interim.

Common Injuries in Ultimate

Some injuries are not what they appear. What feels like a heel bruise can actually be inflammation at the point where the Achilles tendon or plantar fascia attaches to the bone. Sometimes you do have to play through pain, but don't just ignore that pain and figure you can rest after the season. See someone who knows more than you do. Here's some basic information on common injuries in ultimate and how they're best treated.

Plantar fasciitis—add arch support, stretch, ice, play through it as well as you can.
Achilles tendinitis—take an anti-inflammatory, stretch lightly, ice, rest if it doesn't improve.
Tight iliotibial track—stretch, do some strength exercises.
Bone spur—see a doctor as soon as you can.

Torn ACL—get surgery and rehab aggressively.
Meniscus—needs arthroscopic surgery.
Pulled hamstring—rest, ice on and off, light jogging, stairs.
Pulled quad—ice on and off with knee bent, light jogging.
Pulled groin—wait it out (no playing).
Separated shoulder—needs surgery.
Dislocated shoulder—see a doctor (some people keep playing for a time but often are forced to retire due to repeated injury).
Common cold—play through it but rest a lot afterward.

Diet

You don't need us to tell you about proper dieting. In a nutshell, avoid foods high in fat. Don't eat lots of sweets and fried foods. Weight gain affects your play immediately. Avoid excessive drinking during the season. Aside from being bad for you, too much alcohol leads to a cascade of other bad conditions, including tardiness to practice, skipped training runs, improper hydration, and resentment and animosity from your teammates. Ultimate players pride themselves on their health and fitness. Don't be a hypocrite. If you say you're going to be serious about training, then take your training seriously. A big part of this is eating right.

Training Regimen

The following regimen is designed for a male in his 20s to 30s who plays a 12-week season on a national-caliber ultimate team. The regimen is based on experience and consultation with players, runners, and other athletes. Remember—this routine was *not* created by a physician. Consult your doctor before starting this or any program of exercise. A basic level of conditioning at the start is assumed (say, you can run six miles and do some sprinting but might feel it a bit the next day). The program begins by establishing a good level of cardiovascular fitness, then later adds explosive strength aspects, particularly, plyometrics and sprinting. This is only one of many possible routines. In fact, even if you ignore most advice but train and play hard during the season, you'll probably develop a good cardiovascular base and some speed—but your performance won't be optimal. Before we discuss the regimen, let's first review its components.

Warm-Up and Cool-Down

The warm-up and cool-down are important parts of any workout. The warm-up gets your muscles loose and functioning at peak levels. The cool-down helps prevent soreness and promotes recovery. Every workout should begin with a warm-up and end with a cool-down. These routines are essential, as they allow you to achieve good mechanical form, help your muscles work at their peak, and aid in injury and soreness prevention. Stretching is particularly important at the track and for plyometrics. Arrive at least 30 minutes before your scheduled run, and begin with a light jog once or twice around the track. Then stretch your major muscle groups for 20 minutes or so, and take several short bursts at varying degrees of intensity, paying close attention to how tight your muscles are. Mind your hamstrings! You might notice that some muscles are a problem right from the outset. This might not necessitate a day off but could prevent you from doing the shorter bursts. For example, you might have to substitute one 400-meter lap for two 200-meter dashes. After a track workout, take two laps at a slow pace, then repeat your warm-up stretching routine. Shorter warm-ups and cool-downs are appropriate for strength-training workouts but should not be omitted. Finally, at the end of your cool-down, relax! Enjoy the hard work you've done. You'll find that even simple conversations carry an extra sweetness, especially after a shared hardship at the track.

Agility Training

Agility training can be as simple as setting up cones and running back and forth between them. Or it can mean plyometrics, which is a series of exercises focused on developing explosiveness in your muscles.

Plyometric routines are strength-developing exercises that use your own body as weight resistance. These exercises develop explosive speed and are often high impact. Most plyometric exercises should not be attempted until you're well into a training regimen. Stretch thoroughly before a plyometrics routine, and monitor your muscles closely for pulls and strains. In the regimen prescribed below, we're assuming a level of fitness at the start, so we start plyometrics somewhat earlier than might be right for you. Check with your doctor or fitness trainer.

Most plyometric leg exercises involve lunging, jumping, hopping, skipping, or bounding for about 30 yards, resting enough to recover (usually about a minute) and then repeating for a total of three times. The motion should not be rushed (it's not a race), but should be explosive. For example, "lunges" in the table means taking an exaggerated step forward, landing on the front leg and bending it to 90 degrees at the knee, then powering the back leg up and forward before landing on it. Lunging looks like a low, long, exaggerated version of walking. "Hops" means jumping off of one leg and landing on the same leg, striving for height (not speed) with each hop. Count the number of hops it takes to go the 30 yards.

Training the abdominal muscles, torso, arms, and shoulders can also be incorporated into a plyometric workout, though we're fine with referring to all such routines as "push-ups" and "sit-ups" (for example, using table 18.1, you can substitute a 10-minute abdominal workout for 150 sit-ups). The phrase "10-minute death" in table 18.1 refers to three sets of the following routine: 1 minute of sit-ups, 15 seconds rest, 40 seconds of push-ups, 15 seconds rest, 1 minute of jumping (40 seconds of jumping jacks straight into 20 seconds of jumping off both feet, bringing knees up high). Allow 15 seconds between sets. The workout takes exactly 10 minutes. If you are indoors and unable to jump, substitute 1 minute of wall sits (sitting with your back against a wall and your knees bent at 90 degrees, with no chair). You can also add 2 minutes of sit-ups on your sides and abdomen at the end, or add a fourth set.

Gym

Speed demands strength, so you must work to build and then maintain strength. Where this happens is the gym. Gym workouts are a great way to maintain strength or develop additional strength in the off-season and preseason. Shortly into a 12-week season, gym workouts should give way to plyometrics and other agility training. Table 18.1 refers to muscle groups to focus on in the gym. The typical gym exercise involves three sets of 10 to 12 repetitions (16 to 18 reps for legs), with three minutes between sets. Sets should be grouped in series, such as three for the calves followed by three for the quads. You should be struggling toward failure during the last few reps.

Going to the gym during preseason and off-season is an excellent way to build and maintain strength and agility.

Track

Go to any ultimate tournament and you can easily spot the team that works out at the track. Track workouts build a combination of speed, strength, endurance, recovery, and grit that no other workout can give. They bring a team together in common struggle. Track workouts also directly train for the athletic skill most needed in the game of ultimate—running. If you're serious about the game, you'll go to the track and work hard. The track workouts in table 18.1 will test your strength of will. Rise to the challenge.

In table 18.1, rest times appear in parentheses. Larger numbers represent time in seconds between sprints, whereas numbers such as 3.5 or 4 represent time in minutes between sets. For example, in the track entry for week 1, "3 sets 3 × 400 (80, 4), 4-min rest, 1 mile" means doing three sets of three 400-meter dashes, with 80 seconds between dashes, and 4 minutes of rest between sets, then resting 4 minutes and running a full mile (about 4 laps).

Pacing

Don't be the guy whose successive 400 times are 68, 71, 80, 78, 80, and 82. It's bad enough that you have ruined your own workout (a runner who posts such times basically gets the workout equivalent of just two quick 400s rather than six strong ones), but others might keep up with you on your first two laps and ruin their workout as well. Similarly, don't hold back so much early on that your final lap is five seconds faster than all the others. Over the course of the season, learn to calibrate yourself so you can deliberately run at the pace you want. Before you go to your first 400 workout at a pace of, say, 74 seconds, run a few timed 100s and 200s until you know what a 74-second 400 pace feels like. Then, when you're in your workout and the aforementioned rabbit at his 68-second pace gets 30 yards ahead of you, you can confidently keep to your pace, knowing you'll be able to maintain it throughout your workout.

TABLE 18.1

Week	Track	Gym/plyometrics/ agility	Other
Week 1	3 sets 3 × 400 (80, 4), 4-min rest, 1 mile	Squats, calf presses, hip-flexor lifts, hamstring curls, bench press, curls	100 push-ups, 150 sit-ups, 2-mile jog
Week 2	3 sets 3 × 400 (80, 3.5), 4-min rest, 1 mile	Squats, calf presses, hip-flexor lifts, hamstring curls, bench press, curls	100 push-ups, 150 sit-ups, 2-mile jog
Week 3	3 sets 3 × 400 (80, 3.5), 3-min rest, 1/2 mile, medium pace	Bench press, legs, plyometrics (lunge, bound, jump, skip, abs)	100 push-ups, 150 sit-ups, 2.5-mile jog
Week 4	3 sets 3 × 400 (75, 3), 3-min rest, 1 mile	Plyometrics (lunge, bound, jump, skip, abs)	100 push-ups, 150 sit-ups, 2.5-mile jog
Week 5	3 × 400 (75), 3.5-min rest; 2 sets of 1 × 400, 4 × 200 (75, 45, 3.5), 3.5-min rest, 1 mile	Plyometrics (as above)	150 push-ups, 200 sit-ups, curls, wall sit, 3-mile run
Week 6	3 × 400 (75), 3.5-min rest; 6 × 200 (45), 3.5-min rest; 2 × 400, 2 × 200 (75, 45), 3.5-min rest, 1 mile	10-minute death, agility	150 push-ups, 200 sit-ups, curls, wall sit, 3-mile run
Week 7	1 mile, 5-min rest; 6 × 100, jogging curves, 3-min rest; 1 mile, 5-min rest; 6 × 100, jogging curves, 3-min rest, 1 mile	10-minute death, agility	150 push-ups, 200 sit-ups, curls, wall sit, 3-mile run
Week 8	4 sets 1 × 400, 3 × 200, 2 × 100 (80, 45, jogging curves), 3-min rest between sets.	10-minute death, agility (cones, cuts, jumps)	150 push-ups, 200 sit-ups, 3-mile run
Week 9	4 sets 1 × 400, 2 × 200, 4 × 100 (80, 45, jogging curves) 3-min rest between sets.	Agility (cones, cuts, jumps)	150 push-ups, 200 sit-ups, 3-mile run
Week 10	4 sets 1 × 400, 3 × 200, 2 × 100 (80, 45, jogging), 3-min rest between sets.	Agility	100 push-ups, 150 sit-ups, 3-mile run
Week 11	3 sets 4 × 200 (45, 3.5)	Stationary bike, stair-stepper	100 push-ups, 150 sit-ups, 3-mile jog
Week 12	3-mile jog	None	At least two 2-mile jogs

Table 18.2 shows some times for you to shoot for in your workouts. Your pace will vary depending on your conditioning and your top speed. These times assume a modest amount of recovery in between reps, as in the workouts above. Don't pay much attention to differences of less than half a second because you probably have that much error in the timing.

183

TABLE 18.2

	400 meters	200 meters	100 meters
Men—fast	68-70 seconds	30 seconds	<15 seconds
Men—slower	74-77 seconds	33-35 seconds	15-15.5 seconds
Women—fast	75-80 seconds	35 seconds	16-17 seconds
Women—slower	85-90 seconds	40-42 seconds	18-19 seconds

Variation

Try not to vary your track workout from whatever routine you set for yourself. It's very tempting to adjust the workout while you're at the track and suffering, but at that point you're not of sound mind. Decide on your workout while thinking clearly and reasonably. Neither underdo it nor overdo it. At the track, think only of completing it. Of course, you should listen to your body. If you feel completing the workout poses a risk to your health, then by all means quit. But if you're just feeling a bit tired, persevere.

With the exception of your track routine, it's okay to vary your workout somewhat. When lifting weights, some variety helps beat boredom and work different parts of the same muscle. Your variation can be something as simple as a twist at the top of your lift or a slight change in your lifting angle. But don't vary your workout just to make it easier on yourself. For example, in the middle of a set of 50 sit-ups, don't suddenly decide to do the remaining sit-ups lying on your side.

Here are a few tips for the track. If you divide up a conditioning task into quarters, the third one is the most difficult. If you're sprinting around the track, say, you'll likely get off to a strong start. You won't have given up by the second quarter, either, and surely by the last fourth you have the end in sight. It's in that third quarter where the mind starts wandering, forgets the priorities, and turns its attention to life after the workout or the evening's excitement—or suddenly finds itself fascinated by the intriguing number of lanes (eight) on the track. Know this and avoid the third-quarter slide. When you're tempted to slack, focus on keeping your stride length or your stride rate up.

No team wins on talent alone. Winning takes hard work and dedication. Conditioning is probably the least pleasant aspect of playing the sport at the top level, but it's vital to success. So, how can you push yourself hard enough? Know this—speed and strength in themselves are valuable assets for ultimate, but a player who combines them with intelligence becomes simply unstoppable. When you understand this yourself, and when you internalize it, your motivation comes from within.

Glossary

alley—The areas of the field near the sideline, particularly on the strong side, into which many long comeback cuts flow.

anticut—Motion to bring a defender away from an area of the field, with the intent of clearing space for another cutter.

around pass—A breaking pass that travels around the breakside of the marker, such as a backhand thrown to the backhand side in a force forehand.

attacking end zone—The end zone in which one's team on the field tries to score.

away—In the downfield directional; the side of the field that is not home.

away cut—A midrange downfield cut originating close to the disc.

back—(verb) To defend by positioning oneself on the downfield side of an offender.

backfield—The area or direction toward the defending end zone.

bailout—A nondump cut intended to maintain possession when the stall count is high; any successful nondump cut or pass that maintains possession when the stall count is high.

bait—To give extra space to an offender to draw a blockable throw.

behind cut—A cut toward the back side of a defender.

bid—An attempt to catch or block the disc.

bite—To fall for an opponent's fake.

blade—A forehand or hammer throw in which the plane of the disc is nearly vertical.

break (or break-mark)—To complete a pass in the direction that the marker is trying to prevent; any successful such completion.

breakdown—A situation where the intended play can't be completed as planned; any situation where there's offensive confusion.

breakside (or break-mark side)—The side of the field obstructed by the marker.

Buddy—The player who cuts after "the Man" in a standard sequence.

burn—To get open against a defender, usually by a significant amount.

cag—A handler who trails play in the backfield to set up a strategic dump or a reset.

center stack—The standard stack formation along the middle of the field.

chain—A string.

check—A signal that play can begin, as a "tap in" (defense touches disc) or a "ground check" (offense touches disc to ground).

cheat—Moving slightly closer to (or farther from) an offender, as in "cheat in" or "cheat out."

clam—A defensive formation in which three defenders cover the three offenders nearest the disc, while four downfield defenders cover cuts to any of four assigned areas.

clear—To run out of the cutting area.

clog—To remain too close to the disc or to obstruct an important throwing lane.

comeback—A cut from originating downfield and traveling directly toward the thrower.

contain—A force-middle zone formation; defensive mindset to prevent big plays at the expense of conceding shorter gains.

continuation cut—A cut made to continue an offensive plan, especially one to complete a swing.

cover—To defend an offender, especially to do so successfully.

crash—To cut into the cup of a zone.

crossfield—(adjective) From one side of the field to the other.

cup—A defensive structure in zone defense formed by the two points and the middle-middle.

cutter—An offensive player running with the intent of receiving a pass.

deep—(adjective) Far downfield; (noun) a position in zone defense responsible for covering deep cuts; (noun) position in zone offense responsible for making deep cuts.

deep-deep—A position in zone defense covering long cuts.

dominator—Weave.

downfield—The area or direction toward the attacking end zone.

downfielder—Downfield player.

dump—A short pass toward the backfield.

face guard—(verb) To front.

fake—A misdirection.

fast break—A quick-moving offense immediately following a turnover, intended to capitalize on the opposing team's positional or mental disadvantage at the point of turnover; any offense modeled in this style.

fill—To cut into space created by another cut.

flare—To move from the middle of the field toward the sideline.

flood—To put several offenders in one area of the field.

flow—A quality of steady offensive progress in which every pass is closely succeeded by another.

FM—Force middle.

force—A defensive formation in which the marker attempts to prevent throws released in a predetermined direction.

force backhand—A defensive formation in which the force direction is toward the right side of the field (as looking toward the defending end zone).

force forehand—A defensive formation in which the force direction is toward the left side of the field (as looking toward the defending end zone).

force middle—A defensive formation in which the force direction is toward the sideline farther from the disc.

force side—The side of the field left unobstructed by the marker.

45 cut—A cutback to the thrower whose direction of motion forms a 45-degree angle with a downfield (or with a horizontal) line, especially one such cut when the thrower stands near the cone of the attacking end zone.

front—(verb) To defend by positioning oneself between offender and thrower.

gainer—A yardage-gaining pass.

give and go—An offensive play in which the thrower immediately cuts for the disc (and receives it) after throwing a pass.

greatest—A play in which a receiver jumps from in bounds to catch the disc, then releases a successful (completed) throw before landing out of bounds.

guarding—Defending a downfield offender, especially in a one-on-one defense.

hammer—A type of throw employing the forehand grip, in which the disc is released upside down from above the head.

handler—A position on zone offense primarily responsible for initiating and governing offensive progress.

heckle—To good-naturedly taunt on-field players, especially as a spectator.

high-release throw—A throw whose point of release is higher than usual.

high stall count—Any stall count nearing 10 seconds.

hitch—An extra pass that can be inserted at the start of a string or set offensive play, usually as a delay or to initiate motion; the offensive player designated to receive the first pass from the pull.

ho—Horizontal (used only in reference to positioning during a layout, as in the call, "Get ho!").

home—The side of the field where the team supplies are kept.

horizontal stack—A stack formation oriented laterally across the field.

huck—A long pass.

hyzer—An angle describing the disc's trajectory that, for a smoothly flying disc, is formed between the disc and the horizontal plane while viewed head on in the direction of motion; the tilt of a disc.

I-formation—A configuration of the deeps in the zone where one is deep and the other is short.

inside-out—(noun) A breaking pass that travels around the strong side of the marker; (adjective) a curl of the flight path (from the forehand side to the backhand side for a backhand or from the backhand side to the forehand side for a forehand).

invert throw—An inside-out throw.

iso—An isolation play; a play call to a specific player.

juke—A jolty motion by an offender to misdirect or unbalance his defender.

junk—Any defensive formation that's not strictly one-on-one or zone defense; any defense that the offense has not recognized.

Kring ("The Kring")—A defense that leads to offensive confusion.

last back—The most downfield defender (or offender) on a team; a defensive policy in which the most downfield defender prepares to switch to cover long cuts.

layout—A dive.

leading (pass)—Any pass that a receiver has to run to catch up to.

line—The offensive assignments; the offensive plan at the start of a point.

loose cup—An expanded cup formation.

mac—A tip of the disc that alters the flight path, especially a tip that alters the trajectory only slightly.

man—One-on-one defense.

Man ("The Man")—the primary cutter.

man to man—One on one.

marker—The defender covering the thrower.

middle (of the field)—The line halfway between the sidelines.

middle-middle—A position on zone defense at the top of the cup, primarily responsible for covering throws through the cup.

midfield—The line halfway between the goal lines.

milk—To extend the range of a pass by running along with the disc.

Moses—A split.

offender—Offensive player.

offensive triangulation—The act (by a thrower) of having the triangle formed by himself, the intended receiver, and the intended point of reception in sight.

off-point—A point on the zone not marking the disc.

one-on-one—A style of defense in which each defender is assigned to one opponent.

on-point—A point on the zone who is marking the disc.

open side—Force side.

outside-in—A curl of the flight path (from the forehand side to the backhand side for a forehand or from the backhand side to the forehand side for a backhand).

oyster—A fake clam; a clam for zero passes.

pancake—A method of catching in which the disc is sandwiched between two clapping hands.

person (as a defense)—One on one.

person to person—One on one.

poach—The act by a defender of intentionally moving away from her to help out with defense somewhere else on the field.

point—A position on zone defense forming either of the two ends of the cup.

point block—A defensive block by the marker occurring immediately after the release.

popper—A position on zone offense primarily responsible for cuts in and behind the cup.

power position—A position ideal for a long pass, when a thrower catches the disc running laterally across the field or downfield and his defender is behind him.

pull—The throw that initiates a point.

push pass—A type of throw in which no backswing is used.

rail—A wing in a zone offense.

rebound—The path of the disc after a player tips it while attempting to catch it.

receiver—Person in process of catching the disc; cutter.

Red Sea—A split.

red zone—The part of the playing field proper near the attacking end zone.

release—The point at which the disc leaves the thrower's hand.

reset—A short pass at a high stall count to maintain possession; the act of maintaining possession through a reset pass; a call to revert to the play or defensive set called on the line.

scoober—A type of throw employing the forehand grip in which the disc is released upside down from the backhand side.

second cut—A cut intended to receive the disc from a player currently cutting.

shade—To position (or reposition) oneself defensively in specific relation to the offender (as in, "shade deep").

short-deep—A position in zone defense typically covering an area downfield of the cup.

short stack—A compressed stack formation in which the last in the stack is several yards closer than in the standard stack.

side-middle—A wing position on zone defense.

side stack—A stack formation along one side of the field, creating an enlarged alley.

sky—To jump up and catch the disc, especially in the presence of an opposing player.

split—A set play in which several stack members cut to the sideline, creating a path in the middle of the field, filled by one cutter cutting back to the disc.

split stack—A stack formation in which two groups of players stack on the two side-lines, creating space in the middle of the field.

stack—An offensive formation in which noncutting players form a line in an area of the field (especially in the middle of the field).

stoppage—Cessation of play after a foul, pick, violation, or time-out.

straight up—A defensive formation in which the marker positions herself directly downfield of the thrower.

"strike!"—A call alerting the defense to an open receiver on the near sideline.

string—A series of passes to specific cutters in a specific order.

strong side—Force side.

swill—An errant pass that stays aloft too long; any poor throw.

swing—To move the disc from one side of the field to another with a series of throws; the act of doing so.

switch—A reassignment of defensive roles among two defenders.

thrower—The player with the disc.

throwing lane—The swath of field between the thrower and where receivers are expected to cut.

thumber—A type of throw in which the thumb is placed on the inner rim of the disc.

tight cup—A compressed cup formation.

touch—(noun) The quality of gentleness or finesse imparted to the path of a disc.

transition—The change from one defense to another in the middle of a point; the change from defense to offense (or offense to defense) following a turnover.

trap—Any defensive formation in which a thrower on the sideline is forced in the direction of that sideline, especially an aggressive such formation.

triangulation—The act (by a defender) of keeping the triangle formed by herself, her offender, and the thrower in sight.

turnaround time—The time between reception and release of the next throw; the minimal amount of time it takes a player to receive and successfully release a throw.

underneath—A fill cut back to the disc after a deep cut by another player.

up call—A cry of "Up!" indicating that the disc has been thrown.

weak side—Breakside.

weave—An offense in which only three players move the disc, while other offensive players remain downfield for large gainer possibilities.

wide side—The opposite side of the field in a situation where the disc is near a sideline, but not being trapped.

wing—A position on zone defense primarily responsible for covering an area near the sideline; a position on zone offense primarily responsible for receiving passes near the sideline.

zone—A style of defense in which defenders are assigned to cover areas of the field or throwing lanes, rather than individual opponents.

Index

Note: The italicized letter *f* refers to figures.

About the Authors

Jim Parinella is among the most recognized names in Ultimate. He is one of the leaders and top players of the six-time national and three-time world champion team, Death or Glory (DoG). Parinella is also heavily involved in the Ultimate Players Association (UPA), where he was on the board of directors from 1998 to 2003, serving as president in 2000 and 2001.

In addition, Parinella is a regular contributor to the UPA Newsletter, Ultimate Life Magazine, and other Ultimate publications. He lives in Sudbury, Massachusetts.

Eric ("Zaz") Zaslow has been an Ultimate player since 1977. He played with DoG when they were world champions (in 1996 and 1999) and national champions (in 1996, 1997, and 1998). Currently, he is one of the leaders and top players of another national-caliber team, Chicago's Machine.

Zaz is a current member of the board of directors for the Ultimate Players Association (UPA). He lives in Chicago.